MARCO POLO

Travel with Insider Tips

BE

D0591650

www.marco-polo.com

6 **INSIDER TIPS**
Our top 15 Insider Tips

8 **BEST OF...**
- Great places for free
- Only in Berlin
- And if it rains?
- Relax and chill out

12 **INTRODUCTION**
Discover Berlin!

18 **WHAT'S HOT**
There are lots of new things to discover in Berlin

20 **IN A NUTSHELL**
Background information on Berlin

26 **SIGHTSEEING**
29 Mitte 41 Tiergarten 47 Prenzlauer Berg/ Friedrichshain 50 Kreuzberg 53 Charlottenburg/Wilmersdorf 56 In other districts 61 Excursions

64 **FOOD & DRINK**
Top culinary tips

76 **SHOPPING**
For a fun-filled shopping spree!

SYMBOLS

INSIDER TIP Insider Tip
★ Highlight
●●●● Best of...
Scenic view
Responsible travel: for ecological or fair trade aspects
(*) Telephone numbers that are not toll-free

PRICE CATEGORIES HOTELS

Expensive	over 140 euros
Moderate	90–140 euros
Budget	under 90 euros

Prices per night for two people in a double room with breakfast

PRICE CATEGORIES RESTAURANTS

Expensive	over 25 euros
Moderate	15–25 euros
Budget	under 15 euros

Prices for an average main course without drinks

On the cover: A stunning island just for art p. 38 | Stay cool at night p. 89

86 **ENTERTAINMENT**
Where to go?

98 **WHERE TO STAY**
From low budget to luxury

106 **DISCOVERY TOURS**
106 Berlin at a glance
110 Where the Wall once stood
114 Through Berlin's history: the Spandauer Vorstadt
116 Bike tour into nature
119 Cruise through the city by ship

122 **TRAVEL WITH KIDS**
Best things to do with kids

124 **FESTIVALS & EVENTS**
All dates at a glance

126 **LINKS, BLOGS, APPS & MORE**
Plan ahead and use on the go

128 **TRAVEL TIPS**
From A to Z

132 **USEFUL PHRASES**

136 **STREET ATLAS & STREET INDEX**

172 **INDEX & CREDITS**

175 **DOS & DON'TS**

DID YOU KNOW?
Berlin on the water → p. 35
Relax & enjoy → p. 44
Floating swimming pool → p. 58
Keep fit! → p. 61
Gourmet restaurants → p. 68
Local specialities → p. 72
Books & films → p. 94
Sporting fever → S. 96
Luxury hotels → p. 102
Budgeting → p. 129
Currency converter → p. 130
Weather → p. 131

MAPS IN THE GUIDEBOOK
(138 A1) Page numbers and coordinates refer to the street atlas
(0) Site/address located off the map
Coordinates are also given for places that are not marked on the street atlas

(🗺 A–B 2–3) refers to the removable pull-out map

INSIDE FRONT COVER:
The best Highlights

INSIDE BACK COVER:
Public transportation route map

The best MARCO POLO Insider Tips

Our top 15 Insider Tips

INSIDER TIP In memoriam

Micha Ullman's *memorial* to the Burning of the Books on Bebelplatz under the Nazi dictatorship draws our gaze downwards. Below the sheet of glass empty bookcases can be seen that symbolise the 20,000 books burned here on 10 May 1933 → p. 31

INSIDER TIP The village within the city

Surrounded by apartment blocks in Neukölln, the historical village of *Rixdorf* looks from another era with its church, blacksmith and barns → p. 59

INSIDER TIP Telling history

Former inmates guide visitors through the *prison* run by the former East German State Security (Stasi) and tell their personal stories of solitary confinement and psychological terror → p. 59

INSIDER TIP Stalinist glory

The 90m-wide *Karl-Marx-Allee* in Friedrichshain with its monumental, Moscow-style housing blocks is impressive (photo above) → p. 37

INSIDER TIP Paddling in the Spree

In the *Freischwimmer* restaurant and water lounge (photo right) you can either enjoy the romantic location on the river bank or you can rent a canoe or kayak and explore the Spree. Life jackets available for children → p. 69

INSIDER TIP Hip design

The shop *Aus Berlin* presents more-or-less useful – and many weird – things created by around 270 Berlin designers. If you are after pills to cure lovesickness, bookends in the shape of pieces of the Berlin Wall or a Television Tower lollipop, this is the place for you → p. 80

INSIDER TIP A good night story

The breakfast room doubles up as a library. Readings with famous or still-unknown authors are held regularly in the lounge of the *Literaturhotel* in the suburb of Friedenau. Some literature Nobel Prize winners live(d) just round the corner → p. 102

INSIDER TIP A drink with a view
You can enjoy the magnificent view from the roof of the *Park Inn Hotel* (40th floor) opposite the Television Tower – and sip a cocktail at the same time. There are even deckchairs waiting for you → p. 102

INSIDER TIP Nostalgia for nerds
Excellent interactive exhibition in the *Computerspielemuseum* (computer games museum) featuring lots of games you might remember from your childhood → p. 30

INSIDER TIP "There ain't much better than a life on a cutter"
The *deckhouse* of an old stern-wheel tug on the Spree is the perfect place to get your teeth into some sprats or Berlin-style hamburgers → p. 69

INSIDER TIP Second-hand Beatles
Music fans and vinyl freaks will find 200,000 singles and countless other records at *Platten Pedro*, Berlin's largest antiquarian record shop → p. 78

INSIDER TIP Turkish delights
Try the finest Turkish sweets from one of Turkey's best confectioners right in the city centre at the *Confiserie Orientale* → p. 78

INSIDER TIP Loft camping
Overnight in a caravan at the *Hüttenpalast* located on a factory floor in Neukölln – a unique and extremely comfortable experience! → p. 104

INSIDER TIP The BVG's convertible trains
Public transport with a difference: travel the underground in carriages with the roof down – an experience not to be missed! → p. 122

INSIDER TIP Don't get dizzy
The fastest lift in Europe will whisk you to the top of the *Kollhoff Tower* on Potsdamer Platz. There you will not only be able to admire the view but also have a coffee or enjoy your breakfast in comfort → p. 45

BEST OF...

GREAT PLACES FOR FREE

Discover new places and save money

FOR FREE

Lunchtime concerts

From September to June, you will be able to enjoy a free lunchtime concert every Tuesday in the *Philharmonie*. The performing ensembles are first-rate and include the Berlin Philharmonic and scholarship holders from the orchestra's academy → p. 95

Wall art

The *Eastside Gallery* (photo), the longest open-air gallery in the world, is located to the south of the Ostbahnhof railway station. Take a look at what artists have left for future generations on a 1,316 m (4,317 ft) long piece of the former Berlin Wall → p. 48

New Berliner bike tours

Hop on the saddle and away you go. The Allgemeine Deutsche Fahrrad Club (ADFC) offers *free city tours* on bike. Bikes can be hired first at a low cost for example from *Next-Bike (www.nextbike.de)* → p. 129

Rock for free

Free admission on Thursdays from 7pm at the *Sageclub* in the Heinrich-Heinrich-Straße underground station! Dance the night away or just enjoy being a part of the scene → p. 90

Déjeuner sur l'herbe

In summer, the Berliners pack their picnic baskets and make a pilgrimage to the *English Garden* in Tiergarten to relax and listen to free concerts of jazz and Klezmer music. Join in the fun! → p. 41

Life on the border

Get a vivid impression of life behind the wall at the *Gedenkstätte Berliner Mauer* (Berlin Wall Memorial) at the Nordbahnhof station: with mine patrols (without any mines though), eyewitness accounts, observation tower, documentary films etc. – and what's best: admission to everything is free → p. 35

ONLY IN BERLIN
Unique experiences

Quadriga with twelve legs
The *Brandenburger Tor* is an absolute must. Not only the street artists let their hair down here, there are also many hobby photographers. Who can take the most beautiful picture of this city landmark? → p. 41

"TV asparagus"
This is the name the people of Berlin have affectionately given the *Fernsehturm* on Alexanderplatz. You will really miss out on something if you don't visit the viewing platform 203 m (666 ft) above street level – it's the best view in Berlin → p. 34

Wall taxi
A taxi will take you to all remnants of the Berlin *Wall* in the city. The driver will point out the most important places and garnish his stories with his personal experiences in the former divided city → p. 130

Curry 36
Cheap but tasty – that's all a Berlin currywurst needs to be, with some chips or a bread roll to go along with it. The Berliners queue up at *Curry 36* in Kreuzberg for a grilled sausage with curry powder → p. 74

Sophisticated shopping
Time and time again, the *Ku'damm* has been pronounced dead, but the many customers in the fashionable boutiques on the elegant boulevard cannot all be wrong. This is where Berlin is at its most glamorous in a setting of magnificent old buildings: typical of Berlin – but sometimes beautiful can be expensive → p. 54

Don't forget your swimsuit...
You will feel like you are at the seaside: deck chairs and sand as far as the eye can see. The wide expanse of water at *Wannsee* is an inviting place to sunbathe or swim, and a snack bar is never far away (photo) → p. 24

Jazz in a beer garden
Real Kreuzbergers don't give a hoot about the yuppies in Mitte or Friedrichshain when they sit back with a pint in their hands in one of the beer gardens – listening to live jazz in *Yorckschlösschen*, for example → p. 94

BEST OF...

AND IF IT RAINS?

Activities to brighten your day

Under water

The sharks and crocodiles in the *Zoo-Aquarium* become especially popular when it's raining cats and dogs outside. You will find it much more peaceful upstairs among the snakes and tarantulas → p. 56

Museumsinsel

Fancy the Processional Way in Babylon, Caspar David Friedrich or Nefertiti? You will be really spoilt for choice trying to decide between the five museums on the *Museumsinsel* with their magnificent collections → p. 38

Expedition to the tropics

You will feel like you are in a jungle in the tropical plant glasshouse in the *Botanischer Garten* it is so warm and humid among all the palms, ferns and lianas → p. 56

In a tent

The tent-like roof at Potsdamer Platz is not only a protection from the rain. The *Sony Center* (photo) also offers a huge range of entertainment and culinary delights. The setting is particularly impressive in the evening when the coloured LEDs in the ceiling start to glow → p. 45

RAIN

Shopping under cover

A creative factory charm and original pop-up stores selling quirky accessories and fashion by Berlin designers make *Bikini Berlin,* the city's new alternative department store, the perfect hang-out on bad weather days → p. 81

Vertical garden

The tropical plant wall in the café at *Dussmann's* cultural department store' is a fantastic setting for a break when it's raining outside. Try their delicious cakes and snacks. You can also browse around the store's massive selection of books and music media → p. 82

RELAX AND CHILL OUT

Take it easy and spoil yourself

CHILL OUT

● ***Dream away***

You float in salt water and listen to underwater music in a kind of grotto. The sauna, steam bath and massages in the *Liquidrom* next to the Tempodrom are pure bliss → **p. 44**

● ***A cup of tea***

Taking part in the Chinese tea ceremony in the *Berghaus zum Osmanthussaft* calms down even the most hectic person. The world's noise simply is left outside the door → **p. 56**

● ***Beach bar***

In summer, you can lie back in a deck chair in *Strandbar Mitte* with a view of the Spree and Bodemuseum. In the evening, join in a dance and indulge in a pizza from the wood-fired oven → **p. 89**

● ***Sweating Turkish style***

Let yourself be pampered in true oriental fashion in the *Sultan Hamam* in Schöneberg – hamam and Turkish massages → **p. 44**

● ***Fairy-tale figures***

The water splashing out of fountains and fairy-tale figures is tremendously soothing and the fresh air performs miracles. You can regain your stamina at the *Fairytale Fountain* in the Volkspark in Friedrichshain → **p. 50**

● ***Pfaueninsel***

This idyll on the outskirts of town is easy to reach with the BVG's double deckers and a ferry. Wide stretches of grass are the perfect place to relax or have a picnic, and peacocks roam areound freely → **p. 58**

● ***Breath of fresh air***

Tired of the big city? The best way to relax is to take a stroll around the *Tempelhofer Feld,* the site of one of the city's former airports. Watch kites flying in the skies above and let the sound of the wind drown out big city noises. It feels like being in the countryside (photo) → **p. 60**

INTRODUCTION

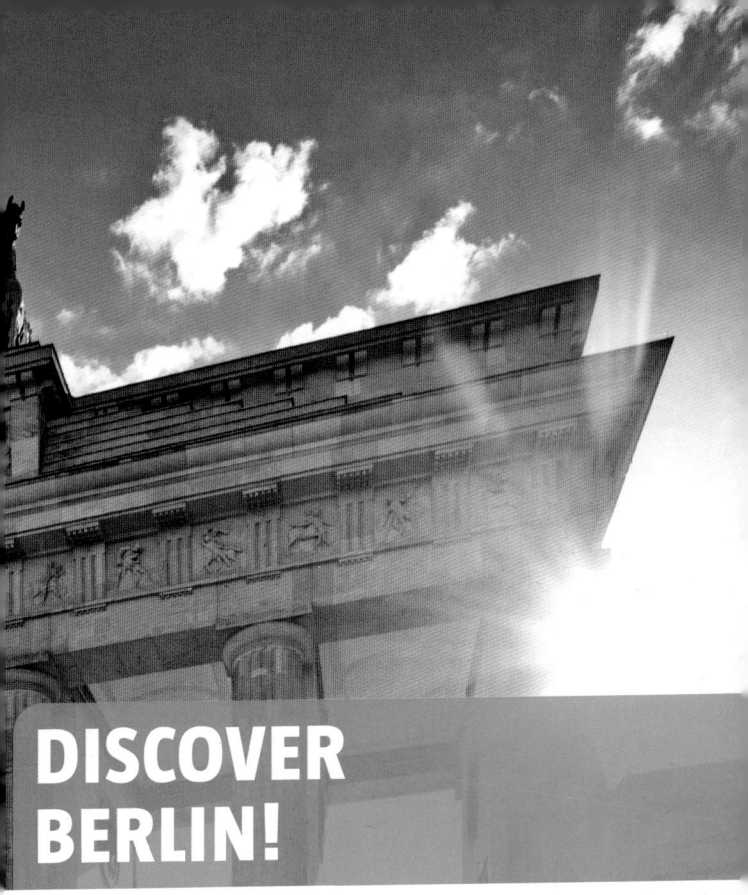

DISCOVER BERLIN!

Berlin attracts creative people from all over the world as if by magic and is ***one of the most popular cities of the world***. No other city in Europe has as much art and culture to offer! No matter whether it is art, dance, theatre or music, the cultural scene in Berlin provides a stage for international stars and also acts as a breeding ground for talented youngsters to develop their skills and become the real avant-garde themselves. With its more than 150 concert halls, theatres and other stages, three opera houses and around 200 museums and art collections, Berlin has an enormous variety of cultural institutions.

Apart from the Museumsinsel with its magnificent exhibits, the treasures found in the more than 440 small galleries are equally unique. This has made Berlin one of the most important cities in the ***art-business world***. For the people of Berlin, culture is not merely the Staatsoper and Philharmonie but also the countless concert clubs and tiny theatres "round the corner" where superb performances are often held and seats are cheap. Berlin is famous worldwide for its ***feverish nightliefe*** with more than 200 clubs, innumerable bars, cafés and pubs. There are no set closing times and most places stay open until the early hours of the morning – if they close at all. The "in" districts of Mitte,

Photo: Brandenburger Tor

Friedrichshain, Kreuzberg and Prenzlauer Berg, with their varied theatre, club and pub scene, are typical of this metropolis' international orientation.

Today, you hardly ever get the feeling that this city was ***once divided by a wall***. In the past, however, you didn't need a compass to work out where the East stopped and the West began. The wall that ran through the centre of the city from 1961 to 1989 could really not be missed. In the one half there was East Berlin, the capital city of the German Democratic Republic that came under the influence of the Soviets and, in the other half, the walled-in city of West Berlin under the protection of the western allies France, Great Britain and the USA. Now, 25 years after the Fall of the Wall, visitors to the city can barely see the difference in a cityscape that once developed differently as a result of the two political systems. Many of the prefabricated concrete buildings which were typical of the GDR in the eastern part of the ctiy have been revamped. They look so surprisingly modern and cosy that living on the 8th floor of a building on Alexanderplatz is now considered chic. And, when you stand at Checkpoint Charlie – the erstwhile Allied border crossing on Friedrichstraße – you will see that the former eastern sector is dominated by luxurious business premises and boutiques while a certain dreariness has spread across the west.

Despite the burden of history Berlin is growing back together again

With a population of around 3.4 million, the new – and old – capital Berlin is still in a period of upheaval. Enormous efforts have been made since the reunification of

Unter den Linden boulevard ends at the Schlossbrücke – with the Berliner Dom in the background

Germany to create an ***architecturally representative capital city***. There have been continuous building, restoration and revitalisation activities everywhere. Potsdamer Platz was Europe's largest building site in the 1990s but has since successfully established itself as a new city centre. The Sony Center's tented roof is now regarded as one of the city's landmarks. Berlin is exceedingly proud of its ***glass main railway station*** – Europe's largest – that was opened in 2006. Since 2008, an ***enormous multi-purpose indoor arena***, the Mercedes-Benz Arena (thus rechristened in 2015; formerly O_2 World) at the GDR's former main station – the Ostbahnhof – has drawn huge crowds for pop concerts and the basketball games of the first-division team Alba Berlin. A new office and commercial district is growing up around it. After the demolition of the Palast der Republik, the former seat of the East German parliament, plans are underway for the former ***royal palace*** to rise from the ashes until 2020 and become the home of the "Humboldt Forum" with museums for non-European cultures and a range of other scientific institutions and libraries as an extension of the Museumsinsel.

Even sceptical Berlin residents are proud of the ***successful architectural solutions*** devised for the government district. From the dome of the Reichstag you can see to Potsdamer Platz in the south, the monumental glass roof of the main station to the north, the Federal Chancellery to the west and the offices of the MPs to the east. Many politicians and their advisers walk to their parliamentary debates and you will be surprised at how many famous people you will come across in the nearby restaurants and cafés. And, there is something else that is only possible in a city like Berlin: first and foremost, people are thought of as people. Whether somebody is famous or not is purely secondary. ***Live and let live*** – that's Berlin's motto. Berliners expect to be treated as an individual and are prepared to treat others as such.

In the new seat of power

People of 186 nationalities live in Berlin. Especially young people from all over the world are attracted to Berlin. English, the globetrotter language, is becoming the only language spoken in increasingly more bars and cafés. Since the financial crisis, the city has become a popular destination for Spaniards and Israelis also enjoy immersing themselves into the ***creative Berlin scene*** to transform their ideas into reality. At least 200,000 Russians and Poles, together with Ukrainians and Czechs live in Berlin where it can be witnessed first hand how a divided country is growing together and how Europe is becoming more unified as well – after all, Berlin is the only capital city in Europe that is located both in the east and west! Many Russians and Ukrainians who have settled in Berlin are Jewish and this has led to ***everyday Jewish culture*** once again finding its rightful place in the city. If you stroll around the area near Oranienburger Straße in Mitte, you will come across a Jewish school and cafés and restaurants serving Jewish and oriental specialities. On the other hand, life in the former western inner-city areas, especially Kreuzberg, Neukölln and Wedding, is characterised by the ***Turkish way of life***. You can see large Turkish families bartering for crates of aubergines and grapes at the markets or discussing things with friends while traders praise their goods at the top of their voices. Quite an experience!

Throughout Berlin's 777-year history newcomers to the city have often brought innovative ***cultural and economic impulses*** with them. Be it Huguenots, Bohemians or Silesians, their customs and traditions have left a mark on the city, especially on the culinary sector. *Bouletten* (or *Buletten*) for example is a French word for meatballs that have become a Berlin speciality. In the past, people facing religious persecution in particular were drawn to the Spree as Prussia's regents were known far and wide for their ***religious tolerance***. In 1701, during the reign of Friedrich I, a church was built for the Protestant Huguenots – the French Cathedral – and the St.-Hedwigs-Kathedrale was built at the end of the 18th century as a Catholic house of worship for the Silesians. In 1886, Europe's largest synagogue – with seating for 3,200 people – was opened on Oranienburger Straße. This was destroyed in World War II and has only been partially reconstructed.

Over the years, Berlin has played a ***central role in world history*** on many an occasion. Memories of the Nazi dictatorship, the persecution of the Jews and the terrible consequences of World War II are kept alive with countless memorials and remembrance sites. Although the inner city was badly bombed, many historical buildings have been preserved or reconstructed. The Staatsoper Unter den Linden, Berliner Dom, the Schauspielhaus, as well as the German and French Cathedrals on Gendarmenmarkt are magnificent examples of this. And, there is the Museumsinsel with its ***unique ensemble of stately Classicist buildings*** with archaeological and art collections that are now all open to the public after the completion of lengthy reconstruction work.

Of course, the ***recent past*** has also left its mark. Many of the young people who live in, or visit, Berlin never experienced the divided city themselves. This makes memorials such as the Wall Documentation Museum on Bernauer Straße or the Allies Museum in Zehlendorf even more important than ever before. The drone of a Douglas DC 3, a transport plane from the time of the airlift in 1948/49, when supplies to the western sector of the city had to be masterminded completely from the air as a result of the Soviet blockade, brings back memories of that period whenever it takes off – on special occasions – for flights over Berlin. French, English, Russian and American educational institutions and cultural centres still bear witness to the former presence of the ***four Allied occupying powers***. Some Berlin children visit a French music school while others attend a college with a pronounced emphasis on Russian studies. The 400,000 trees that were planted along the streets to make life in the walled-in city more bearable have also remained to this day.

This green metropolis adds quality of life

In fact hardly any other comparable city has ***as many parks and green spaces*** as Berlin. And the residents of Berlin are similarly "green" when they think about the quality of life in their city. More than 40 per cent of all their journeys are made on foot or by bike and 26 per cent use public transport. Only half of all households have a car. An increasing number of visitors to Berlin can now be seen pedalling hard around the city and there are an enormous number of places where bikes can be rented. Berlin is also the secret ***organic food capital*** with more specialist shops per head than any other German city.

An institution on Berlin's nightlife scene: Clärchens Ballhaus

The only problem is the economy. Dealing with the results of 40 years as a divided city is not as easy to come to grips with as many people had hoped. And progress is painfully slow. In the past, the city was kept alive under two opposing political systems and, today, Berlin is still finding it difficult to exist without a stable, efficient economy that has evolved over decades. In spite of the rapidly increasing number of jobs in the service sector, Berlin has to live with a current unemployment rate of 11 per cent. However, the city is making the most of its potential as a ***base for scientific institutions***. The universities, specialist colleges, research and scientific organisations are important employers providing around 200,000 jobs. Business in the ***creative sector is also booming*** – especially in the IT field and design branch. Innovative fashion labels are attracting attention outside Berlin and upcycling is the latest craze, i.e. of transforming old materials into new fashion. Today many companies in the capital are focusing on creating a sustainable and ecological business. Time and time again people from Berlin have been successful in establishing themselves as avant-garde businesses and product designers. There are ideas everywhere, but Berlin is where they become reality. And you may well feel the same as many local residents who, despite seeing their city day in, day out, continuously discover exciting new things around about and are often surprised at how much they didn't know before. ***Berlin is like a lucky-dip*** – you never know what you're going to come across next!

The perfect place for the adventurous and creative

WHAT'S HOT

1 Multicultural delights

Exotic bites to eat *Markthalle Neun (Eisenbahnstr. 9 | www.markthalleneun.de) (photo)* in Kreuzberg transforms into a world snack bar on Thursdays from 5pm at its *Street Food Thursday* event: Thailand tapioca dumplings, Mexican tacos, German cheese noodle specialities, Peruvian ceviche, Nigerian fufu and Korean buns are all on the menu. A street food market is also held on Sundays (4pm–10pm) in two old railway buildings on the RAW site (*Reichsausbesserungswerk | Warschauer Str. | Friedrichshain).*

2 Upcycling

Old into new The trend of transforming waste into creative items has now spread to fashion in Berlin. Stylish products made from old materials are available at the *Upcycling Fashion Store (Anklamer Str. 17 | Mitte | upcycling-fashion.com) (photo)* and the *Schmidttakahashi label (www.schmidttakahashi.de)* by Eugenie Schmidt and Mariko Takahashi at *Oukan (Kronenstr. 71 | Mitte).* Accessories and toys made from waste can also be found at *Upcycling deluxe (Kastanienallee 22 | Mitte | www.upcycling-deluxe.com).*

3 Ready for takeoff?

Playground for everyone You don't need water to do water sports; sailing or kite surfing can be done on asphalt. Take your board and kite out to the *Tempelhofer Feld* (see p. 60) where you can really hit high speeds *(photo).* The *Berliner Kiteschule (www.berliner-kiteschule.de)* offers courses. If you prefer to take things easier, book a unicycle session at *Dingadu (dingadu.de)* or hire a Segway from *Steckdose Berlin (Tempelhofer Damm entrance | www.steckdose-berlin.de).*

There are lots of new things to discover in Berlin. A few of the most interesting are listed below

(Electro)mobile in Berlin

4

Like a rocket People in Berlin like to be on the move – but not if the environment has to pick up the bill. They swing themselves onto an electric *erockit* motorbike *(www.erockit.net) (photo)*. It is driven by muscle power – but also has a built in "amplifier". Your own energy gets multiplied by 50! The faster you pedal, the faster the bike goes. You can also hire bikes from *Lautlos (Wilhelmstr. 93 | Mitte | Tel. 030 88 76 62 34 | www.berlin.lautlosdurch-deutschland.de)*. The car sharing enterprise *Multicity* also has 350 e-cars to hire for approx. 25 cents a minute; you can recharge these small Citroën C-Zeros at over 200 charging stations around the city. The electricity used is from 100% regenerative energy sources. Multicity customers in Berlin also have access to the *Flinkster* and *e-Flinkster* vehicles and the "Call a bike" service (see p. 129) from the Deutsche Bahn. BVG customers are also entitled to other benefits such as a discount registration fee and free minutes.

5

Action speaks...

...louder than words The *Haus der guten Taten, Coeco* ("Good Deed House") at Schlossstraße 1 *(www.coeo-berlin.de)* really lives up to its name. The welfare organisation sells products made in special workshops by handicapped people; the profits flow back into social projects The *Guerrilla-Gardeners (www.facebook.com/guerillagardening) (photo)* come armed with bulbs and rakes. Their aim? To beautify the city and green public spaces for the benefit of all – and, if there is a need, this can even be in a building skip or at the former Tempelhof airport.

IN A NUTSHELL

ALTERNATIVE CULTURE

Off theatres, small hip clubs and concert venues in hidden courtyards: you can discover Berlin's real charm if you venture beyond the highly-subsidised cultural palaces. Only those who have been to a performance in the *Theater zum Westlichen Stadthirschen* (Western City Deer Theatre) or listened to a punk band in *Schokoladen* (Choc Shop) will know what this means. This is where locals and newcomers have fought for some cultural freedom to make it possible for them to experiment with new kinds of performing arts way off the beaten track. This is where you can get a close-up view of the origins of new movements in music, theatre and art! Berlin's nightlife always has something novel to offer: the trendy clubs in abandoned buildings or old factories are often not officially registered; their addresses are passed on almost on the sly. The best way to find out what is going on is to ask a local or look at Facebook. Once you have got your hands on one of these secret addresses you'll be the proud owner of a piece of insider information – but only for a short time. Like nomads, most of the clubs soon move on to a new location.

ART METROPOLIS

With its more than 440 galleries and numerous collections, Berlin is one of the most important art markets in the world, with an annual turnover of 500 million euros. Collectors fly in regularly to buy new works. Street art is also of major

Photo: Fashion Week, Showcase Lena Hoschek

Bars on the banks of the Spree, the rebuilding of the royal palace, the charm of East Germany in your hotel room – anything is possible

importance. In the city centre, you can admire works by street artists like Alias or Emess on every corner. Compared to the total number of residents, Berlin has the largest percentage of freelance artists in Germany – six per cent. This number has increased by more than 40 per cent since 2000; around 5,000 artists are working in Berlin today! This is partly due to the fact that it is comparatively cheap to rent studios. And – unlike in Paris, London or New York – even young artists can live comfortably in Berlin.

BERLIN PALACE

Severely damaged in World War II, its ruins blown up on the orders of the East German authorities, the royal palace originally on this site is now about to rise from the ashes. The facade is being constructed at the moment; inside, there will be space for the *Humboldt Forum* housing museums focusing on non-European cultures, the State Library and collections owned by *Humboldt-Universität*.

COURTYARD ARCHITECTURE

Berlin is famous for its courtyard ensembles. It is not at all rare to find between two and eight blocks of flats, one behind the other, connected by courtyards and passageways. This style of architecture, typical to Berlin, has regained its former fame partly thanks to the revamped Hackesche Höfe in Mitte. Other examples of skilful courtyard redevelopment in Mitte are the Heckmann-Höfe on Oranienburger Straße, the Sophie-Gips-Höfe on Sophienstraße and the Kurt-Berndt-Höfe on Neue Schönhauser Straße. The latter was built for the Metropol Palast Company in 1911/12. After being given back to its former owners, the building was remodelled and modernised in the late 1990s.

DEMONSTRATIONS

Berlin is not only the seat of government but also where Germans like to protest. Roughly seven demos are registered daily. Yet among them are reoccurring events such as the march in remembrance of the socialist leaders Rosa Luxemburg and Karl Liebknecht in January, several 1 May demos and the gay and lesbian parades on Christopher Street Day in June. On some days, the traffic in the city has a hard time; this can be the case when farmers drive their tractors into town to protest against agricultural polices while students take a stand against the austerity programme of the State of Berlin and parents hold a rally for free kindergarten places for their children in front of the Town Hall.

DESIGN

Unesco has recognised Berlin as a "City of Design", making it the first German city to be included in a global network of creative centres, the "Creative City Network", founded by the organisation. Other member cities in this illustrious club include Buenos Aires, as another "City of Design", and Edinburgh as a "City of Literature". Currently, nine educational institutions, including two art academies and three fashion schools, provide training for designers and, according to the Economic Senate, around 3,000 students are taking advantage of these offers. Approximately 8,000 designers and artists are actively involved in the creative sector where they produce furniture, coat stands, lamps, fashion. In Berlin, artists and designer firms generate a turnover of approximately 800 million euros a year – a growing market that is acknowledged internationally. The branch's showcase event is the annual *DMY International Design Festival Berlin (www.dmy-berlin.com)* with exhibitions and experimental designs focusing on a specific subject.

DIALECT

"They don't mince their words" is one of the most common explanations for the – frequently, quite brusque – rhetoric of the locals from Berlin. If you get on a bus and ask the driver the best way to somewhere, be prepared for a stroppy answer ("Do you think I'm an information office, or something?"). There are definite limits to friendliness; but if you don't take the gruff exterior too seriously and have a quick-witted riposte on hand, you will soon be accepted. Although you might already know some words in German, remember: in Berlin bread rolls are called *Schrippen* not *Brötchen*, and doughnuts are definitely not *Berliners* but *Pfannkuchen*.

FASHION

The trend scouts of the major fashion firms regularly come to Berlin to get inspiration from the imaginative, daring outfits worn by those living in the "in" districts

Mitte, Prenzlauer Berg and Friedrichshain. Fashion is a big issue, not least because of the *Fashion Week* (end of Jan and beginning of July). Some Berlin designers sew one-off garments in backrooms and sell them out front. But the man on the streets does not pay much attention to fashion. Most people in Berlin are more interested in being comfortably dressed. And in some districts you could almost believe that tracksuits and flip-flops are considered chic...

GREEN, GREENEST

Berlin residents really know how to save energy. According to statistics, they produce less CO_2 per inhabitant than anywhere else in Germany! And only every second household – that means every third resident – has a car. Several large companies and state institutions, including the federal buildings and German Bundestag, obtain their heat from power stations fired with vegetable oil and their water is warmed by solar energy. The federal headquarters of the Christian Democratic Party and the new premises of the Green Party's Heinrich Böll Foundation are also equipped with photovoltaic panels. If you are interested, you can take a tour in a solar boat *(tel. 0151 54 22 80 44 | www.solarpolis.de)* to become acquainted with the sights and buildings from the water – and save energy at the same time. Many locals also try to make sure that their groceries are organic and come from the region. Countless large and small organic markets are flourishing although, compared to the average in Germany, the net household income in Berlin is rather modest. Europe's largest organic supermarket is located on Senefelderplatz in Prenzlauer Berg and has a total retail area of almost 17,000 sq ft. Its nutrition-conscious customers are drawn by 18,000 different products including 200 different wines and 180

Skies over Berlin – Hackesche Höfe at the Hackescher Markt

varieties of cheese. There are also two vegan supermarkets in Prenzlauer Berg *(Schivelbeiner Str. 34)* and Friedrichshain *(Warschauer Str. 33)*.

LOVE OF ANIMALS

People in Berlin seem to be crazy about anything on four legs. Dogs in particular are real favourites and pedestrians always have to look at least one step ahead to avoid treading on a "stinking landmine". But dog poo is not the only problem; our canine friends simply do not have enough space to run about in. The legal exercise areas in the Volkspark in Friedrichshain and Hasenheide in Kreuzberg are notoriously overcrowded. That not everybody is capable of dealing with this becomes clear if you visit the animal shelter on the north-eastern outskirts of the city. Covering an area of 40 acres – including a pet cemetery – it is the largest of its kind in Europe. As many as 12,000 animals are cared for by a staff of around 75 every year.

MAJOR AIRPORT

There is no end to the squabbling over the expansion of Schönefeld Airport to create a new major airport. After 25 years of planning and construction, there is still no end in sight and the people of Berlin are already manning the barricades to protest about flight paths. South Berlin will be especially subjected to aircraft noise. Local residents rightly fear not only a decrease in their quality of life but also in the price of their property. Their neighbours in the north, on the other hand, can heave a sigh of relief. The closure of Tegel Airport means that, from 2018 or so onwards, after more than 45 years, it will be possible to sleep more peacefully in Spandau and Reinickendorf.

MULTICULTURAL

People from 186 nations can be found in Berlin. Some streets – particularly in Neukölln, Kreuzberg, Moabit and Wedding – are dominated by Arab and Turkish culture. But, life in the city would not be the same without the supermarkets, bakeries, cafés and restaurants of the Russians (mainly in Charlottenburg and Marzahn), Poles and the workers formerly contracted to help out in East Germany – the Vietnamese. Unemployment is especially high among migrants. Many Turks who came to Berlin as immigrant workers almost 50 years ago found themselves out of work after the Reunification of Germany and factories and firms closed down one after the other. There are hardly any jobs for unskilled workers without a school leaving qualification and it is disastrous that 15 per cent of the young people from migrant families living in Berlin are unable to start an apprenticeship because they lack this basic qualification. The Berlin Senate is attempting to solve this problem through new education campaigns such as making it compulsory to attend a day-care centre with special language training before starting school.

ON THE WATERFRONT

Hardly any other city in Europe is blessed with as many lakes, rivers and canals as Berlin. There are more than 500 km (310 miles) of shoreline where you can go for a walk, sunbathe and even live! Most of the restaurants and clubs with a view of the water are located near the Oberbaumbrücke in Friedrichshain. Beach bars with deck chairs on the shores of the Spree and, of course, a vast number of places where you can swim in summer – all boasting a water quality standard from good to excellent – invite you take a break. A highlight is the more than 100 year old ● *Strandbad Wannsee (April–Oct daily 10am–6pm, in*

For Berliners with green fingers: urban gardening in the Prinzessinnengärten

summer until 8/9pm | admission 5.50 euros | www.strandbadwannsee.de | S 1, 7 Nikolassee), Europe's biggest continental lake swimming bath. Guests get the feeling of being at the Baltic Sea with its fine sand and wicker beach chairs with a hood.

SCIENCE

Did you know that Berlin is one of the leading cities for science in Europe? Around 200,000 scientists, students and other specialists teach, study and carry out research in four universities, the Charité Medical University, eight specialist colleges, three art academies, 18 private universities and more than 60 research institutes. Every year in June, they join up forces and organise an evening of events that gives an interesting insight into the achievements of individual institutes and research centres.

URBAN GARDENING

Spinach and leek can be seen growing in the city and remind inhabitants of how vegetables are actually grown. A lot of Berlin's wasteland has been transformed into vegetable plots such as the Prinzessinnengärten *(prinzessinnengarten.net)* at the Moritzplatz in Kreuzberg. The gardens also have their own café which uses the freshly picked vegetables in their delicious soups and bakes in summer. On the Neukölln side of the city's former airport, Tempelhofer Feld, you'll also see pumpkins and courgettes growing in abundance. Corn and red cabbage are also grown and harvested even on main city thoroughfares such as Torstraße in the Mitte district. In this way at certain times in late summer, Berliners can live from hand to mouth.

SIGHTSEEING

WHERE TO START?
Alexanderplatz (141 F2–3) *(🗺 L3–4)* is the ideal place to start your visit of Berlin and it is easy to reach by underground (U 2, 5, 8) or on the district line (S 3, 5, 7, 75). The entrance to the public car park for 600 vehicles is off the central strip of the Alexanderplatz 6 street. The Rotes Rathaus, the seat of the Lord Mayor of Berlin, is also right on "Alex" and it's just a short walk to reach the Museumsinsel with the Cathedral, the Pergamon and Bode Museums and many other institutions.

Even Berliners sometimes have difficulties recognising certain parts of their city. Those who haven't been into the city centre for several months will find new buildings have popped up on what were empty pieces of land, new bridges have appeared where there was no crossing before, and newly-opened museums waiting for them to explore. No other European city is changing so quickly!

The construction boom has also taken hold of the western sector of the city; new hotels are springing up everywhere, rundown buildings on Kurfürstendamm – such as the famous Kranzlereck – have simply been demolished and modern structures have taken their place. The airy buildings in the government district never fail to captivate viewers and visitors have to queue up to

Photo: Eastside Gallery: "My God, Help Me To Survive This Deadly Love" by Dmitri Vrubel

Berlin is changing at a breathtaking pace. New museums, whole streets and buildings make the city like a fascinating kaleidoscope

see inside the Reichstag with its glass dome. There is still plenty of scope for inspired architecture and new ideas, for example at the Ostbahnhof where a new commercial district has been built. And then there is the reconstruction of Berlin's former royal City Palace; the Palast der Republik that replaced the Baroque edifice on the site has been demolished. A new residential and office district for many thousand people is being developed near the main station, the largest in Europe, that was opened in 2006.The inner city is gradually starting to show itself at its best and anybody who walks through the restored Brandenburger Tor today will find it difficult to believe how desolate Pariser Platz behind it was for so many years. Many visitors see a city that didn't exist in this form 25 years ago and don't even notice it. Whether on Potsdamer Platz or Friedrichstraße, the architects have been successful in at least one aspect: the postmodern architecture has been assimilated perfectly into the cityscape almost everywhere and only a few make fun of the fact that Berlin still does not have skyscrapers.

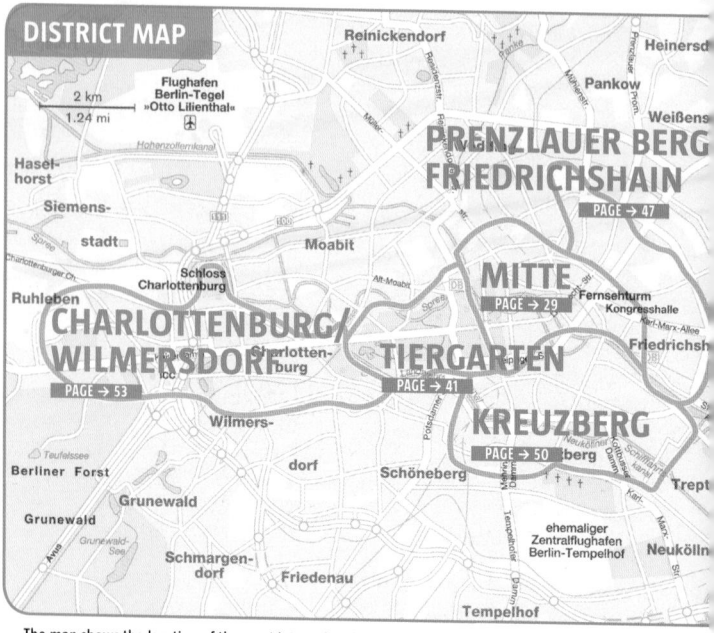

The map shows the location of the most interesting districts. There is a detailed map of each district on which each of the sights described is numbered.

The residents of Berlin prefer to keep things within reasonable limits and there is still not enough economic power to warrant a business district like the one in Frankfurt am Main.

On the other hand, culture ranks very highly in Berlin. With over 200 museums, collections and archives, Berlin has a superlative museum landscape. Painting, everyday culture, technical and local history – there is such a great variety that it would take months even to get some sort of general overview. And, on top of that, there is always something new.

The courage to take cultural risks has a long tradition in Berlin. Does any other city have a museum specially built for an excavated altar? It is not without reason that the Pergamon Museum, opened in 1930, is one of the most popular in the city and attracts around 1 million visitors annually (but it is closed until 2017). And that can be said about the entire *Museumsinsel*, too. The ensemble of five museums houses artistic treasures that can only be matched worldwide by the Louvre in Paris and the Hermitage in Saint Petersburg. It was Crown Prince Friedrich Wilhelm came up with the idea of a centre for art and history. The *Old Museum* (Engraving Collection), the *New Museum*, *Bodemuseum* and *National Gallery* (European and German 19th century painting) and *Pergamon Museum* (Collection of Antiquities, Middle-Eastern Museum, Museum for Islamic Art, Main Archives and Library) developed between 1825 and 1930. The New Museum has been remodelled to plans by the British

architect David Chipperfield and, since autumn 2009, is home to the collection of the Egyptian Museum which was formerly displayed in the Old Museum. The Bodemuseum, with its impressive dome, presents exhibits from the Museum for Byzantine Art and sculptures. The *Stiftung Preußischer Kulturbesitz* (Prussian Cultural Property Foundation) developed out of Friedrich Wilhelm III's "royal museum" and now includes the Berlin State Museums, State Library, Secret State Archives and the Ibero-American Institute, as well as the Institute for Music Research with its Musikinstrumenten-Museum. The latter has its home in the Culture Forum in Tiergarten, the West Berlin counterpart to the Museumsinsel. Entrance fees to the Berlin State Museums range from 8 to 12 euros but higher prices are charged for special exhibitions such as those at the Neue Nationalgalerie. Information on all museums, guided tours and special exhibitions: *tel. 030 24 74 98 88* or *www.museumsportal-berlin.de.*

MITTE

The treasures on Museumsinsel are considered highlights from the history of art by experts around the world, the Television Tower with its 203 m (666 ft) high viewing platform is a real crowd-puller on sunny days, and taking a photo of the city's most important landmark – the Brandenburger Tor – is a must. *Mitte* has, by far, more sights than any other district of Berlin. Take a walk along Unter den Linden and you will discover the historical heart of the city. The *Humboldt-Universität*, for example, where famous scientists such as Albert Einstein and Rudolf Virchow taught. Or the *Zeughaus*

MARCO POLO HIGHLIGHTS

★ Fernsehturm
Best view of the city in the former centre of Berlin → p. 34

★ Gendarmenmarkt
The city's most beautiful square with buildings from the 18th and 19th centuries → p. 36

★ Museumsinsel
Impressive ensemble consisting of five huge museums → p. 38

★ Unter den Linden
Boulevard with magnificent historical buildings → p. 40

★ Brandenburger Tor
Berlin's symbol on Pariser Platz now shines in all its glory → p. 41

★ Sony Center
Spectacular: vibrant, urban complex on Potsdamer Platz → p. 45

★ Tempelhofer Feld
A former airfield open to everyone as an urban playground → p. 60

★ Reichstag
A successful mix of old and new along with a wonderful view from the top of the glass dome → p. 46

★ Jüdisches Museum Berlin
A gripping exhibition of Jewish culture in the "lightning bolt" building designed by star architect Daniel Libeskind → p. 52

★ Schloss Charlottenburg
Baroque architecture with a magnificent park → p. 55

★ Schloss Sanssouci
Potsdam's Prussian jewel – a total work of art with palaces, pavilions and landscaped gardens → p. 62

Hold on tight – the Berliner Dom as seen from a cruise ship

with the German Historical Museum. There is also plenty of action in the evening between Gendarmenmarkt, the Nikolai District and Neue Synagoge: the restaurants, bars and clubs will make sure that you'll enjoy yourself until the early hours. The best place to go shopping is around the *Hackescher Markt*. That is where Berlin designers have set up their studios and shops. Modern art is mainly sold north of the Neue Synagoge; the density of international galleries is quite impressive.

1 BERLINER DOM (141 E3) *(🗺 K–L4)*
The cathedral, constructed between 1894 and 1905 under the supervision of the architect Julius Carl Raschdorf, was severely damaged in World War II. The main section of the building only became available for services in the mid-1990s after extensive reconstruction work had been completed. The altar with the Apostle Wall, the baptismal font and two candelabras are still from the old cathedral. The Hohenzollern crypt is the resting place for around 90 monarchs and members of the Prussian nobility. There is a INSIDER TIP wonderful view of the Museumsinsel and the newly built palace from the dome! *April–Sept Mon–Sat 9am–8pm, Sun noon–8pm; Oct–March Mon–Sat 9am–7pm, Sun noon–7pm (no visits during services) | admission 7 euros (three children up to 18 years free) | prayers Mon–Sat 12–12:30pm, Mon–Fri 6–6:30pm, services Sun 10am, 6pm | several guided tours daily | Am Lustgarten | www.berlinerdom.de | S 3, 5, 7, 75 Hackescher Markt | bus 100 Schlossplatz*

2 INSIDER TIP COMPUTERSPIELEMUSEUM (153 A2) *(🗺 N4)*
An oversized Atari joystick, the first 3-D glasses and lots of game consoles can be tried. 300 exhibits spread over an area of 600 m² (0.15 acres) document the 40 year history of the digital game culture from Pong to Zelda. *Wed–Mon 10am–8pm | admission 8 euros | Karl-Marx-Al-*

lee 93a | www.computerspielemuseum.de | U 5 Weberwiese

3 DDR-MUSEUM (141 E3) *(🗺 L4)*
Those that actually experienced it have mixed feelings about this review of everyday life in East Gemany with its restricted range of food, tacky jeans, nudist holidays, Erika typewriters and music by Karat and City that can be heard once again over headphones. The history of life in the GDR over more than 800 m²/8,611 sq ft. *Daily 10am–8pm, Sat until 10pm | admission 7 euros, online from 5 euros | Karl-Liebknecht-Str. 1 | Spreepromenade | www.ddr-museum.de | S 3, 5, 7, 75 Hackescher Markt*

4 INSIDER TIP DENKMAL DER BÜCHERVERBRENNUNG (141 D4) *(🗺 K4)*
This memorial on Bebelplatz near the Staatsoper created by the Israeli artist Micha Ullman commemorates the Burning of the Books on 10 May 1933. Works by Erich Kästner, Bertolt Brecht, Kurt Tucholsky and other authors who the Nazis did not approve of were flung onto the fire. The memorial in a former tram tunnel is conceived as a cleared out library with room for 20,000 books. You look into the empty bookcases through a sheet of glass in the ground. *Bebelplatz | bus 100 Staatsoper*

5 DEUTSCHES HISTORISCHES MUSEUM (141 D3) *(🗺 K4)*
The core of the permanent exhibition that was reopened in the Zeughaus in 2006 is formed by the so-called "epoch rooms". The visitors wander through them from the beginnings of German history to the present. Temporary exhibitions are shown in the new building designed by Ieoh Ming Pei. *Daily 10am–6pm | admission 8 euros (children under 18 free) | Zeughaus (old building) | Unter den Linden 2 | www.dhm.de | S 3, 5, 7 Hackescher Markt*

6 DOROTHEENSTADT CEMETERY (140 A6) *(🗺 J–K3)*
Many of the greats from the world of art and culture have found their final resting place here. Among them are the former Federal President Johannes Rau, Heinrich Mann, Bertolt Brecht, Helene Weigel, Anna Seghers, Heiner Müller, Karl Friedrich Schinkel, Johann Gottlieb Fichte and Georg Wilhelm Friedrich Hegel. The remains of the French cemetery that was set up for the Huguenots in 1780 can also be found within the walls. The old trees

LOW BUDGET

Free exhibitions by prize-winning natural photographers as well as special shows of quality works of art are presented in the basement of the VW-Showroom in the Automobil-Forum **(140 C4)** *(🗺 K4). Daily 10am–8pm | Mitte | Unter den Linden 21 | U/S Friedrichstraße*

You will have a trip past many of the sights in Berlin for the price of a bus ticket by simply taking bus no. 100 from Bahnhof Zoo to Alexanderplatz. Stops at the Siegessäule, Schloss Bellevue, Reichstag and Brandenburger Tor.

There is a magnificent view over the city from the roof of the *Park Inn Hotel* **(141 F2)** *(🗺 L3) (daily noon–10pm, 2–6pm in winter | Mitte | Alexanderplatz 7)* on Alexanderplatz. Entrance to the panorama terrace on the 40th floor is only 4 euros.

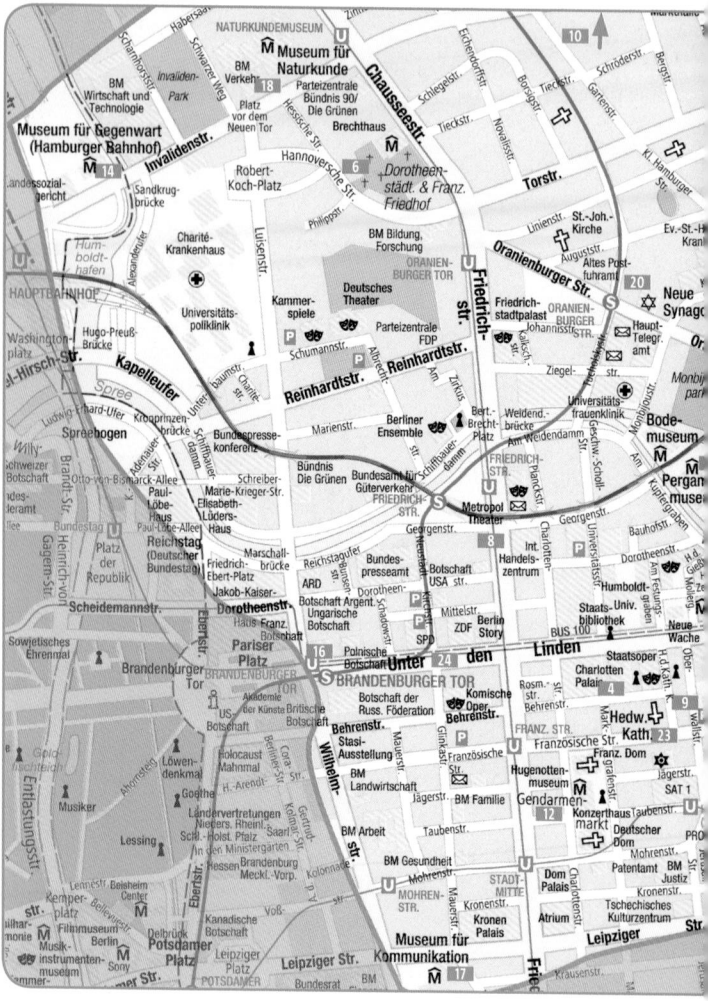

SIGHTSEEING IN MITTE

1. Berliner Dom
2. Computerspielemuseum
3. DDR-Museum
4. Denkmal der Bücherverbrennung
5. Deutsches Histor. Museum
6. Dorotheenstadt cemetery
7. Fernsehturm (TV tower) and Alexanderplatz
8. Friedrichstraße
9. Friedrichswerdersche Kirche
10. Gedenkstätte Berliner Mauer
11. Gedenkstätte Stille Helden
12. Gendarmenmarkt
13. Hackesche Höfe
14. Hamburger Bahnhof
15. Karl-Marx-Allee
16. Madame Tussauds Berlin

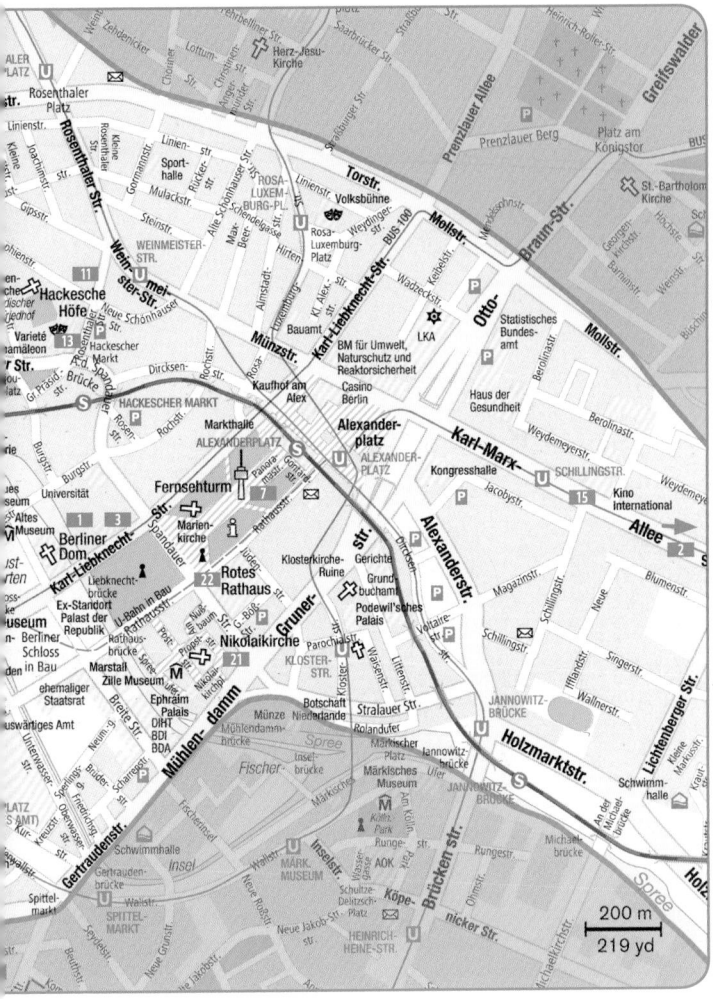

pedestrian zone

17 Museum für Kommunikation
18 Museum für Naturkunde
19 Museumsinsel
20 Neue Synagoge
21 Nikolai District
22 Rotes Rathaus
23 St.-Hedwigs-Kathedrale
24 Unter den Linden

World-time clock at the base of the Fernsehturm on Alexanderplatz

make this a quiet spot to escape from the mad rush of the city and catch your breath. *Chausseestr. 126 | U 6 Naturkundemuseum*

7 FERNSEHTURM AND ALEXANDERPLATZ (141 F2–3) *(Ⓜ L3–4)*

The ★ ● *Fernsehturm* is the second highest television tower in Europe and one of the city's landmarks. Built between 1966 and 1969, the tower with its glass sphere and overall height of 365 m (1,197 ft) can be seen from almost everywhere in the centre of the city. It is hard to find a place on the platform 203 m (666 ft) above the ground on cloudless days. An SMS service makes it possible for you to not have to queue or wait: visitors are sent an SMS when it is their turn. Then the express lift will catapult you up to the platform in a mere 40 seconds. The restaurant *Sphere (tel. 030 24 75 75 87 5 | Moderate)* above the viewing platform revolves around its own axis twice an hour. If it is a clear day, you will be able to see a good 40 km (25 miles). *Nov–Feb daily 10am–midnight, March–Oct 9am–midnight | admission 13 euros, VIP ticket 23 euros (no waiting time!) | Panoramastr. 1a | www.tv-turm.de*

Alexanderplatz at the base of the television tower (on the other side of the railway tracks) was named in honour of Tsar Alexander I in 1805 and formerly used as a parade ground and market. Today, it is overrun with people on a shopping spree and visitors to the television tower. The square completely changed its appearance after it was restored, the *Kaufhof* department store renovated, and *C&A* moved into the listed Berolinahaus completed in 1929. Only the *World-time Clock* and *Friendship between Nations Fountain* bring

back memories of life in former East Berlin. The *Neptune Fountain* is located near the Rotes Rathaus (red Town Hall): the god of the sea, balancing with his tripod on a large shell seems to want to get a better view of things. Stretched out beneath him are four female figures representing the Rivers Oder, Weichsel, Rhine and Elbe. When Kaiser Wilhelm II. was presented with the fountain as a gift by its sculptor Reinhold Begas, the Emperor had it erected in front of the City Palace. It was only given this place near the Town Hall after it was restored in 1969. *Alexanderplatz | U/S Alexanderplatz | bus 100 Spandauer Straße*

8 FRIEDRICHSTRASSE (140 C1–6) *(🗺 K4–5)*

Friedrichstraße was already the place to go for some fun in the 1920s. The street, some 3.5 km (2 miles) long, that crosses the Mitte district from north to south is lined with theatres, cabarets and bars. Before the Reunification, the Berlin Wall cut the street in two and the border crossing here was the famous Checkpoint Charlie. Today, there are only a few sandbags piled up high and a control booth to remind you of this. Stylish business premises, such as the *Quartier 206* with its exclusive boutiques, now dominate the skyline. The *Galeries Lafayette*, with its glass atrium, is another architectural highlight. The *Friedrichstadtplast* was already famous for its revues when this area was still part of East Germany. *U/S Friedrichstraße*

9 FRIEDRICHSWERDERSCHE KIRCHE (141 D4) *(🗺 K4)*

Karl Friedrich Schinkel created one of the major German, neo-Gothic works with this church that was built between 1824 and 1830. Statues from the early 19th century line the interior. The main focus is on Classicist sculptures by Johann Gottfried Schadow, Christian Daniel Rauch and others. *Closed at the moment for structural engineering reasons | Werderscher Markt | U 2 Hausvogteiplatz*

10 GEDENKSTÄTTE BERLINER MAUER ● (146 B5) *(🗺 K2)*

A section of the original wall has been left standing. On the open-air site, listening stations offer information about tragic escape efforts and the former line of the border. The documentation centre shows an exhibition (newly devised in 2014) on everyday life on Bernauer Straße in the walled city that is no longer

BERLIN ON THE WATER

The most pleasant way to discover the historic Mitte or government districts is by taking a cruise. Numerous ships chug up and down the Spree all year long. The stops include the Museumsinsel, Friedrichstraße and the Haus der Kulturen der Welt. A round trip from Mitte via Kreuzberg to Charlottenburg and back to Mitte along the Spree and Landwehr Canal is particularly interesting. On this three-hour tour you will not only see most of the main sights in the city, the onboard "cityscape guide" (most of the time the captain himself) will also give you lots of information about everyday life and customs of the people of Berlin. *Information on sailing times and prices: tel. 030 5 36 36 00 | www.sternundkreis.de.*

Karl-Marx-Allee – the city's former monumental socialist boulevard

in Mitte but already part of the district of Wedding. *Tue–Sun April–Oct 9:30am–7pm, Nov–March 9:30am–6pm | admission free | Bernauer Str. 111 | www.berliner-mauer-gedenkstaette.de | S1, 2, 25 Nordbahnhof*

11 INSIDER TIP GEDENKSTÄTTE STILLE HELDEN (141 E2) *(🗺 L3)*

This impressive archive uses multimedia technology to present the biographies of Jews and those who protected them in the Third Reich. *Daily 10am–8 pm | admission free | Rosenthaler Str. 39 |www.gedenkstaette-stille-helden.de | S3, 5, 7, 75 Hackescher Markt*

12 GENDARMENMARKT ★ (141 D4–5) *(🗺 K4)*

With its buildings from the 18th and 19th centuries this is considered the most beautiful square in the city. The *Schauspielhaus*, which was built by Karl Friedrich Schinkel between 1818 and 1821 and now serves as a concert hall, and the Schiller Monument are framed by the Französische and Deutsche Dom. The *French Cathedral (tower April–Oct daily 10am–7 pm, Nov–March daily 10:30am–6:30pm, organ recital Tue–Fri 12:30pm, Huguenot Musem Tue–Sun noon–5pm | admission tower 3 euros, Huguenot Museum 2 euros | Gendarmenmarkt 5)* suffered severe damage during the war and was reconstructed in 1983. It was built between 1701 and 1705 for the 8,000 Huguenots living in the city at that time. An exhibition in the cathedral provides an information on the life of these Calvinist Protestants.

The 70 m (230 ft) high tower was built from 1780–85 and you have a magnificent view over the historical heart of Berlin from the top. The *German Cathedral* at the opposite side of the square is no longer used as a church today but as an exhibition space on German democratic history. *www.gendarmenmarkt.de | U6 Stadtmitte*

13 HACKESCHE HÖFE
(141 E2) *(🗺 L3)*

The Hackesche Höfe were built between 1905 and 1907 and this labyrinth of interconnecting courtyards has since become an architectural highlight. Restaurants, cinemas, galleries, a cabaret and boutiques have been set up in them. Many Jews used to live in the area with its long tradition as a centre of craft and retail businesses. The partially restored *New Synagogue* (see p. 38) on Oranienburger Straße bears witness to this past. *S 3, 5, 7, 75 Hackescher Markt*

14 HAMBURGER BAHNHOF
(151 E1) *(🗺 J3)*

The former railway station has been transformed into a museum with a total area of 140,000 square feet where especially art from the past 60 years is on display; most of the works were provided by the collector Erich Marx. The core of the collection is formed by works by Robert Rauschenberg, Roy Lichtenstein, Andy Warhol, Cy Twombly, Anselm Kiefer and Joseph Beuys and added to this an excellent permanent loan from the Flick Collection is shown in special exhibitions. *Tue–Fri 10am–6pm, Sat/Sun 11am–6pm | admission 8 euros, with special exhibitions 14 euros | Invalidenstr. 50/51 | www.hamburgerbahnhof.de | S/UHauptbahnhof*

15 INSIDER TIP KARL-MARX-ALLEE
(153 D–F 2–3) *(🗺 M–O 3–4)*

Not only the architecture of this boulevard, the longest listed ensemble of its kind in Germany, points towards Moscow. Socialist realism, also called the "Stalinist gingerbread style", can be seen on both sides of this impressive road built between 1952 and 1960 that is nearly 90 m (295 ft) wide. Only rubble was left of what was once Frankfurter Straße after the war. The symbol of this impressive avenue, with its housing blocks that are nearly 300 m (984 ft) long and up to 9 storeys high, are the two towers at Frankfurter Tor that were modelled on the towers of the cathedrals on Gendarmenmarkt. The buildings were mainly built using the rubble of bombed houses. On 17 June 1953, the worker's revolt that was brutally crushed flared up on this street which was called "Stalinallee" until 1961. *U 5 Frankfurter Tor*

16 MADAME TUSSAUDS BERLIN
(140 B4) *(🗺 J4)*

The famous wax museum near Brandenburger Tor has around 80 life-sized models, ranging from Berlin's former Lord Mayor Klaus Wowereit to Johnny Depp, Madonna and The Beatles, football stars and Angela Merkel. *Daily 10am–7pm (Aug until 8pm) | admission 22.95 euros, online ticket from 13.50 euros (tickets are up to 5 euros cheaper from the BVG ticket machines!) | Unter den Linden 74 | www.madametussauds.com | U/S Brandenburger Tor*

17 INSIDER TIP MUSEUM FÜR KOMMUNIKATION (140 C6) (Ⓜ K5)

The Museum for Communication is considered the oldest postal museum in the world. The visitor is presented with a fascinating exhibition including a computer gallery, interactive exhibits, robots, Philip Reis' first telephone apparatus and the most famous stamps ever: the red and the blue Mauritius. *Tue 9am–8pm, Wed–Fri 9am–5pm, Sat/Sun 10am–6pm | admission 4 euros | Leipziger Str. 16 | www.mfk-berlin.de | U 2, 6 Stadtmitte*

18 MUSEUM FÜR NATURKUNDE (140 A1) (Ⓜ J3)

This collection with more than 25 million zoological, paleontological, mineralogical and geological objects is world class. After its restoration, the famous INSIDER TIP original skeleton of the Brachiosaurus brancai – 23 m (75 ft) long and 13 m (43 ft) high – can once again be seen in all its glory. Hundreds of specimens provide an overview of our indigenous fauna. *Tue–Fri 9:30am–6pm, Sat/Sun 10am–6pm | admission 6 euros | Invalidenstr. 43 | www.naturkundemuseum-berlin.de | U 6 Naturkundemuseum*

19 MUSEUMSINSEL ★ ● (141 D–E 2–3) (Ⓜ K–L 3–4)

All museums *daily 10am–6pm, Thu until 8pm, Alte Nationalgalerie, Altes Museum, Bodemuseum closed Mon | www.smb.museum | S 3, 5, 7, 75 Hackescher Markt*

Etruscan, Greek and Roman art and sculpture is shown in the *Old Museum*. Stone sculptures and figures made of clay and bronze, friezes, vases, gold jewellery and precious silver will make you fully aware of the magnificence of this culture.

The restored *Bodemuseum*, with its splendid collection of sculptures, the Museum for Byzantine Art (with pictures from the early medieval period until the late 18th century) and collection of 500,000 rare coins, is the pride and joy of Berlin's residents.

After extensive restoration, the *National Gallery*, with its valuable paintings and sculptures from the 19th century, is now one of the most beautiful museum buildings in Berlin. Works by artists such as Menzel, Schadow and Blechen tell us a lot about the architecture, fashion and spirit of the Imperial period.

The *Pergamon Museum* was built between 1910 and 1930 specifically to house the Pergamon Altar that the engineer Carl Humann had discovered in Turkey in the 19th century and spent 20 years restoring. The sculptural frieze, 113 m (370 ft) long, is one of the great masterpieces of Hellenist art and shows the battle of the gods against the giants (closed until 2019 for restoration work). The majestic market gate from Milet (130 AD), a showpiece of Roman architecture, can be seen in an adjacent hall. The collections of Islamic and Near-Eastern art are also unique in the world. The almost 100-foot long tiled Processional Way of Babylon with its ornate depictions of lions is simply outstanding.

Since 2009, the world-famous, more than 3,000-year-old, bust of Nefertiti has been on display in the *Neue Museum* along with the Egyptian collection of the Prussian Cultural Property Foundation. The museum, which is one of the city's loveliest, was reconstructed and combined with modern elements to plans drawn up by David Chipperfield. The museum, built by Friedrich August Stüler between 1843 and 1855, was severely damaged in World War II and remained empty for 60 years. The partially restored wall paintings inside are another highlight.

20 NEUE SYNAGOGE (141 D2) (Ⓜ K3)

When it was consecrated in 1866, this was the largest synagogue in the world with

seating for 3,200 people. Today, the building on Oranienburger Straße is only used as a memorial site, for exhibitions and as a place of prayer. Once you have passed through security, you will find yourself in front of a glass wall which gives you a view of the former place of worship – today, this is a gravelled, open space. The synagogue was only saved from being burned to the ground on 9 November 1938 by the courageous intervention of a Berlin policeman. In 1943, a bombing raid almost completely destroyed it. The façade and golden dome, with a staircase leading up to it, were renovated since 1988. *March–Oct Sun/Mon 10am–8 pm, Tue–Thu 10am–6pm, Fri 10am–5pm (until 2pm Fri in March and Oct), Nov–Feb Sun–Thu 10am–6pm, Fri 10am–2pm | admission 3.50 euros, dome 2 euros | Oranienburger Str. 30 | www.cjudaicum.de | S 1, 2, 25 Oranienburger Straße*

21 NIKOLAI DISTRICT (141 E–F 3–4) *(🗺 L4)*

The *Nikolaiviertel* with the Nikolai Church to the south-east of Alexanderplatz is considered the birthplace of the city; this is where the first houses were built in the 13th century. At first glance, it appears that the buildings there today were constructed in the 18th and 19th centuries but most of them were actually built in the 1980s. *U 2 Klosterstraße*

22 ROTES RATHAUS (141 F3) *(🗺 L4)*

You can see the red-brick building that was built between 1861 and 1870 on Alexanderplatz from afar. The main building is in the style of the Italian Renaissance while the bell tower is modelled on Laon Cathedral in France. 36 panels depicting the history of Berlin can be seen on the first floor. The town hall suffered severe

Magnificent setting for a large collection: Egyptian section in the Neuen Museum

damage in World War II and became the seat of the East Berlin Council in 1958, the Senate of West Berlin taking up office in Schöneberg Town Hall. Since the Reunification of Germany, the Red Town Hall has once again become the seat for all Berlin. *Rathausstr. 15 | tel. 030 902 624 11 | www.berlin.de | U/S Alexanderplatz*

23 ST.-HEDWIGS-KATHEDRALE (141 D4) *(🗺 K4)*

At the beginning of the 18th century there were only 700 Catholics in Berlin. This increased to around 10,000 just 30 years later. They had fled to liberal Berlin in the wake of the Silesian Wars and, for that reason, the foundation stone for a new church, designed by the architect Jean Legeay together with the royal building director Johann Boumann the Elder, was laid in 1747. It was not until 1773 – almost 30 years after building had started – that the Baroque church could be used. It is modelled on the Pantheon in Rome. The cathedral suffered severe bomb damage in World War II but was reconstructed relatively quickly (1952 to 1963). *Mon–Sat 10am–5pm, Sun 1pm–5pm | free admission | Bebelplatz | U 2 Hausvogteiplatz | bus 100 Staatsoper*

24 UNTER DEN LINDEN ★ (140–141 B–D 3–4) *(🗺 J–K4)*

The boulevard, which begins at *Brandenburger Tor* and ends at *Berliner Dom*, has still not lost any of its importance as Berlin's intellectual and artistic centre – this is not least due to the Museumsinsel. Starting in the 18th century, this was the site of the *Kronprinzenpalais*, the *Zeughaus*, as well as the *Staatsoper* and today's *Humboldt-Universität*. At the end of the 19th century, the *Berliner Dom* was constructed in the Wilhelmine style. The boulevard was completely devastated during World War II. With the exception of the royal City Palace whose remains the East Berlin city council had blown up

Form and function in harmony: Bauhaus-Archiv in the Tiergarten

in 1950, all other buildings have been restored or replaced. The palace on the banks of the Spree was replaced by the *Palast der Republik*; during the East German era this was an important national cultural centre. It has now been demolished and the former royal palace is being reconstructed on its original site. The information centre *Humboldtbox* provides information on the building site and shows a INSIDER TIP model of the city centre. *U/S Brandenburger Tor*

TIERGARTEN

Joggers' favourite park, parliament buildings and a shopping paradise – hardly any other district is as varied as Tiergarten.

You have the best panoramic view of the city from the dome of the Reichstag building from where you can see the striking tented roof of the Sony Center on Potsdamer Platz and the Quadriga, the chariot that crowns Brandenburger Tor. To the west, the golden goddess Victoria on Victory Column beckons over the treetops. Berlin's "green lung", the park which gives this district its name, not only offers the city's stressed residents recreation but also cultural highlights such as the Philharmonie and ● INSIDER TIP concerts in summer in the *English Garden* or Indian pop bands in the House of Cultures of the World.

1 BAUHAUS-ARCHIV (151 D5) *(Ⓜ H5)*

Fascinating collection on the history of the Bauhaus: furniture, works of art, design by Ludwig Mies van der Rohe, Walter Gropius and others. Gropius designed the museum itself in 1964. *Wed–Mon 10am–5pm | admission Sat–Mon 7, Wed–Fri 6 euros | Klingelhöfer Str. 14 | www.bauhaus.de | bus 100 Lützowplatz*

2 EMBASSY DISTRICT (150–151 C–D 4–5) *(Ⓜ G–H5)*

Many embassies have been re-established to the south of the Tiergarten. Diplomats resided here before World War II but only the renovated Japanese and Italian embassies still keep up the tradition from that time. The new embassies of Sweden, Norway, Iceland, Denmark and Finland are architectural highlights in their own right. They share a building complex (Embassies of the Nordic Countries) that also has a community house, restaurant and exhibition rooms. The Mexican Embassy next door, on the other hand, is an avant-garde building with a 18 m (60 ft) high foyer, a rooftop garden and a spectacular façade. All of these embassies consider a cultural programme that is available to the general public as being particularly important and organise regular exhibitions, concerts and readings. *Embassy of the Nordic Countries (Community House Mon–Fri 10am–7pm, Sat/Sun 11am–4pm | Rauchstr. 1 | tel. 030 5 05 00 | www.nordicembassies.org); Embassy of the United States of Mexico (exhibition hall Mon–Fri 9am–4:30pm | Klingelhöferstr. 3 | tel. 030 2 69 32 30 | embamex.sre.gob.mx/alemania | bus 100 Nord-Botschaften)*

3 BRANDENBURGER TOR ★ ● (140 A–B4) *(Ⓜ J4)*

A million spectators cheered when Berlin's landmark was unveiled on 3 October 2002 after years of restoration work. The people of Berlin are really attached to the emblem of their city that was first named "Peace Gate". The 20 m (66 ft)high monument has adorned Pariser Platz since 1791; it was built to plans by the architect Carl Gotthard Langhans who took the Acropolis in Athens as a model. The Goddess of Victory, driving her four horses onwards, is regarded as the harbinger of peace.

After his successful campaign, Napoleon humiliated Berlin in 1806 by taking the Quadriga back to Paris. It was not until eight years later, after the War of Liberation, that it was returned to its original location. Victoria was decorated with an Iron Cross, laurel wreath and Prussian eagle in memory of the battle against Napoleon.

Brandenburger Tor was severely damaged during World War II and the city administrations of East and West Berlin used old plaster models to create a copy of the Quadriga. However, the East German government insisted that the Iron Cross and Prussian eagle be removed and a staff with a wreath of oak leaves placed in the Goddess of Victory's hand. Only after the Reunification of Germany could the old symbols be reinstated. *Pariser Platz | U/S Brandenburger Tor*

The four horses on Brandenburger Tor pulling the Goddess of Victory's chariot

4 DENKMAL FÜR DIE ERMORDETEN JUDEN EUROPAS (140 A–B 4–5) *(🕮 J4)*

The Holocaust Memorial was inaugurated in 2005. Following plans drawn up by the New York architect Peter Eisenman, 2,711 rectangular columns of various heights, called steles, were set up in rows covering an area of just over 4½ acres. You can enter the complex from all sides and its wave-like shape is perceived differently from wherever you are. A detailed and moving exhibition in the underground *information centre (April–Sept Tue–Sun 10am–8pm, Oct–March 10am–7pm)* is a must. *Wilhelmstr. 1/Behrenstr. | www.stiftung-denkmal.de | U/S Potsdamer Platz*

5 GEDENKSTÄTTE DEUTSCHER WIDERSTAND (151 D5) *(🕮 H5)*

A new permanent exhibition gives an insight into how individuals and groups struggled against the Nazi dictatorship 1933–45

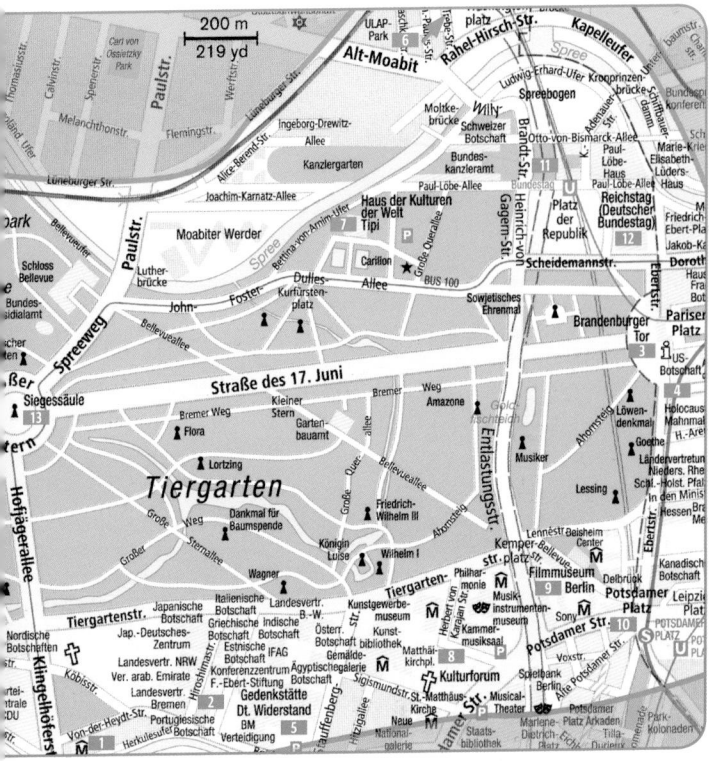

SIGHTSEEING IN TIERGARTEN

1. Bauhaus-Archiv
2. Embassy district
3. Brandenburger Tor
4. Denkmal für die ermordeten Juden Europas
5. Gedenkstätte Deutscher Widerstand
6. Hauptbahnhof (main station)
7. Haus der Kulturen der Welt
8. Kulturforum
9. Mus. für Film und Fernsehen
10. Potsdamer Platz
11. Regierungsviertel
12. Reichstag
13. Siegessäule

and made use of the limited possibilities they had. *Mon–Wed, Fri 9am–6pm, Thu 9am–8pm, Sat/Sun 10am–6pm | admission free | Stauffenbergstr. 13 | www.gdw-berlin.de | U 2 Mendelssohn-Bartholdy-Park*

6 HAUPTBAHNHOF (151 E2) *(🕮 J3)*

The largest station in Europe opened in 2006 and was built to designs by the Hamburg architectural practice Gerkan & Partner. Glass and steel are the main elements of the imposing multi-storey building with its many shopping malls and underground tracks running from north to south. More than 1,000 trains pass through here every day; 300,000 passengers and visitors crowd the place. *Europaplatz | U/S Hauptbahnhof*

7 HAUS DER KULTUREN DER WELT (151 E3) *(🕮 H4)*

This former congress hall was erected for the 1957 Building Exhibition and aroused international interest with its daringly curved roof that led to Berlin residents giving it the nickname of the "pregnant oyster". The building has been used by the Federal Government as the "House of the Cultures of the World" since 1989. Its culture festivals and events focussing on individual countries have underscored its high international reputation. *John-Foster-Dulles-Allee 10 | www.hkw.de | bus 100 Haus der Kulturen der Welt*

8 KULTURFORUM (151 E 4) *(🕮 H5)*

All museums: *admission 6–10 euros | www.smb.museum | U/S Potsdamer Platz*

Several of the most important works of European painting from the 13th to 18th centuries are united in the *Gemäldegalerie (Tue–Fri 10am–6pm, Thu until 8pm, Sat/Sun 11am–6pm | Stauffenbergstr. 40)* opened in 1998. The individual artistic landscapes and epochs are presented in 72 main rooms and smaller exhibition spaces with 1,400 works of art. The main focus of the collection is on Italian painting from the 14th to 18th centuries (including works by Caravaggio, Botticelli and Raphael) and 15th and 16th century Dutch art.

Treasures from Baroque art, Delft faïence and Baroque glass are just a few of the highlights displayed in the *Kunstgewerbemuseum (Tue–Fri 10am–6pm | Tiergartenstr. 6)*. European porcelain – especially Meissen and KPM – decorative utensils and tableware from the Rococo, Classicist and Jugendstil periods, gold and silver articles as well as costumes and silks can also be marvelled at.

Around 800 of the more than 3,000 European musical instruments from the 16th to 20th centuries in the collection have been on display in the *Musikinstrumenten-Museum (Tue–Fri 9am–5pm, Thu until 8pm, Sat/Sun 10am–5pm | Tiergartenstr. 1)* since 1984. The ensemble of wind instruments from St Wenzel zu Naumburg from the first half of the 17th century is unique, as is one of Bach's harpsichords. You can even try out some instruments and there is a performance on the more than 80-year-old Wurlitzer cinema organ every Sunday at noon.

RELAX AND ENJOY

The ● *Liquidrom* **(152 A5)** *(🕮 J5–6) (Sun–Thu 10am–midnight, Fri/Sat 10am–1am | day ticket 29.50 euros | Kreuzberg | Möckernstr. 10 | tel. 030 2 58 00 78 20 | www.liquidrom-berlin.de | U 1, 7 Möckernbrücke)* in the Tempodrom not only scores with its unique architecture. You can float weightlessly in a saltwater tub in a kind of grotto and listen to the dulcet tones of the water that coloured lights turn all colours of the rainbow. In the evening, DJs work the turntables at the edge of the pool – the music ranges from classical to downbeat.

An Oriental Turkish-style steam bath on 1000 m² of space at the ● *Sultan Hamam* **(159 E1)** *(🕮 H6) (Tue–Sat 9:30am–11pm women only, Mon noon–11pm for men, Sun family day noon–11pm | 3 hrs 16 euros | Schöneberg | Bülowstr. 57 | tel. 030 21 75 33 75 | U 2 Bülowstraße)*. Bath towels and slippers can be borrowed.

Roof-covered plaza: Sony Center at the Potsdamer Platz

20th century European painting and sculpture, from classical modern art to the 1960s, is the main focus of the exhibition in the *Neue Nationalgalerie (closed until 2018 | Potsdamer Straße 50)* that is housed in a low building designed by Mies van der Rohe. Works by Kirchner, Picasso, Klee, Feininger, Dix, Kokoschka and other masters are on display. Particular emphasis is placed on Cubism, Expressionism, the Bauhaus and Surrealism.

9 MUSEUM FÜR FILM UND FERNSEHEN (140 A6) *(🗺 J5)*

The museum exhibits costumes, props, posters, photos, film footage etc. from the beginnings of the German film industry to the modern day. It also focuses on modern film animations, special effects and virtual worlds. In the TV section, you can rediscover old TV series and quiz shows from the last 60 years! *Tue–Sun 10am–6pm, Thu until 8pm | admission 7 euros | Potsdamer Str. 2 | tel. 030 3 00 90 30 | www.deutsche-kinemathek.de | U-/S Potsdamer Platz*

10 POTSDAMER PLATZ (140 A–B6) *(🗺 J4)*

This complex in the heart of the city with a shopping centre, cinemas, a musical theatre, casino, hotels and film museum on the west side of Potsdamer Platz was first opened in 1995 – the original buildings on the site were bombed flat during World War II. The tent-like roof Helmut Jahn designed for the ★ ● *Sony Center* is stunning. Depending on the weather, this is the perfect place for people-watching or for simply sitting on one of the café terraces. In the *Kollhoff Tower*, Europe's fastest lift propels visitors up to the INSIDER TIP viewing platform *(daily 10am–8pm; until 6pm in winter | 6.50 euros)* with a panorama café *(www.panoramapunkt.de)* 93 m (305 ft) above the ground in a mere 20 seconds. *U/S Potsdamer Platz*

11 REGIERUNGSVIERTEL (140 A–B 3–4) (🗺 J4–5)

A string of modern government buildings has sprung up to the west and east of the Reichstag. Plans for the Federal Chancellery (completed in 2001) were drawn up by the architects Axel Schulte and Charlotte Frank who were also responsible for the overall plan of the government district. Its box-like design has led to the Chancellery becoming popularly known as the "Federal (or Chancellor's) washing machine". The four interlinked arms of Eduardo Chillida's 18-foot-high steel sculpture "Berlin" in front of the portal symbolise German unity. The *Paul Löbe House* to the north of the Reichstag building was named after the Reichstag President in the years 1924–32. It has 21 conference halls and 550 rooms for the 275 members of parliament and their staff. Its counterpart on the other side of the Spree is the *Marie Elisabeth Lüders House*. It was named after a Reichstag representative, is currently being expanded and houses the Parliament Library – the third largest of its kind in the world. The so-called *Ministers' Garden* to the north-east of Potsdamer Platz, where several of the federal states have their delegations, is also architecturally interesting.

12 REICHSTAG ★ (140 A3–4) (🗺 J4)

The glass dome, added to the Reichstag building that was originally built by Paul Wallot between 1884 and 1894, has made it a real crowd-puller since the mid-nineties. Visitors have to register in advance with the *Bundestag* for a tour or reserve a table in the *Käfer Restaurant* on the roof if they want to enjoy a walk up the spiral slope inside the dome. From up there, you have a

Architecture for the 21st century: the office buildings for the members of the Bundestag

fantastic view over the government district, the main railway station and the rest of Berlin, particularly spectacular after nightfall. Down below, members of the German parliament hold their debates and you can watch them at work through the glass roof. The Reichstag was set ablaze in 1933 and severely damaged in battles to regain control of Berlin. It was reconstructed between 1961 and 1972 to house an exhibition on German history, now on display in the German Cathedral. In 1990, the first parliament of a reunified Germany was constituted here. The architect Norman Foster's plans for the building led to it being gutted and crowned with a glass dome to make it suitable for its modern-day purpose. *Daily 8am–midnight, last admission 10pm; visits to the dome only by appointment (best online) at least 2 hours in advance, also possible on site | Bundestag Visitors' Service (guided tours and visits to plenary sessions) | Platz der Republik 1 | tel. 030 22 73 21 252 | www.bundestag.de | bus 100 Reichstag*

13 SIEGESSÄULE (150 C4) *(🗺 G4)*

The 67 m (220 ft) high national monument once adorned the square in front of the Reichstag. In order to have more space for his "Reichshauptstadt Germania", Hitler had the golden statue of Victoria – which is affectionately known as "Gold Else" – moved to the Große Stern in Tiergarten. The Victory Column was designed by Heinrich Strack to commemorate the victory over the Danes and erected between 1864 and 1873. There is a fine view of the city from the observation platform. *April–Oct Mon–Fri 9:30am–6:30pm, Sat/Sun 9:30am–7pm, Nov–March Mon–Fri 10am– 5pm, Sat/Sun 10am–5:30pm | admission 3 euros | Großer Stern | bus 100 Großer Stern*

PRENZLAUER BERG/FRIEDRICHSHAIN

There are more organic-ice cream shops here than anywhere else and, in summer, the playgrounds are so crowded you will feel like you are in China.

It comes as no surprise that statistics show that the districts of *Prenzlauer Berg* and *Friedrichshain* are among those with the most children in Europe. You will see large numbers of young people – not least because of the exciting nightlife, especially in Friedrichshain. Hardly anywhere else in the city will you find as many bars, restaurants, clubs and pubs. Students and an increasing number of well-heeled professionals live in Friedrichshain, and Prenzlauer Berg has

long been one of the preferred residential areas for highly paid academics. Many of the inhabitants of the two districts flock to the Volkspark in Friedrichshain on weekends to chill out, skate, go for a walk or have a game of beach volleyball.

1 EASTSIDE GALLERY ●
(154 B2) *(🗺 N5)*
The largest open-air gallery in the world stretches from the Ostbahnhof to Oberbaum Bridge. 118 artists have immortalised themselves here on 1,316 m (4,318 ft) of Berlin Wall. The best-known works are "My God, Help Me To Survive This Deadly Love" by Dmitri Vrubel and Gerhard Lahr's "Berlin–New York". *Friedrichshain | Mühlenstraße | www.eastsidegallery.com | U/S Ostbahnhof*

Buskers in Friedrichshain

2 KOLLWITZPLATZ (147 D4) *(🗺 L–M2)*
Avoiding destruction almost completely, this ensemble of houses around the square is one of the loveliest groups of historical buildings in Berlin. The square was named after the painter and graphic artist Käthe Kollwitz who lived here with her husband from 1891 to 1943. In a small park, a monument created by the sculptor Gustav Seitz in 1958, modelled on a self-portrait, acts as a memorial to the famous resident. Many other famous people live or have lived on Kollwitzplatz, which is also known for its weekly market and its many cafés and restaurants. *Prenzlauer Berg | U 2 Senefelderplatz*

3 KULTURBRAUEREI (147 D4) *(🗺 L2)*
The former Schultheiss Brewery has established itself as a cultural centre. The courtyard ensemble is alive day and night thanks to its large cinema, its halls for concerts and other events, as well as any number of clubs, restaurants and shops. Interesting: the new INSIDER TIP *Documentation centre of everyday culture of the GDR (Tue–Sun 10am–6pm, Thu 10am–8pm | free admission)*. The building, constructed in yellow brick that is so typical of Berlin, was erected between 1890 and 1910 to plans drawn up by the royal architect Franz Schwechten who also designed the Kaiser Wilhelm Memorial Church. *Prenzlauer Berg | Knaackstr. 75–97 | U 2 Eberswalder Straße*

4 MAUERPARK
(146 C3–4) *(🗺 K–L 1–2)*
Many dogs and many more adults and children have a great time in this park on what used to be the border between East and West Berlin. Today, graffiti artists try out their talents on a remaining piece

200 m
219 yd
Schmeling-Halle
Fried.-Ludwig-Jahn-Sportpark
Eberswalder Str.
Danziger Str.
Schönhauser Allee
Kulturbrauerei
Kollwitzplatz
Wörther Str.
Prenzlauer Allee
Senefelder-platz
Metzer Str.
Greifswalder Str.
Prenzlauer Berg
Platz am Königstor
Volkspark Friedrichshain
Märchenbrunnen
Platz der Vereinten Nationen
Helmholtz platz
Planetarium
Rathaus Prenzlauer Berg
Städtisches Krankenhaus
Ellaskirche
Stadtbibliothek
Ernst-Thälmann-Park
Zionskirche
Herz-Jesu-Kirche
Immanuel-kirche
Wasserturm
Jüdischer Friedhof
Segenskirche
Pfefferberg
St.-Bartholom.-Kirche
Schwimmhalle
Statistisches Bundesamt
BM für Umwelt, Naturschutz und Reaktorsicherheit
Haus der
Kaufhof am Alex
Hackescher Markt
HACKESCHER MARKT
Neue Schönhauser
Rosa-Luxemburg-Platz
Torstr.
Mollstr.
Otto-Braun-Str.
Münzstr.
Weinmeister Str.
Linienstr.
Volksbühne
Sportpalast
Stadtbibliothek
Arbeitsamt
Fröbelplatz
Kollwitzstr.
Knaackstr.
Husemann
Christburger
Marienburger Str.
Winsstr.
Raabestr.
Heinrich-Roller-Str.
Kolmarer Str.
Belforter
Dieterichstr.
Mühlstr.
Esmarchstr.
Hufelandstr.
Käthe-Niederkirchner-Str.
Bötzowstr.
Lessing-Str.
Hermann-Str.
Saarbrücker Str.
Straßburger Str.
Lottum-Str.
Christinen-Str.
Rykestr.
Choriner Str.
Oderberger
Kremmener Str.
Fürstenberger Str.
Wörther Str.
Grüntaler Str.
Schwedter Str.
Kastanienallee
Zionskirchstr.
Fehrbelliner Str.
Teutoburger Platz
Senefelder-Platz
SENEFELDER-PLATZ
Greifswalder Str.
Prenzlauer Allee
Schönhauser Allee
Danziger Str.
Eberswalder Str.
Oderberger
Kulturbrauerei
Knaackstr.
Husemann
Kollwitzstr.
Sredzkistr.
Christburger
Choriner Str.
Wörther Str.
Kollwitz-platz
Handw.-kammer
Jüdischer Friedhof
Wasserturm
Immanuel-kirche
Belforter
Kolmarer Str.
Mühlstr.
Raabestr.
Winsstr.
Heinrich-Roller-Str.
Metzer Str.
Straßburger Str.
Saarbrücker Str.
Teutoburger Platz
Pfefferberg
Senefelder-platz
SENEFELDER-PLATZ
Herz-Jesu-Kirche
Zionskirche
Segenskirche
Lottum-Str.
Christinen-Str.
Rykestr.
Choriner Str.
Oderberger
Kremmener Str.
Fehrbelliner Str.
Zionskirchstr.
Greifswalder Str.
Prenzlauer Allee
Prenzlauer Berg
Platz am Königstor
BUS 200
Am Friedrichshain
Volkspark
Friedrichshain
Märchenbrunnen
Schwimmhalle
St.-Bartholom.-Kirche
Hochstr.
Friedenstr.
Weinstr.
Bänningstr.
Büschingstr.
Georgen-kirchstr.
Mollstr.
Otto-Braun-Str.
Statistisches Bundesamt
BM für Umwelt, Naturschutz und Reaktorsicherheit
LKA
Casino Berlin
Haus der
Kaufhof am Alex
Hackescher Markt
HACKESCHER MARKT
Neue Schönhauser
Münzstr.
Dircksen
Torstr.
Rosa-Luxemburg-Platz
Linienstr.
Volksbühne
Sportpalast
Stadtbibliothek
Arbeitsamt
Fröbelplatz
Kollwitzstr.
Knaackstr.
Husemann
Christburger
Marienburger Str.
Winsstr.
Raabestr.
Heinrich-Roller-Str.
Kolmarer Str.
Belforter
Dieterichstr.
Mühlstr.
Esmarchstr.
Hufelandstr.
Käthe-Niederkirchner-Str.
Bötzowstr.
Lessing-Str.
Hermann-Str.
Saarbrücker Str.
Straßburger Str.

where Friedrichshain, Treptow and Kreuzberg merge. *Eichenstr. | S Treptower Park*

6 OBERBAUMBRÜCKE (154 B2) *(Ⓜ N5)*

The bridge with its elevated railway tracks, street and covered walkway over the Spree unites Friedrichshain and Kreuzberg. It is considered a masterpiece of 19th century architecture and was constructed for a trade exhibition in 1896. The name "Oberbaum", "upper barrier", comes from the days when customs officials blocked shipping lanes here with a barrier so that they could collect their tolls. The Spanish architect Santiago Calatrava designed the new middle section when the bridge was renovated in the 1990s. *Friedrichshain | U1 Schlesisches Tor*

7 VOLKSPARK FRIEDRICHSHAIN (153 F 1) *(Ⓜ M–N3)*

The 128-acre Volkspark Friedrichshain in the north is where people go to race their skateboards through the half-pipe while their parents and younger brothers and sisters relax near the ● INSIDER TIP *Märchenbrunnen*. Not only children love this fountain that was first filled with water in 1913; arches frame stone bowls with cascades, characters from Grimm's fairy tales and balustrades with animal figures. An open-air cinema at the park's east side attracts visitors to the park at night in summer. You can also enjoy a Pils in the beer garden or coffee and cake in its restaurant *(www.schoenbrunn.net)* at the park's Schwanenteich (swan pond). *Friedrichshain | bus 142, 200 Am Friedrichshain*

KREUZBERG

There is a touch of the exotic in the air: the Turkish way-of-life dominates in the north-east of the district in particular – with Turkish cafés (for men only), vegetable shops, markets and bakeries.

The Oberbaumbrücke connects Kreuzberg and Friedrichshain

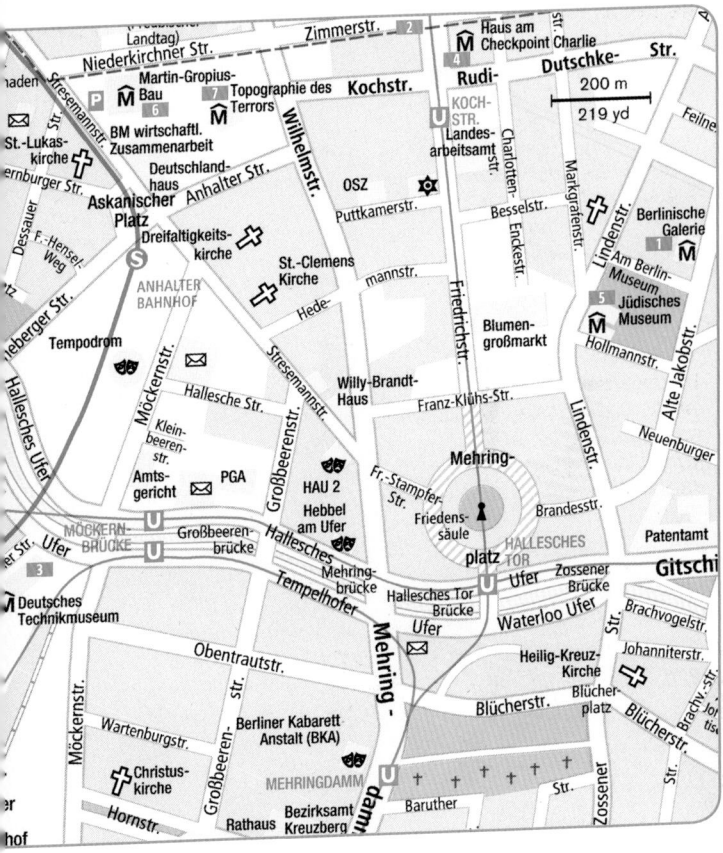

SIGHTSEEING IN KREUZBERG

1 Berlinische Galerie
2 Black Box Kalter Krieg
3 Deutsches Technikmuseum
4 Haus am Checkpoint Charlie
5 Jüdisches Museum
6 Martin-Gropius-Bau
7 Topographie des Terrors

pedestrian precinct

And, in between, there are any number of bars, restaurants and clubs for German-Turkish bohemians to let their hair down. Many young people live in the area around Oranienstraße and Oranienplatz – a centre of West Berlin alternative culture while the wall was still standing – and the choice of bars and pubs is correspondingly large.

Well-off academics have moved into the chic, renovated factory lofts along the river banks on Fraenkel and Paul-Linke Ufer. A large weekly market is held on Tuesdays and Fridays on the other side of the river, on Maybachufer. The many Turkish stall-holders and their customers create a bazaar-like atmosphere.

1 INSIDER TIP BERLINISCHE GALERIE (152 C5) (🗺 K5)

You will be dazzled by the works of the so-called "Neue Wilden" that evolved around Rainer Fetting, and those of the "old"Expressionists in the State Gallery for Modern Art. New Realism is represented with works by Otto Dix and George Grosz. Also special exhibitions. *Wed–Mon 10am–6pm | admission 8 euros | Alte Jakobstr. 124–28 | www.berlinischegalerie.de | U 1, 6, 15 Hallesches Tor*

2 BLACK BOX KALTER KRIEG (152 B4) (🗺 K5)

A 240 square yards big black information box documents the recent German history: starting with the allied victory, followed by the armament and ending with the fall of the communist regime. A map shows the division of Berlin into four sectors by the victorious powers. *Daily 10am–6pm | admission 5 euros | Friedrichstr. 47/ corner of Zimmermannstr. | www.bfgg.de/zentrum-kalter-krieg | U 6 Kochstraße*

The Jüdische Museum also tracks the fates of individuals

3 DEUTSCHES TECHNIKMUSEUM (151 F6) (🗺 J6)

Young and old will be delighted by this collection of historical vehicles, instruments and inventions. You will really need more than a day if you want to visit the engine shed with its historic locomotives and the shipping section with 1,500 exhibits. In *Spectrum (Möckernstr. 26)* 150 experiments explain technical principles. The large plane collection in the aviation section is really impressive. *Tue–Fri 9am–5:30pm, Sat/Sun 10am–6pm | admission 6 euros | Trebbiner Str. 9 | www.sdtb.de | U 1, 2 Gleisdreieck*

4 HAUS AM CHECKPOINT CHARLIE (140 C6) (🗺 K5)

Permanent exhibition on the construction of the Wall and division of the city. Documentation of attempts to escape and the vehicles used for this: from mini-submarines to a hot-air balloon. *Daily 9am–10pm | admission 12.50 euros | Friedrichstr. 43 | www.mauer-museum.com | U 6 Kochstraße*

5 JÜDISCHES MUSEUM BERLIN ★ (152 B–C5) (🗺 K5)

The permanent exhibition in the spectacular building designed by the New York architect Daniel Libeskind that is connected to the old Baroque building shows 2,000 years of Jewish culture. Multimedia technology, lighting effects and the unorthodox layout of the exhibition rooms create an emotional connection between the visitors and exhibits. One of the many subjects dealt with is the history of the persecution of Jews in Germany from the early Middle Ages to

the present day. The glass plaza was created in 2007 by roofing over the former central courtyard. *Mon 10am–10pm, Tue–Sun 10am–8pm | admission 8 euros | Lindenstr. 9–14 | www.jmberlin.de | U 1, 6, 15 Hallesches Tor*

6 MARTIN-GROPIUS-BAU (152 A4) *(🗺 J5)*

Originally a museum for arts and crafts, this magnificent building with its beautiful reliefs and mosaics which was erected between 1877 and 1881 to plans drawn up by Martin Gropius (Walter Gropius' great-uncle) and Heino Schmieden, now serves as an atmospheric location for art and history exhibitions. *Wed–Mon 10am–7pm | different admission fees for the various exhibitions | Niederkirchner Str. 7 | www.gropiusbau.de | S 1, 25 Anhalter Bahnhof*

7 TOPOGRAPHIE DES TERRORS (152 A4) *(🗺 J5)*

An open-air exhibition on the site of the former centre of power of the National Socialist, SS police state provides information on the atrocities that were planned and organised here. There are display boards showing pictures of executed politicians and resistance fighters. A new documentation centre was opened here in 2010. *Daily 10am–8pm | free admission | guided tours by appointment | Niederkirchner Str. 8 | www.topographie.de | S 1, 25 Anhalter Bahnhof*

CHARLOTTENBURG/WILMERSDORF

Shopping district, gourmet quarter and culture – all of this is concentrated in the districts of Charlottenburg between KaDeWe and Schloss Charlottenburg, and Wilmersdorf to the south of Ku'damm. The number of restaurants around Savignyplatz must break all records, while the castle park is teeming with joggers and museum visitors. Kurfürstendamm is still the traditional shopping strip for the better-heeled, while the younger crowd gather in the shade of the Memorial Church and shop in the new designer shop centre Bikini-Haus. With the Theater des Westens, Schaubühne, German Opera and Schiller Theatre (the State Opera's temporary home until at least 2016), Charlottenburg competes with the theatres in the east of the city. Wilmersdorf attracts people with its numerous traditional, speciality shops.

1 FUNKTURM (148 B5) *(🗺 C5)*

Modelled on the Eiffel Tower in Paris, but considerably smaller, the Berlin counterpart was erected on the Fair grounds in 1926 and was considered the modern landmark of Berlin for many years. Especially in the divided city the 138 m (453 ft) "beanpole" – as the locals called it – became a symbol for the inhabitants of West Berlin. There is a restaurant 55 m (180 ft) above ground level and a viewing platform 71 m (233 ft) feet higher up. The transmission mast at the top of the tower is used for the police radio. As the tower is often closed for servicing, it is wise to call before you make a visit. *Mon 10am–8pm, Tue–Sun 10am–11pm | admission 5 euros | Charlottenburg | Messedamm | tel. 030 30 38 19 05 | www.funkturm-messeberlin.de | S 7, 41, 42 Messe Nord | U 2 Kaiserdamm*

2 KAISER-WILHELM-GEDÄCHTNIS-KIRCHE (139 E4) *(🗺 G5)*

The bleak ruins of the tower of the church erected between 1891 and 1895 in memory of Kaiser Wilhelm I point into the sky like a warning finger. After it was almost completely destroyed in World War II, church

officials decided to at least leave its tower standing. Between 1958 and 1961 a modern octagonal church constructed of 16,000 blue glass bricks, designed by Egon Eiermann, was erected adjacent to it. There is an exhibition on the history of the church on the ground floor of the tower. *Daily 9am–7pm, Memorial Hall Mon–Fri 10am–6pm, Sat 10am–5:30pm, Sun noon–5:30pm, church concert Sat 6pm | Charlottenburg | Kurfürstendamm 237 | www.gedaechtniskirche-berlin.de | U/S Zoologischer Garten*

3 KURFÜRSTENDAMM ●
(149 D–F6) *(🗺 D–F 5–6)*

Before Reunification, this shopping boulevard was the epitome of (West) Berlin's metropolitan flair. Recently, many eyesores from the 1960s have been demolished and new complexes including the *Kranzlereck*, with offices, shops and a café, have since opened. New hotels and trendy shops are attracting young people back to the shopping mile. The boulevard was laid out as a 3.5 km (2 miles) ride

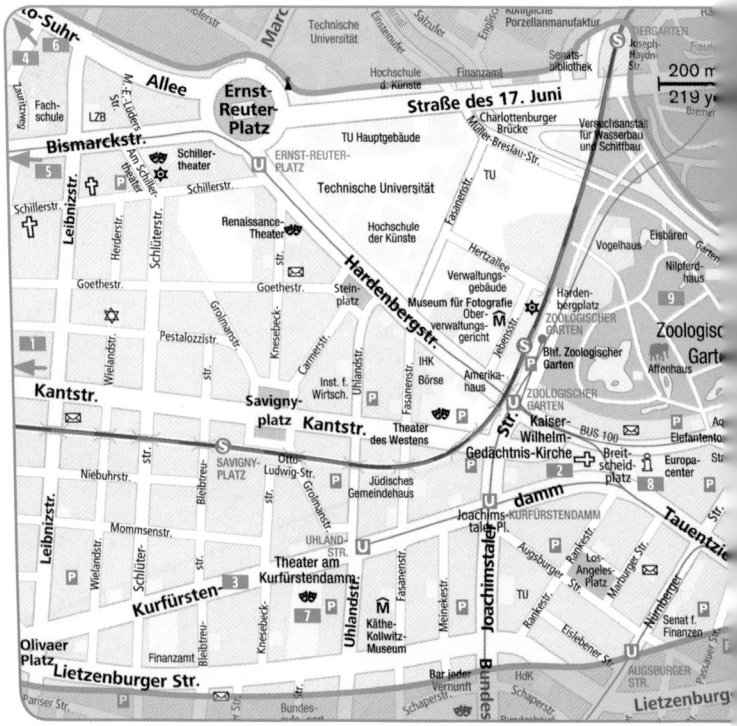

SIGHTSEEING IN CHARLOTTENBURG AND WILMERSDORF

1 Funkturm
2 Kaiser-Wilh.-Gedächtniskirche
3 Kurfürstendamm
4 Museum Berggruen
5 Olympiastadium
6 Schloss Charlottenburg
7 The Story of Berlin
8 Weltkugelbrunnen
9 Zoologischer Garten

between 1883 and 1886 and some houses still bear witness to the opulent turn-of-the-century architecture around 1900. *Charlottenburg | U 1, 9 Kurfürstendamm*

4 MUSEUM BERGGRUEN (148 C3) *(🗺 D4)*

Works by Picasso and Paul Klee form the core of this collection assembled by the art dealer Heinz Berggruen. Early works, as well as paintings, sculptures and works on paper, are exhibited under the title "Picasso and his Time" on three floors in this magnificent building designed by Stüler. Beautiful sculpture garden. *Tue–Fri 10am–6pm, Sat/Sun 11am–6pm | admission 10 euros | Charlottenburg | Schlossstr. 1 | www.smb.museum | S 41, 42 Westend*

5 OLYMPIASTADIUM (164 C3) *(🗺 A–B4)*

Germany's second largest stadium has space for 75,000 spectators. It was built to plans by the architect Werner March for the 1936 Olympic Games and, today, is mainly used for the games of the Hertha BSC football club. The National Socialist architecture had suffered greatly over the years and the stadium was completely renovated for the 2006 Football World Championship. All seats are now protected from the weather. *Daily 9am–7pm, in winter until 4pm, June–15 Sept 9am–8pm | tours of the stadium daily 11am, end of March–Oct also 1pm, 3pm, June–Aug also 5pm, except when Hertha BSC is playing or other events are on | admission without tour guide 7 euros, including guide 10 euros | Charlottenburg | Olympischer Platz 3 | tel. 030 25 00 23 22 | www.olympiastadion-berlin.de | U 2 Olympiastadion*

6 SCHLOSS CHARLOTTENBURG ★ (148–149 C–D 2–3) *(🗺 D4)*

The more than 300-year-old summer residence of the Electress Sophie Charlotte not only impresses with the French-style landscape architecture of its garden but with its grand architecture from the 17th and 18th centuries. The apartments of Friedrich I and his wife are open to the public. The mausoleum of Queen Luise, the wife of Friedrich Wilhelm III, is at the far end of the park. *Old Palace April–Oct Tue–Sun 10am–6pm (Nov–March until 5pm), New Wing April–Oct Wed–Mon 10am–6pm (Nov–March until 5pm), Belvedere (KPM Porcelain Collection) and Mausoleum April–Oct Tue–Sun 10am–6pm, New Pavilion (art and crafts of the Romantic movement) Tue–Sun 10am–5pm, in summer until 6pm | admission: Palace 12 euros, New Wing 6 euros, Belvedere 3 euros, New Pavilion 4 euros, Mausoleum 2 euros |Charlottenburg | Spandauer Damm 10–22 | www.spsg.de | Bus 145 Luisenplatz*

Gedächtniskirche with the modern extension designed by Egon Eiermann

7 THE STORY OF BERLIN (150 A6) *(🗺 F5)*
Going around the 24 rooms will seem like a journey through time during which you will find out a great deal about the history of Berlin. Young people in particular will be fascinated by all the hi-tech and multimedia installations. *Daily 10am–8pm, last admission 6pm | admission 12 euros | Charlottenburg | Kurfürstendamm 207 | www.story-of-berlin.de | U 1 Uhlandstraße*

8 WELTKUGELBRUNNEN (139 E4) *(🗺 G5)*
The Berlin sculptor Joachim Schmettau created this fountain on Breitscheidplatz in 1983. It has since become a popular spot not far from the Memorial Church and Europacenter. Its massiveness led locals to christen it the "Water Meatball". However, the granite globe with its arched openings is not particularly clunky at all. Instead, a dazzling spectacle is created by the interaction of flowing water, figures and cascades. *Charlottenburg | U/S Zoologischer Garten*

9 ZOOLOGISCHER GARTEN (139 E–F 3–4) *(🗺 F–G5)*
The 160-year-old zoo is the oldest in Germany and – with its 13,700 animals of 1,388 species – the most diverse in the world. Just one highlight: the ● *aquarium* with the crocodile section. *Daily 9am–7pm, until 5pm in winter | admission 13 euros, with aquarium 20 euros | Charlottenburg | Budapester Str. 5 | www.zoo-berlin.de | U/S Zoologischer Garten*

IN OTHER DISTRICTS

ALLIIERTENMUSEUM (162 B3) *(🗺 C9)*
The subject is the history of the western powers and Berlin in the years from 1945 to 1994. There is an impressive documentation of the Berlin Airlift in 1948/49 and you can even inspect one of the planes the local residents called "raisin bombers" parked outside. The museum is expected to relocate into Hangar 7 of the former Tempelhof airport (see *Tempelhofer Feld, p. 60)* in 2017. *Thu–Tue 10am–6pm | free admission | Zehlendorf | Clayallee 135 | www.alliiertenmuseum.de | U 3 Oskar-Helene-Heim*

BOTANISCHER GARTEN ● (163 E2–3) *(🗺 E9–10)*
The whole natural world can be found on this 1,070-acre site: Siberian steppe grass, Japanese cherry trees and common or garden vegetables located in a spacious park in Steglitz. Highlights include the huge old buildings housing tropical plants, giant water-lilies, bamboo and palm trees; the orchid hall and cactus collection are also superb. *Daily 9am to nightfall | admission 6 euros | Dahlem | Königin-Luise-Str. 6–8 | second entrance: Steglitz | Unter den Eichen | www.bgbm.org | S 1 Botanischer Garten*

BRÜCKE-MUSEUM (162 B1) *(🗺 C8)*
This idyllically located building in Grunewald houses an impressive collection of works by those artists who came together in Dresden in 1905 to form the "Brücke" (Bridge) group including Ernst Ludwig Kirchner, Erich Heckel, Karl Schmitt-Rottluff, Max Pechstein and Emil Nolde. *Wed–Mon 11am–5pm | admission 5 euros | Dahlem | Bussardsteig 9 | www.bruecke-museum.de | bus 115 Pücklerstraße*

GÄRTEN DER WELT (165 E3) *(🗺 0)*
Europe's largest *Chinesischer Garten*, covering an area of 6¾ acres, presents a rocky landscape with waterfalls, a lake with bridges, pavilions and many other attractions. Relaxing: the tea ceremony in the ● *Berghaus zum Osmanthussaft (chinese tea ceremony, reservations only, 8 euros |*

The big splash: in the hippo hall of the Berlin Zoo

tel. 0179 3 94 55 64). Included in the grounds are a *Japanischer Garten (Mon–Fri from noon, Sat/Sun from 9am),* an Oriental, a Balinese and a Christian monastery garden as well as a maze. In 2017, the Gärten der Welt will be part of the International Garden Show (IGA) and a new visitors centre, new playgrounds and recreational facilities will be built for the occasion. A cable railway linking the Neue Grottkauer Straße underground station over the Kienberg to the Gärten der Welt is also being planned. *Daily from 9am, April–Sept until 8pm, March, Oct until 6pm, Nov–Feb until 4pm, guided tours April–Oct Tue–Fri 11am, 2pm | admission 4 euros, in winter 2 euros | Marzahn | Eisenacher Str. 99 | www.gruenberlin.de | U 5 Cottbusser Platz, then Bus 195 Erholungspark Marzahn*

GLIENICKER PARK

(164 B4) *(🗺 0)*

A wonderful place to go for a stroll, just as in the days when the prince electors and princesses held hands in the shade of the oak trees and admired the view over the River Havel. Laid out by Lenné and Schinkel at the beginning of the 19th century, the 290-acre English landscaped park is divided into a Northern European, an Alpine and a Mediterranean section. The well-tended trees, a Classicist house, Italian pavilions, fountains, pergolas and arcades will make your walk fly by. The round temple with its Corinthian columns that Schinkel designed in 1835 is a real highlight. Spies were exchanged between East and West on Glienicker Bridge at the southern end of the park during the Cold War. *Wannsee | Königstr. | Bus 316 Glienicker Brücke*

GRUNEWALD

(156 A5–6, 162 A–B 1–2) *(🗺 A–C 5–10)*

When the city was divided by the Wall, Grunewald was the epitome of a recreation area. Today, it is much more peaceful. Several lakes including *Teufelssee* (Devil's Lake) as well as the River Havel will tempt you to take a swim. Teufelssee is also the

site of *Ökowerk (tel. 030 3 00 50)* which offers a natural garden, beehives and survival courses for children. The 16th century *Jagdschloss Grunewald (April–Oct Tue–Sun 10am–6pm, at other times Sat/Sun 10am–4pm | admission 6 euros)* on the banks of Lake Grunewald has a beautiful Renaissance hall, a valuable collection of paintings and a hunting museum. The 120 m (394 ft) high *Teufelsberg* (Devil's Mountain) in the north was created from the mass of rubble from buildings destroyed during the war. *Grunewald | S 7, 9 Grunewald*

HOUSE OF THE WANNSEE CONFERENCE (164 B4) *(Ⓜ 0)*

On 20 January 1942, representatives of the Nazi regime and the SS met in this mansion with a view of the lake to finalise the organisation of the genocide of the Jews based on a decision that had been made previously. An exhibition on the ground floor provides information on the conference, the events leading up to it and its horrific consequences. *Daily 10am–6pm | free admission | Wannsee | Am Großen Wannsee 56–58 | tel. 030 805 00 10 | www.ghwk.de | S Wannsee, then bus 114 Haus der Wannseekonferenz*

JÜDISCHER FRIEDHOF WEISSENSEE (165 D3) *(Ⓜ O–P 1–2)*

More than 115,000 Berlin Jews have found their final resting place here. This makes the cemetery, which was established in 1880, the largest Jewish graveyard in Europe. The brick building and layout of the burial areas were designed by Hugo Licht. A memorial stone has been erected in remembrance of the 6 million Jews who were murdered by the National Socialists. The publishers Samuel Fischer and Rudolf Mosse, as well as the painter Lesser Ury, are among the prominent people buried here. Men must wear a *kippa* head covering (can be borrowed at the entrance). *April–Oct Sun–Thu 7:30am–5pm, Fri 7:30am–2:30pm, Nov–March until 4pm, Fri until 2:30pm | Weißensee | Herbert-Baum-Str. 45 | tram 12 Albertinenstraße*

PFAUENINSEL ● (164 B4) *(Ⓜ 0)*

Originally, the 165-acre Pfaueninsel (Peacock Island) was the site of the zoo that Friedrich Wilhelm III had set up at the beginning of the 19th century. Today, only the peacocks in the wild and the romantic park are a reminder of the island's original purpose. The little white castle looks like

FLOATING SWIMMING POOL

Since 2004 the hull of a barge filled with water has been used as a floating swimming pool on the Spree. The water doesn't come from the river but from the tap. The walls of the ship have been lined with blue plastic like any other swimming pool. When it's sunny, the jetties and beach nearby the *Badeschiff* **(154 B5)** *(Ⓜ 06)* are bursting with party people. In the evenings, DJs work the turntables. On summer weekends it is often so full that it can take a while before you get a turn to jump into Berlin's biggest bath tub. In winter, the pool is roofed over and combined with a sauna. *Easter–Sept daily 8am–midnight, in winter 10am–midnight | admission 5 euros, in winter with sauna (3 hrs.) 12 euros, entrance up until 3pm 8 euros | Treptow | Eichenstr. 4 | tel. 030 53 32 03 82 | www.arena-berlin.de | S Treptower Park*

Swim with a view: the floating swimming pool at the Osthafen

a film set. It was built for Wilhelmine Enke, the paramour of Friedrich Wilhelm II. Take a look at the *dairy* and the hall in the style of a Gothic Revival church where parties were held. *Castle: April–Oct Tue–Sun 10am–5:30pm, guided tours only; dairy: April–Oct Sat/Sun 10am–5:30pm, Nov/Dec Sat/Sun 11am–3:30pm | admission 3 euros | Wannsee | Pfaueninselchaussee | ferry daily | 3 euros | www.spsg.de | tel. 030 80 58 68 31 | bus 218 Pfaueninsel*

INSIDER TIP RIXDORF (165 D4) *(🗺 N8)*
This small village with its sheds and forges, once founded by the Bohemians, is situated in the middle of the Neuköllner mass of houses. Here you get a feeling of how the Berlin metropole once grew out of many small locations. Pretty: the Bohemian Bethlehem Church and the Bohemian Cemetery. *U 7 Karl-Marx-Straße*

SOWJETISCHES EHRENMAL (155 D4) *(🗺 P7)*
One of the largest Soviet military cemeteries in Germany is located in Treptower Park. Not only the grave slabs in memory of the 7,000 Soviet soldiers who fell in the Battle of Berlin are impressive, the sheer size of the complex is also astonishing: eight walls with reliefs, the monumental 12 m (49 ft) high bronze sculpture of a soldier carrying a rescued German child, as well as the gigantic sculpture "Mother Homeland" that was chiselled out of a 50-ton block of granite. The monument was erected between 1947 and 1949. *Treptow | Alt-Treptow 1 | S Treptower Park*

INSIDER TIP STASI PRISON HOHENSCHÖNHAUSEN (165 E3) *(🗺 Q2)*
Grey functional buildings, walls and barbed wire give an impression of how political prisoners were kept in solitary confinement. People who actually experienced this guide you through the building and help you understand what people had to suffer who were subjected to the psychological torture of the East German secret police. *Guided tours Mon–Fri 11am, 1pm, 3pm, March–Oct also noon, 2pm, Sat/Sun hourly 10am–4pm | admission 5*

Socialist pathos: Soviet memorial in Treptower Park

euros | Hohenschönhausen | Genselerstr. 66 | tel. 030 98 60 83 30 | www.stiftung-hsh.de | tram 6 Genslerstraße

TEMPELHOFER FELD ★ ●
(160–161 B–E 3–6) *(🗺 K–M 7–9)*

Even today Europe's biggest office building, the central building of the *Tempelhof airport,* with a length of 1,300yd and 5,000 rooms, gives an impression of the monumental architecture of the National Socialism. Opened in 1936 for the Olympic Games in Berlin, an international flying hub and the seat for the air ministry was planned. This airport is no longer in use since 2008. The site is to be kept as a recreational space for the long-term; it is used during the day by joggers, skaters and walkers. Segways can be hired at the site's west entrance (Tempelhofer Damm) and small allotments have been created at the east end (urban gardening). On *Platz der Luftbrücke* a monument pays homage to the Berin Airlift during the soviet Berlin blockade 1948/49. Counterparts can be seen at Frankfurt Airport/Main and in Celle. *Guided tours of the building Mon–Fri 4pm, Fri also 1pm, Sat/Sun 11am, 2pm | 12 euros| Tempelhof| Platz der Luftbrücke | www.tempelhoferfreiheit.de | U 6 Platz der Luftbrücke*

TIERPARK FRIEDRICHSFELDE
(165 E3) *(🗺 S5–6)*

Enjoy this spacious zoo which houses around 7,500 animals of over 800 species, located in what was once a castle park designed by the famous landscape architect Peter Joseph Lenné. Highlights include the walk-in Vari-Wald (lemurs from Madagascar), the elephant nursery and the Malayan bear house. The early-Classicist *Friedrichsfelde Castle (Tue, Thu, Sat, Sun 11am–5pm)* from 1690 is open again now that the renovations have been completed; concerts are frequently held in the main hall. *Daily 9am–7pm, until 5pm in winter | admission 12 euros | Lichtenberg | Am Tierpark 125 | www.tierpark-berlin.de | tel. 030 51 53 10 | U 5 Tierpark*

EXCURSIONS

KÖPENICK (165 E4) *(🗺 0)*

In the German-speaking world, this waterside town to the south-east of Berlin is known due to a story about a bogus captain who confiscated the city's treasury in 1906. Köpenick has been part of Greater Berlin since 1920 but has managed to preserve its own charm. Along with its pretty old town and castle, Müggelsee is the perfect destination for a relaxing day trip away from city life.

The best way to get to Köpenick is on the water. In summer, boats run by the *Stern- und Kreisschifffahrt (www.sternundkreis.de)* leave Treptow harbour every hour. The excursion boats take 60 minutes to steam upstream along the Spree, past the industrial complexes of former East Germany, the Plänter Forest and idyllic shoreline properties. Visitors for Köpenick should disembark at Am Luisenhain in the heart of the old town. The famous red-brick *town hall* is directly opposite. In 1906, one year after it was opened, the unemployed shoemaker Wilhelm Voigt decided to gain entry into the town hall wearing a captain's uniform, arrest the mayor and steal the borough's coffers. An exhibition in the town hall *(Mon–Fri 8am–6pm, Sat/Sun 10am–6pm | admission free)* documents the story that inspired the author Carl Zuckmayer to write his famous play "The Captain of Köpenick". The events are re-enacted in front of the town hall at 11am on Wednesdays and Saturdays.

The magnificent and beautifully restored *Köpenicker Schloss*, a moated 17th century castle, is located around 200 m (655 ft) to the south of the town hall and was originally built for the later King Friedrich I of Prussia. It houses the *Kunstgewerbemuseum (Tue–Sun 10am–6pm | admission 6 euros)* and an exhibition of historical craftsmanship. The castle park, with its delightful café, is an ideal place to take a

KEEP FIT!

Aspria Spa & Sports **(149 D6)** ***(🗺 D5)*** *(Mon–Fri 6am–11pm, Sat 8am–10pm | day ticket 27–85 euros | Charlottenburg | Karlsruher Str. 20 | tel. 030 8 90 68 88 60 | www.aspria-berlin.de | U 7 Adenauerplatz)*) is a fantastic fitness and wellness temple spread over 16,000 m2. With a 25 m/82 ft pool and offering a wide range of courses even for day visitors as well as a children's sport programme and sauna.

At its opening in 1930, the *Stadtbad Mitte* **(146 B6)** ***(🗺 K3)*** *(closed mid-June–mid-Sept, ask for current opening times by phone | admission 3.50–5.50 euros depending on the time of day | Gartenstr. 5 | tel. 030 30 88 09 12 | www.berlinerbaeder.de | S 1, 2, 25 Nordbahnhof)* was Europe's most modern swimming pool and is still popular with fast swimmers. Behind a 10 m/33 ft high glass front and under a glass-covered roof, the pool is 50 m/164 ft long and the water stays at a pleasant 28 degrees Celsius.

Jogging around the city: sport enthusiasts can practise their hobby along the Spree and some even manage the distance from the Reichstag to Schloss Charlottenburg. If the way back seems too strenuous, hop onto one of the many cruise ships sailing past.

break with a view of *Frauentog*, a bay on the River Dahme. Here you'll find the *Solarbootpavillon (March–Oct Mon–Fri noon–7pm, Sat/sun 10am–7pm, during the summer holidays daily 10am–7pm | tel. 0160 6 30 99 97 | www.solarwaterworld.de):* This is where you can rent a solar-boat from 10 euros an hour and glide silently over the Spree and Dahme. From your boat you will be able to see the *Fischerkietz* (Fisherman's District) – a lovely settlement with historical fishermen's houses and the *Flussbad Gartenstraße (May–Sept daily 1pm–5:30pm | admission 3 euros)* – on the eastern shore of the Frauentog.

Excursion boats sail on further from the Luisenhain dock to *Müggelsee*. You can also reach Berlin's largest lake by tram (lines 60 and 61 in the direction of "Altes Wasserwerk") in around 20 minutes. Get off at the Bölschestraße/Am Wasserwerk stop and walk about 300 m (984 ft) to the lake with its beer garden, beach bar and small – but first-rate – French restaurant *Domaines (www.domaines-berlin.de | Moderate)*. The Spreetunnel leads to the west shore of the lake where there are several places to go swimming. A stroll along the lakeside will take you to the popular, rustic *Rübezahl* inn. During summer, ships depart from here for Friedrichshagen. The quickest way back to the centre of Berlin is then by district line from Friedrichshagen station. Information: *Tourist information Köpenick (Mon–Fri 9am–6:30pm, Sat 10am–4pm, in winter only until 1pm on Saturdays | Alt-Köpenick 31–33 | Am Schlossplatz | tel. 030 65 57 55 01 | www.berlin-tourismus-online.de)*

POTSDAM (164 B4–5) *(Ⓜ 0)*

The capital of Brandenburg attracts many visitors with its chic villas, magnificent castle grounds and Prussian history. It is located to the south-west of Berlin on the opposite bank of the Havel and can be easily reached on the district line *(line 7, every 10 minutes)*.

Today, what used to be the royal seat of the Prussian kings is a town with a unique cultural and park landscape. Since 1990, large sections of Potsdam have been declared a Unesco World Heritage Site. These include Sanssouci park, the Neuer Garten, Babelsberg and Glienicke (on the Berlin side of the Havel) with their respective castles. ★ *Schloss Sanssouci* park is a magnificent example of French and Italian landscape garden architecture. The *Expressbus X 15 (mid-April–Oct., in winter bus 695)* will take you to the park from Potsdam-Stadt station where the district line from Berlin arrives; get off at the Schloss Sanssouci stop. Originally, the park was only a terraced garden that Friedrich II (the Great) had laid out in 1744 to cultivate fruit and wine. He then fell in love with the view from the hill to such an extent that he had a palace built above the terraces as his summer residence. The single-storey palace, barely 100 m (328 ft) long, was constructed by Georg Wenzeslaus von Knobelsdorff in a mere two years (1745–47). Schloss Sanssouci (which means "without a care") is relatively small and was intended to serve the young king as a place where he could relax. This is where the king spent his summers studying philosophy, music and literature and receiving guests.

Friedrich II had several other buildings, including the *Neue Palais* und the *Chinesisches Teehaus*, erected in addition to the palace. The *Neue Palais* was the last and, at the same time, largest 18th century construction project in the park at Sanssouci. It was built for Friedrich the Great between 1763 and 1769 to show that he had not been financially ruined by the Silesian wars. A stroll through the park will take you past the *Orangery* and several gardens devoted to specific themes.

Fruit and wine used to be grown on the terraced gardens at Schloss Sanssouci

A 15-minute, signposted, walk from the park exit leads you back to town. The INSIDER TIP *Holländisches Viertel*, erected for Dutch immigrants between 1732 and 1742, is located at Nauener Tor. The soldier-king Friedrich Wilhelm I recruited them as he needed well-trained craftsmen to carry out extensions to his garrison city. Today "Little Amsterdam" is popular for its mixture of shops and pubs. The Russian colony *Alexandrowka*, with 14 small, decorated wooden houses from the early 19th century, is located to the north of the Dutch Quarter. This is where the Russian singers the Tsar had given to King Friedrich Wilhelm II as a present were housed.

Bus 692 from Nauener Tor will take you to *Schloss Cecilienhof (April–Oct. Tue–Sun 10am–6pm, Nov–March Tue–Sun 10am–5pm)* where the Potsdam Conference was held by the Allies in 1945. The palace not only includes an exhibition on the conference but also houses a hotel with a good restaurant *(closed until 2017 for renovations)*. Cecilienhof was constructed between 1914 and 1917 in style of an English country house for Crown Prince Wilhelm and his wife Cecilie; it was the last palace built by the Hohenzollern family.

Another attraction worth visiting is the *Neue Garten* which houses the Schloss Cecilienhof, an English-style landscape garden at the Heiligen See where you can also swim in summer. A stone's throw away is the *Marmorpalais (Nov–March Sat/ Sun 10am–4pm, 6pm in April, May–Oct Tue–Sun 10am–6pm | admission 5 euros)* which Friedrich Wilhelm II. had built between 1787–92. The architects were Carl von Gontard and, from 1789, Carl Gotthard Langhans who also designed the Brandenburger Tor in Berlin. Information*: Tourist Information (April–Oct Mon–Fri 9:30am–6pm, Sat/Sun 9:30am–4pm, Nov–March Mon–Fri 10am–6pm, Sat/Sun 9:30am–2pm | Brandenburger Str. 3 | tel. 03312755 88 99 | www.potsdam.de) and inside the main railway station (Mon–Sat 9:30am–8pm, Sun 10am–4pm)*

FOOD & DRINK

Berlin is a gourmet's paradise. There is a wide choice of places to eat ranging from internationally acclaimed restaurants with Michelin stars to excellent Turkish and Russian cuisine.

Alpine cuisine – with all the classics such as Wiener schnitzel, boiled beef and potato salad – is especially popular on the banks of the Spree. So-called lounge restaurants are also much in demand. If you want to eat well without ruining your holiday budget, do this at lunchtime when some of the gourmet restaurants offer attractive set meals at relatively inexpensive prices.

But, you will also find local food at acceptable prices in Berlin. Both locals and visitors like substantial meals with fresh ingredients from the area. Increasingly more restaurants cater for vegans and the latest craze is stone-age cuisine (paleolithic food) which avoids using cereal and dairy products. In contrast, burgers are very popular right now and you can't go anywhere in the city without finding them. Many pubs and snack bars now sell freshly made ones. The large number of Italian restaurants also provides a good choice for a quick meal. Interestingly, many are owned by Turks and you will hardly hear a word of Italian coming out of the kitchen. But, in most cases the pizzas and pasta are up to standard and there might only be some discussion about the salads; uninteresting glasshouse produce and ready-made dressings are unfortunately wide-spread. Seeing that Berlin has around 200,000 Turkish residents, there are surprisingly

Photo: Desserts at Fischers Fritz

A city of gourmet restaurants and snack bars: everything from currywurst to sushi – Berlin caters to all culinary tastes

few Turkish restaurants. However, you can find a döner kebab stand on most corners. Most people are not aware that pita bread filled with meat and salad is just as much a Berlin invention as currywurst.

And then there are the Russians – not only in the form of their own clubs and bars but also their culinary culture. *Beef stroganoff*, *borscht* and *pelmeni* taste especially good washed down with vodka. Asian cooking is still popular although many Chinese restaurants don't come anywhere near the quality of those in their original country. On the other hand, modern Asian cooking with lemon-grass soup and paeng chicken has many admirers especially now that many restaurant owners have moved away from the kitschy pseudo-Asian interior decoration of former days. Many restaurateurs have managed to remain successful by switching to pan-Asian cooking: Asian dishes with an American or European touch. Eating is always a matter of what is in fashion – especially in a big city like Berlin.

Viennese coffee house with style and tradition: Café Einstein

CAFÉS & BREAKFAST

CAFÉ EINSTEIN ★ (151 D5) *(🗺 H5)*
Traditional Viennese-style coffee house in the former villa of the silent-film star Henny Porten. The café of the same name in Mitte *(Unter den Linden 42)* is more modern. Both addresses have some things in common; many famous regulars, as well as a good menu (e.g. boiled beef). *Daily 8am–1am | Tiergarten | Kurfürstenstr. 58 | tel. 030 2 63 91 90 | www.cafeeinstein.com | U 1 Kurfürstenstraße*

INSIDER TIP CAFE FREISTIL (165 D4) *(🗺 F9)*
Today, the scent of coffee is in the air at the former Steglitz Baths and the swimmers have been replaced by guests reading newspapers sitting on cushions on tiled benches. Concerts, theatre performances and readings are also held here. *Mon–Fri 10am–6pm | Steglitz | Bergstr. 90 | tel. 030 54 77 31 18 | www.stadtbad-steglitz.de | S 1 Feuerbachstraße*

CAFÉ LIEBLING (147 E3) *(🗺 M1–2)*
Cosy café on Helmholtzplatz with newspapers and exotic warm drinks made with fresh ingredients including orange, ginger and mint tea. First-rate selection of cakes and soups at lunch. *Mon–Fri from 9am, Sat/Sun from 10am | Prenzlauer Berg | Raumerstr. 36a/corner of Dunckerstr. | tel. 030 41 19 82 09 | www.cafe-liebling.de | tram 12 Raumer Straße*

CAFÉ IM LITERATURHAUS (139 D5) *(🗺 F5)*
After a stroll down Kurfürstendamm: Coffee, cakes and freshly-made dishes in this villa with conservatory will get you going again. *Daily 9am–midnight | Charlottenburg | Fasanenstr. 23 | tel. 030 8 82 54 14 | www.literaturhaus-berlin.de | U1 Uhlandstraße*

DACHGARTENRESTAURANT KÄFER IM DEUTSCHEN BUNDESTAG (140 A3) *(🗺 J4)*
The only parliament that is daring enough to have a restaurant on its roof – and that with a fantastic view and the quality Käfer is famous for. Here, you can feast to your heart's content. In summer, the terrace is also open. *Daily 9am–4:30pm and 6:30pm–midnight, breakfast 9am–10am | Mitte | Platz der Republik 1 | www.feinkost-kaefer.de | U/S Friedrichstraße*

DOUBLE EYE
(159 D2) *(Ⓜ H7)*
Galão, cappuccino or a cup of filtered coffee: there is a coffee type to suit everyone in this popular coffee shop in the Schöneberg district. *Mon–Fri 9:30am–6:30pm, Sat 10am–3:30pm | Schöneberg | Akazienstr. 22 | tel. 0179 4 56 69 60 | doubleeye.de | U 7 Eisenacher Straße*

MANOLO
(147 D4) *(Ⓜ L2)*
Observe what's going on at a busy junctions over a caffè latte and a cake – pure big-city bliss! The fine selection of newspapers and comfortable leather benches also will help you feel at home in this self-service café. If your German is up to it, you can play stories by Berlin authors on the CD player. *Daily from 8am | Prenzlauer Berg | Schönhauser Allee 45/ corner of Danziger Str. | tel. 030 24 62 79 58 | U 2 Eberswalder Straße*

MEIN HAUS AM SEE
(146 C5) *(Ⓜ K3)*
This is the place to drink your first – or last – cappuccino at 4 o'clock in the morning. Welcoming design with many sofas and chairs, and street art on the walls. *Daily from 9am | Mitte | Brunnenstr. 197–98 | tel. 030 27 59 08 73 | www.mein-haus-am-see.blogspot.com | U 6 Rosenthaler Platz*

NO FIRE NO GLORY ★
(147 E4) *(Ⓜ M2)*
Some of the city's best baristi show off their skills here, coffee connoisseurs come for the Faema E61, rated as one of the world's best espresso machines. *Mon–Fri 9am–8pm, Sat/Sun 10am–10pm | Prenzlauer Berg | Rykestr. 45 | tel. 030 28 83 92 33 | www.nofirenoglory.de | tram M2 Marienburger Straße*

OXYMORON (141 E2) *(Ⓜ L3)*
Lovely café-restaurant with Art Nouveau charm in the Hackesche Höfe; large selection of breakfast dishes, high-quality Mediterranean cuisine at lunch and, in the evening, good wine and cocktail selection. *Daily from 9am | Mitte | Rosenthaler Str. 40–41 | tel. 030 28 39 18 86 | www.oxymoron-berlin.de | S Hackescher Markt*

MARCO POLO HIGHLIGHTS

★ Café Einstein
Outstanding coffee, polite service and cosy Viennese coffeehouse charm → p. 66

★ Fischers Fritz
Haute cuisine in the hotel's kitchen – not only for fish fans → p. 68

★ No fire no glory
One of the city's best espresso bars and a member of the slow-coffee movement committed to sustainable coffee cultivation → p. 67

★ Clärchens Ballhaus
In the most beautiful courtyard garden of the city centre you can eat meatballs or pizzas served by efficient waiters → p. 69

★ Neni Berlin
Creative cuisine with Mediterranean-Oriental dishes in a great atmosphere with a splendid view over the Tiergarten → p. 73

★ Sage Restaurant
Rough industrial surroundings, white tablecloths → p. 73

PRINCESS CHEESECAKE (152 B1) *(✉ L3)*
Magnificent cakes made with organic ingredients with an emphasis on its namesake. Cheesecake sounds ordinary, the aim here is to reach for higher goals and the results taste damn good! *Daily 10am–7pm | Mitte | Tucholskystr. 37 | tel. 030 28 09 27 60 | www.princess-cheesecake.de | S 1, 2, 25 Oranienburger Straße*

SANKT OBERHOLZ (146 C6) *(✉ L3)*
Popular, "in" café with WiFi connection and tennis-umpire chairs in front of the entrance. Sitting up there, guests have a fine view of one of the liveliest junctions in the city where Rosenthalerstraße, Brunnenstraße and Torstraße meet. It's quieter inside; good selection of coffee specialities. *Mon–Thu 8am–midnight, Fri/Sat 8am–3am, Sun 9am–midnight |*

GOURMET RESTAURANTS

Facil (140 A6) *(✉ K4)*
Enjoy this open air restaurant with specialities such as Loup de Mer and Bread salad with quails on the 5th floor of the *Mandala Hotel.* In summer the glass roof of this gourmet temple is simply slid back. Menus 42–164 euros. *Mon–Fri noon–3pm and from 7pm | Tiergarten | Potsdamer Str. 3 | tel. 030 590 05 12 34 | www.facil.de | U/S Potsdamer Platz*

Fischers Fritz ★ (140 C4) *(✉ K4)*
2-star chef Christian Lohse pampers his guests in the hotel *The Regent Berlin* with slice of turbot with saffron-crustacean jus. Three-course set lunch for 47 euros, four courses in the evening for 130 euros. *Daily from 6:30am | Mitte | Charlottenstr. 49 | tel. 030 20 33 63 63 | www.fischersfritzberlin.de | U 6 Französische Straße*

Reinstoff (146 A6) *(✉ K3)*
The creative cuisine by chef Daniel Achilles in Berlin's historic Edison courtyards has been awarded with two Michelin stars and 18 Gault-Millau points. Garden vegetables in a St George's mushroom and rapeseed stock, crayfish on Heligoland toast or Brandenburg asparagus grown in saliferous clay with spruce shoot and lilac blossom vinaigrette not only impress the food critics. Menus 132–198 euros. *Tue–Sat from 7pm| Mitte | Schlegelstr. 26c | tel. 030 3 08 812 3 14 | www.reinstoff.eu | U 6 Naturkundemuseum*

Restaurant Tim Raue (152 B4) *(✉ K5)*
The famous TV and Michelin-star cook and his wife opened their own restaurant in Kreuzberg in 2010. His cooking is inspired by Asia – at the very highest level. Pork chin, shimeji mushrooms and king crab should bring him his second Michelin star. Set meal (6 courses) 168 euros, lunch menu (three courses) 38 euros. *Tue–Sat noon–3pm, 7pm–midnight | Kreuzberg | Rudi-Dutschke-Str. 26 | tel. 030 25 93 79 30 | www.tim-raue.com | U 6 Kochstraße*

VÄU (141 D4) *(✉ K4)*
The unpretentious atmosphere with Thonet chairs and modern art is perfectly suited to Kolja Kleeberg's masterfully plain menu policy. Main dishes from around 40 euros, three lunch courses 65 euros, six courses in the evening 130 euros. *Mon–Sat noon–2:30pm, 7–10pm | Mitte | Jägerstr. 54–55 | tel. 030 20 02 97 30 | www.vau-berlin.de | U 6 Französische Straße*

Mitte | Rosenthaler Str. 72a | tel. 030 24 08 55 86 | www.sanktoberholz.de | U 8 Rosenthaler Platz

THEODOR TUCHER (140 B4) *(📖 J4)*
Guests who are interested in literature can relax in comfortable chairs and browse through the latest books on the gallery of this literary café near Brandenburger Tor. If all this reading makes you hungry, good German food is served one floor below. *Daily 9am–11pm | Mitte | Pariser Platz 6a | tel. 030 22 48 94 64 | www.tucher-am-tor.de | U/S Brandenburger Tor*

GARDEN RESTAURANTS

CLÄRCHENS BALLHAUS ★
(141 D1) *(📖 K3)*
Its courtyard garden is especially attractive in summer. Organic meatballs, pizza and cakes served with a flourish – and drinks, of course! Dancing in the evening. *Daily from 11am | Mitte | Auguststr. 24 | tel. 030 282 92 95 | www.ballhaus.de | S Oranienburger Straße | Budget*

INSIDER TIP DECKSHAUS
(153 D3) *(📖 L4)*
You sit on the deck of the tug "Jeseniky" in the historical harbour and eat sprats, meatballs and fish specialities. A great place to have a beer and listen to the Spree flowing by. *Tue–Sat 3–10pm, Sun noon–8pm, in the summer longer if the weather permits | Mitte | Märkisches Ufer 1z | tel. 030 21 79 14 04 | www.deckshaus.de | U 2 Märkisches Museum | Budget*

FREISCHWIMMER (154 C3) *(📖 O6)*
Idyllic location on the banks of a so-called "flood channel". Creative summer cuisine. Young crowd. **INSIDER TIP** Canoes and kayaks can be hired! *Mon–Fri from noon, Sat/Sun from 10am | Kreuzberg | Vor dem Schlesischen Tor 2a | tel. 030 61 07 43 09 | www.freischwimmer-berlin.com | U 1 Schlesisches Tor | Budget*

VÄU, a gourmet paradise near the Gendarmenmarkt

SCHOENBRUNN (147 F6) *(📖 N3)*
Families and the "in" crowd from "Prenzelberg" enjoy their pizza, pasta and antipasti in the Friedrichshain Volkspark. Perfect after (or before) a stroll through the park. Large beer garden. *Daily (in winter only Sat/Sun) 10am–6pm | Friedrichshain | Am Schwanenteich 1 | tel. 030 453 05 65 25 | www.schoenbrunn.net | tram 10 Kniprodestraße/corner of Danziger Str. | Budget*

Chef Loriano Mura gives the finishing touches to a dish in the Bocca di Bacco

THE CLASSICS

HENNE (153 E4–5) *(🗺 M5)*
A true classic when it comes to INSIDER TIP crispy chicken. Families, students, intellectuals and long-time residents nibble chicken legs and sip their beer in this unsophisticated hostelry. It is often full and you might have to wait. *Tue–Sat from 6pm, Sun from 5pm | Kreuzberg | Leuschnerdamm 25 | tel. 030 6 14 77 30 | www.henne-berlin.de | U 8, 15 Kottbusser Tor | Budget*

PRATER (147 D4) *(🗺 L2)*
The traditional place for beer and food from the grill. On sunny days, families and students have their supper in the large beer garden. *Daily from noon; in winter, Mon–Sat evenings only | Prenzlauer Berg | Kastanienallee 7–9 | tel. 030 448 56 88 | www.pratergarten.de | U 2 Eberswalder Straße | Budget–Moderate*

WELTRESTAURANT MARKTHALLE (153 F5) *(🗺 M5)*
The right address for Sauerbraten, goulash and co. Unpretentious classics for those who still remember the student protests of '68 and their successors. In the basement: *Auster Club* with music from the 40s to the 60s. *Daily from 10am | Kreuzberg | Pücklerstr. 34 | tel. 030 617 55 02 | www.weltrestaurant-markthalle.de | U 1, 15 Görlitzer Bahnhof | Budget–Moderate*

ZUR LETZTEN INSTANZ (153 D2) *(🗺 L4)*
One of the founding fathers of Berlin's cooking culture. The names of the dishes such as "cross-examination" and "lawyer's breakfast" remind you that the homey pub is not far away from the law court. *Mon–Sat noon–1am, Sun nooon–11pm | Mitte | Waisenstr. 14–16 | tel. 030 2 42 55 28 | www.zurletzteninstanz.de | U 2 Klosterstraße | Budget–Moderate*

RESTAURANTS: EXPENSIVE

BOCCA DI BACCO (140 C4) *(🗺 K4)*
Ravioli with loup de mer in shrimp cream, octopus carpaccio and lamb with a herb crust appeal to business people and politicians alike. Good wine list. The wine cellar, with a long wooden table for 20 guests,

is especially atmospheric (more than 500 wines from Italy alone!). Reservations essential. *Mon–Sat noon–midnight, Sun 6pm–midnight | Mitte | Friedrichstr. 167–168 | tel. 030 20 67 28 28 | www.boccadibacco.de | U 6 Französische Straße*

HORVÁTH (153 E6) *(✉ M6)*
Not especially elegant, but the ingredients and compositions are truly splendid. The chef Sebastian Frank considers quality more important than white tablecloths. No matter whether it is slice of halibut on pumpkin purée or fillet of beef on a ragout of root vegetables in red-wine sauce, you will really savour the cuisine in this restaurant, whose chef holds one Michelin star. *Wed–Sun 6–11pm | Kreuzberg | Paul-Lincke-Ufer 44a | tel. 030 61 28 99 92 | www.restaurant-horvath.de | U 1, 8 Kottbusser Torz*

PARIS-MOSKAU (151 D2) *(✉ H3)*
The home-style gourmet cooking – such as suckling pig and black pudding with pumpkin puree and truffle risotto – tastes particularly good in this small, half-timbered building next to the railway tracks that has managed to survive the remodelling of the government district. *Daily from 6pm; Mon–Fri also noon–3pm | Tiergarten | Alt-Moabit 141 | tel. 030 3 94 20 81 | www.paris-moskau.de | S Hauptbahnhof*

RESTAURANTS: MODERATE

AIGNER (140 C4) *(✉ K4)*
Refined German and Austrian cuisine in classical surroundings: Sauvignon blanc is served with the Palatine "winegrower's salad" and this is followed by black-pudding dumplings on Riesling cabbage accompanied by a Horcher cuvée from Aigner's own vineyards. *Daily noon–2am | Mitte | Französische Str. 25 | tel. 030 2 03 75 18 50 | www-aigner-gendarmenmarkt.de | U 2 Französische Straße*

BANDOL SUR MER (146 B6) *(✉ K3)*
French restaurant with country-style cooking; dishes include stewed beef with black salsify, and loup de mer. Next door there's the lure of the owners' bistro that's also open during the daytime. *Daily from 6pm | Mitte | Torstr. 167 | tel. 030 67 30 20 51 | www.bandolsurmer.de | U 8 Rosenthaler Platz*

INSIDER TIP BIEBERBAU (158 B4) *(✉ G7)*
The dishes get their characteristic touch from a refined amalgamation of German cooking with a touch of the Mediterranean. Pickled knuckle of pork with truffles, pikeperch with taglierini and Maître Philippe's fine selection of cheese to finish with. Delicious. *Tue–Sat 6pm–midnight, kitchen open until 10pm | Wilmersdorf | Durlacher Str. 15 | tel. 030 8 53 23 90 | www.bieberbau-berlin.de | U/S Bundesplatz*

ENGELBECKEN (148 C5) *(✉ D5)*
Seasonal, alpine cuisine, on the lakeside at Lietzensee, homey and substantial: Weißwurst, roast pork with dumplings and red cabbage, gnocchi with sage butter for vegetarians and delicious cakes are tremendously popular. The meat comes from animals that were kept in a humane manner. *Daily; Mon–Fri from 5pm, Sat from 4pm, Sun from noon | Charlottenburg | Witzlebenstr. 31 | tel. 030 6 15 28 10 | www.engelbecken.de | U 2 Sophie-Charlotte-Platz*

ENTRECÔTE (140 C6) *(✉ K5)*
This is the address for steak fans. French specialities from Angus beef, as well as calf's kidneys in Madeira sauce, in charming surroundings with high ceilings and friendly service. *Mon–Fri 11:30am–midnight, Sat/Sun 5:30–midnight | Mitte | Schützenstr. 5 | tel. 030 20 16 54 96 | www.entrecote.de | U 2, 6 Stadtmitte*

LOCAL SPECIALITIES

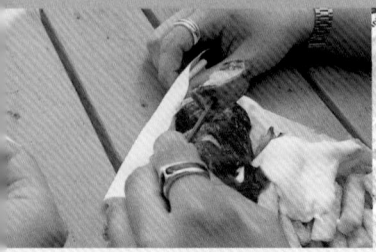

Berliner Weiße – With a shot, a typical drink for the ladies that the lords of creation regard with disdain. Whoever would pour woodruff or raspberry syrup into wheat beer? Women in Berlin like it.
Buletten – Almost every butcher has these meatballs fried and ready to be eaten (photo right) and they are also sold at snack bars as curry-buletten. The word comes from the Huguenots; in French, "boulette" means little ball.
Currywurst – Bratwurst with ketchup and curry powder (photo left) is sold on most street corners in Berlin. The snack-bar owner, Herta Heuwer, came up with the recipe more than 50 years ago.
Döner Kebab – Pita bread filled with grilled veal and salad. A speciality that is just as much at home in Berlin as the currywurst.
Eisbein – Pickled knuckle of pork served with puréed peas. You will need at least one schnapps to go with it...
Kasseler – Smoked rib of pork that does not come from the town of Kassel: a Berlin butcher of the same name is responsible for its fame. A decent serving of sauerkraut to go along with it is almost obligatory.
Quark mit Leinöl – Curd cheese with linseed oil is regularly eaten in many Berlin households. The cheese is mixed with the oil and a pinch of salt and served with boiled potatoes – simple, but delicious!
Schmalzstulle – Pieces of bread with various spreads (Stullen) are once again becoming popular; best of all, hearty and in this case spread with pork dripping and a pinch of salt.
Chocolate – Those with a sweet-tooth should try some Berlin chocolate. Hamann, as well as Fassbender & Rauch, produce first rate quality – and have done so for decades.

GOODTIME GRILL (149 D6) *(Ⓜ E6)*
Highlight: the traditional Japanese Robata grill that lends its typical smoke flavour to Asian-style fish, vegetables and meat (the best US beef fillet). *Daily. noon–midnight |Charlottenburg | Kurfürstendamm 90 | tel. 030 31 99 77 70 | www.goodtime-grill. de | bus M19, M29 Lehniner Platz*

HOSTARIA DEL MONTE CROCE (160 C1) *(Ⓜ K6)*
Italy in the building at the back: the feast begins every evening at 7:30; the cooking

is just like it is in Emilia Romagna. The guests sit at long tables and all enjoy the same nine-course meal. It changes every four weeks. The wine comes straight from the barrel and you can drink as much as you want. Reservation essential. *Tue–Sat from 7pm | Kreuzberg | Mittenwalder Str. 6/2nd courtyard | tel. 030 6 94 39 68 | www.hostaria.de | U 7 Gneisenaustraße*

LA MANO VERDE
(138–139 C–D 4–5) *(🗺 F6)*
Excellent wild herb salads, smoothies: delicious vegan food. *Mon–Sat 5–11pm | Charlottenburg | Uhlandstr. 181 | tel. 030 82 70 31 20 | www.lamanoverde berlin.com | U 1 Uhlandstraße*

NENI BERLIN ★ (139 F4) *(🗺 G5)*
Offering an excellent view onto the Tiergarten (from the 10th floor!), the *25 hour Hotel* restaurant serves exciting dishes with Mediterranean-Oriental influences. Also caters for vegetarians. Fantastic terrace! Book a table in advance! *Mon–Fri noon–11pm, Sat/Sun 12:30–11pm | Charlottenburg | Budapester Str. 46 | tel. 030 120 22 12 00 | www.25hours-hotels.com | U 1, 2, 3 Wittenbergplatz*

NOCTI VAGUS (147 D6) *(🗺 M3)*
Dark restaurant with a show programme to tickle the palate: as your eyes give up their function, your senses of taste and smell increase. The chef leads the guests down new aromatic paths: rabbit in plum-wine sauce or strawberries with green pepper. *Daily from 6pm | Mitte | Saarbrücker Str. 36–38 | tel. 030 74 74 91 23 | www.noctivagus.de | U 2 Senefelderplatz*

RIO GRANDE (154 B2) *(🗺 N5)*
The "big river" here is the Spree: you can enjoy your creamy veal goulash with buttered gnocchi, fried chicken with potato salad and fresh apple strudel with a wonderful view across the water from the beautiful terrace. *Daily 10am–midnight | Kreuzberg | May-Ayim-Ufer 9 | tel. 030 61 07 49 81 | www.riogrande-berlin.de | U 1 Schlesisches Tor*

SAGE RESTAURANT ★
(154 A2) *(🗺 N5)*
This is where industrial architecture meets pizza and fresh brook char: the restaurant landscape in this gigantic brick building on the Spree varies from sophisticated cuisine to home-style cooking. Lovely lounge with a fireplace for smokers. Beach bar on the riverbank. *Tue–Sun from 2pm, in winter from 6pm | Kreuzberg | Köpenicker Str. 18–20 | tel. 030 755 49 40 71 | www.sage-restaurant.de | U1 Schlesisches Tor*

SARAH WIENER IM HAMBURGER BAHNHOF (145 E–F6) *(🗺 J3)*
Cuisine from the alpine countries is served in a side wing of the Hamburger Bahnhof

The chef recommends...

Museum. Beautiful terrace on the bank of the Nordkanal. Other locations: *Chausseestr. 8 (Mitte)* and in the *Museum für Kommunikation* the *Kaffeehaus (Mitte | Leipziger Str. 16). Tue/Wed 10am–6pm, Thu 10am–8pm, Fri 10am–11pm, Sat/Sun 11am–6pm | Mitte | Invalidenstr. 50–51 | tel. 030 70 71 36 50 | www.sarahwiener.de | U/S Hauptbahnhof*

LA SOUPE POPULAIRE (147 D6) *(🗺 M3)*
Art and culinary art combined in the Bötzow brewery: Star chef Tim Raue's creations are inspired by and complimentary to the works being exhibited, with four appetisers, four main courses, and two desserts.

LOW BUDGET

The pizza-like slices (1.50 euros each) with their wonderful toppings at the *Focacceria* **(146 C5)** *(🗺 L2) (daily from 11am | Mitte | Fehrbelliner Str. 24 | tel. 030 44 03 27 71 | U 8 Rosenthaler Platz)* will fill you up quickly.

Schmuck's Restauration
(153 D3) *(🗺 L4–5) (Mon–Fri 7am–6pm | Mitte | Am Köllnischen Park 1 | tel. 030 22 33 65 17 | U 8 Heinrich-Heine-Straße)*, at Märkisches Museum, offers roast chicken, but also "Tafelspitz" and strudel at reasonable prices.

● *Curry 36* **(160 B1)** *(🗺 K6) (daily from 9am | Kreuzberg | Mehringdamm 36 | U 6, 7 Mehringdamm)* is probably the most popular snack bar in Kreuzberg and not only serves currywurst (around 1.50 euros) with chips but also pea soup (2.50 euros). You eat standing up – and that, right through until the early hours.

Cool atmosphere: a mixture between factory and restaurant. *Thu–Sat noon –4am | Prenzlauer Berg | Prenzlauer Allee 242 | tel. 030 44 31 96 80 | lasoupepopulaire.de | tram M2 Prenzlauer Allee/Metzer Straße*

RESTAURANTS: BUDGET

AMPELMANN-RESTAURANT
(141 D2) *(🗺 K4)*
Children love the restaurant's "little green traffic light man" pasta shapes and delicious pizza while adults are also treated to well-cooked food. Sunday brunch *(10am–2pm | 19.90 euros)*. Nice terrace on James Simon Park (banks of the Spree). *Daily 9am–midnight | Stadtbahnbogen 159/160 | tel. 030 84 71 07 09 | ampelmann-restaurant.de | S-Bahn Hackescher Markt*

BABA ANGORA (149 F5) *(🗺 F5)*
First-rate Turkish cuisine with quality lamb dishes, grilled vegetables and seductive desserts. Homey atmosphere, reasonably-priced set meals at lunchtime. Branch at Goltzstr. 32 in Schöneberg. *Daily 11:30am–midnight | Charlottenburg | Schlüterstr. 29 | tel. 030 3 23 70 96 | www.babaangora.de | S Savignyplatz*

BERKIS (159 D1) *(🗺 H6)*
Healthy Cretan cuisine with fresh vegetables, best olive oil and regional organic meat. Branch in the *Wörtherstr. 33 (Prenzlauer Berg). Daily 11:30am–midnight, Sun 1pm–midnight | Schöneberg | Winterfeldtstr. 45 | tel. 030 77 90 04 02 | www.berkis.de | U 1–4 Nollendorfplatz*

INSIDER TIP FISCHSCHUPPEN
(155 D1) *(🗺 P5)*
Small, relaxed bar with beautifully painted walls. Freshly prepared seafood and fish as well as delicious fast food such as fish'n chips on the menu (menu

changes daily). Also sells fish. *Mon–Sat 10am–10:30pm, Sun noon–9:30pm | Friedrichshain | Boxhagener Str. 68 | tel. 030 22 43 50 39 | www.facebook.com/Fischschuppen | S-Bahn Ostkreuz*

GASTHAUS LENTZ (149 D5) *(🗺 E5)*
A classic that not only attracts the old student crowd from '68 who live in the neighbouring flats. Kölsch beer is served, there is no music to disturb your conversation, and there is a variety of lunchtime specials. *Daily from 9am | Charlottenburg | Stuttgarter Platz 20 | tel. 030 3 24 16 19 | www.gasthaus-lentz-berlin.de | S Charlottenburg*

GNADENBROT (158 C1) *(🗺 G6)*
Goulash, roasts and baked potatoes: that is the recipe of this pub in the centre of town. Its proximity to the gay scene in Schöneberg is instantly noticeable. It is like a trip back to the 1970s with self-service, schnitzel, stew, toast "Hawaii". *Daily from 9am | Schöneberg | Martin-Luther-Str. 20a/corner of Motzstr. | tel. 030 21 96 17 86 | www.raststaette-gnadenbrot.de | U 4 Victoria-Luise-Platz*

KIMCHI PRINCESS (153 F5–6) *(🗺 M6)*
"In" restaurant in Kreuzberg with Korean dishes prepared on a barbeque at your table. Creative restaurant design with a red metal wall and wooden tables. *Daily noon–11pm | Kreuzberg | Skalitzer Str. 36 | tel. 0163 4 58 02 03 | www.kimchiprincess.com | U 1 Görlitzer Bahnhof*

INSIDER TIP MERCAN
(153 F5–6) *(🗺 M6)*
Turkish home-style cooking in a simple but friendly atmosphere: the white beans, grilled vegetables, lamb dishes and meatballs are very popular. *Daily from 11am | Kreuzberg | Wiener Str. 10 | tel. 030 61 28 58 41 | U 1 Görlitzer Bahnhof*

Good and reasonably-priced: La Focacceria in Mitte

INSIDER TIP NÖ! WEINGALERIE
(140 C5) *(🗺 K4)*
Small, first-class wine shop with a homey atmosphere and wine-tasting accompanied by cheese and baguette. *Mon–Fri noon–1am, Sat 7pm–1am | Mitte | Glinkastr. 23 | tel. 030 2 01 08 71 | www.cafe-noe.de |*

TOCA ROUGE
(140 C1) *(🗺 K3)*
Over-the-top setting in black. The food is a interesting mixture from all over Asia; pike-perch comes disguised as "A Better tomorrow". "Seven seconds" – roast beef with cucumbers, mushrooms and mustard sauce – is delicious. *Mon–Fri from noon, Sat/Sun from 5pm | Mitte | Torstr. 195 | tel. 030 84 71 21 42 | www.tocarouge.de | S1, 2 Oranienburger Straße*

SHOPPING

WHERE TO START?
Alexa on Alexanderplatz (Mitte) and **Tauentzienstraße** near the Gedächtniskirche (Charlottenburg) will be the first choice for fans of today's fast-selling fashion labels. This is also the home of the **KaDeWe** (Department Store of the West), that is steeped in tradition. Those who are more interested in small boutiques with clothes by Berlin designers will find what they are looking for in the **Hackesche Höfe** and on **Alte** and **Neue Schönhauser Straße**. **Bergmannstraße** (Kreuzberg) is the place for second-hand articles.

Berlin has so many shopping streets that it is impossible to list them all. And, if you are looking for the real shopping heart of the city, you won't be able to pin-point it. There is a simple reason for this: there are shopping areas in almost every district.

In Mitte, this is Friedrichstraße with its exclusive boutiques. The clientele in the *Galeries Lafayette* and *Quartier 206* is just as international as the brand names. On the other hand, Germany's largest Kaufhof department store and the *Alexa shopping centre* attract shoppers to Alexanderplatz. Kurfürstendamm, with its many designer boutiques, and Tauentzienstraße with *Peek & Cloppenburg, Wertheim* and *KaDeWe* department stores are the pride and joy of Charlottenburg's retail world. On

Photo: Quartier 206

Shopping areas and arcades are not just concentrated on the centre – each district has its own shopping centres and specialist shops

Budapester Straße, the new *Bikini Berlin* complex with its designer boutiques has joined this array of shopping opportunities. In Zehlendorf and Steglitz people stroll along Schlossstraße. And, then there are all the resourceful shop-owners in smaller streets such as Goltzstraße in Schöneberg – well-known for its fashion boutiques. Reuterstraße in Neukölln is an eldorado if you are looking for second-hand things. The area around the Hackesche Höfe is renowned for its fashion and design outlets.

ANTIQUE & SECOND-HAND

BERLINER ANTIKMARKT
(140 C3) *(🗺 K4)*
Thirty-five antique dealers offer old dolls, toys, watches, clocks, jewellery and paintings in the arches at Friedrichstraße Station. *Bärenstark* has some fine period teddy bears. *Wed–Mon 11am–6pm | Mitte | S-Bahn-Bögen 190–203 | www.antikmarkt-berlin.de | U/S Friedrichstraße*

Sweet delicacies from Istanbul in the Confiserie Orientale

DÜWAL (138 B4) *(Ⓜ F5)*
Lovers of old books treasure those on offer at this renowned shop. The valuable tomes are stacked to the ceiling. *Mo–Fri 3pm–6pm, Sat 11am–2pm | Charlottenburg | Schlüterstr. 17 | www.duewal.de | S Savignyplatz*

INSIDER TIP PLATTEN PEDRO
(149 D2) *(Ⓜ D–E3)*
Berlin's largest source of old records with around 200,000 singles. The demanding collector will find everything from folk music to hard rock to make his heart beat faster. *Mon–Fri 10am–6pm, in winter until 4:50pm, Sat 10am–2:30pm | Charlottenburg | Tegeler Weg 102 | www.platten-pedro.de | U 7 Mierendorffplatz*

BEAUTY

NIVEA HOUSE (140 C4) *(Ⓜ K4)*
Enormous selection of cosmetics. You can have a quick restoration session in the beauty salon. A facial (25 minutes) costs 25 euros. If you are tense, a neck-and-shoulder massage will loosen you up. *Mon–Sat 10am–8pm | Mitte | Unter den Linden 28 | tel. 030 20 45 61 60 | www.nivea.de | U/S Brandenburger Tor*

THE ENGLISH SCENT
(138 B3) *(Ⓜ E–F5)*
Famous for its somewhat eccentric British perfumes that cannot be found in any other shops in Berlin. Most of the scents come from purveyors by appointment to Her Majesty the Queen. You will receive expert advice if you are not sure which perfume suits you best. *Mon, Tue, Thu, Fri 10am–2pm and 3–6:30pm, Wed from 2pm, Sat 10am–3pm | Charlottenburg | Goethestr. 15 | www.english-scent.de | S Savignyplatz*

DELICATESSEN

INSIDER TIP CONFISERIE ORIENTALE
(140 C1) *(Ⓜ K3)*
One of Istanbul's best confectioners produces exclusively for this small shop which

offers any amount of marzipan and nougat sweets and all sorts of exotic flavours. Try some yourself over a cup of mocha in the shop and then take some home with you all packed up beautifully in little boxes. *Mon–Fri 11am–7pm, Sat/Sun 11am–6pm | Mitte | Linienstr. 113 | www.confiserie-orientale.com | S1, 2, 25 Oranienburger Straße*

FRANZ KARL ★ (147 F5) *(🗺 N2)*
The best cakes and gateaux far and wide make this confectionery run by Franz-Karl Kaufmann a paradise for all fans of Austrian patisserie: individual zebra cakes, Sachertorte, fresh apple strudel, Gugelhupf, blueberry quark cake, raspberry mascarpone cake and, and, and... *Wed–Sun noon–6:30pm | Prenzlauer Berg | Bötzowstr. 15 | www.kuchenkultur-franz-karl.de | tram M10 Bötzowstraße*

GOLDHAHN & SAMPSON
(147 E3) *(🗺 M1)*
Taking a closer look at all of the herbs and spices here is almost like making a journey around the world. Cooking courses are held in the rear section of the shop. A limited – but first-rate – selection of wines and spirits. *Mon–Fri 10am–8pm, Sat 10am–8pm | Prenzlauer Berg | Dunckerstr. 9 | www.goldhahnundsampson.de | U 2 Eberswalderstraße*

VEGANZ
(146 C2) *(🗺 O)*
Europe's first vegan supermarket offers a wide range of organic, ecologically produced groceries and accessories. On Sundays brunch *(10am–4pm)* in the café – try the richness of vegan meals (14.90 euros/pers.). Cooking classes. Branch in Friedrichshain *(Warschauer Str. 33). Mon–Sat 8am–9pm, Sun 10am–6pm | Prenzlauer Berg | Schivelbeiner Str. 34 | tel. 030 44 03 60 48 | www.veganz.de | U-/S Schönhauser Allee*

MARCO POLO HIGHLIGHTS

★ Flea market am 17. Juni
The classic among Berlin's flea markets → p. 81

★ KaDeWe
Even just visiting the gourmet floor is a great experience → p. 82

★ Quartier 206
Sophisticated atmosphere, fine selection, no hurry – welcome to this designer departement store → p. 83

★ 14 oz.
Not only VIPs like shopping here as if they were in a private living room → p. 83

★ Trippen
Wood and leather designer shoes of cult status; the cool showroom looks like a gallery → p. 84

★ Franz Karl
One of the city's best confectioneries with the finest Austrian patisseries and long queues at the counter → p. 79

★ Markt am Maybachufer
Large Turkish families buy vegetables by the crate, the merchants try to outshout each other → p. 85

THIS & THAT

INSIDER TIP AUS BERLIN
(141 F2) *(🗺 L3)*
Products from more than 200 Berlin designers and producers add colour to the drab prefabricated concrete building opposite the Marienkirche. These range from painted storm jackets to heartbreak pills. You can even find Gorbachev Vodka on the shelves – this is produced in Reinickendorf. Sometimes, DJs work the turntables. *Mon–Sat 10am–8pm | Mitte | Karl-Liebknecht-Str. 9 | www.ausberlin.de | U/S Alexanderplatz*

INTERSHOP 2000 (154 C2) *(🗺 O5)*
You will find (almost) everything that was part of everyday life in former East Germany in this erstwhile Konsum shop: Mitropa chinaware, eggcups and Free German Youth (FDJ) pennants. Ideal for rummaging around in the past era of Socialist design. *Wed–Fri 2–6pm, Sat, Sun noon–6pm | Friedrichshain | Danneckerstr. 8 | www.intershop.2000.com | U/S Warschauer Straße*

KPM (139 D–E 1–2) *(🗺 F4)*
Elegant items from the Royal Porcelain Factory (KPM) are not only sold in the magnificently restored old buildings but also displayed in a fascinating way – with demonstration workshops, guided tours, special exhibitions and a café. In an additional room on the other side of the courtyard you can purchase the somewhat cheaper B-goods. *Mon–Sat 10am–6pm | admission KPM Welt 10 euros | Tiergarten | Wegelystr. 1 | www.kpm-berlin.de | S 7, 9, 75 Tiergarten*

LUXUS INTERNATIONAL
(146 C4) *(🗺 L2)*
120 Berlin designers display their latest products and wild ideas in this small shop. You will find everything you can't do without, from cuddly-kebabs to badges for football-haters. One of the hits is a currywurst-stand card game. *Mon–Sat 11am–8pm | Prenzlauer Berg | Kastanienallee 84 | www.luxusinternational.de | U 2 Eberswalder Straße*

MODULOR (153 D5) *(🗺 L5)*
With over 7,000 items of stationery, decoration and model making items, this store is not only popular with DIY enthusiasts and architects. The place to go for corrugated cardboard, perforated sheets, film or paper in varying lengths and strengths – also available in its online shop. With sewing studio and consultation service providing creative ideas. *Mon–Fri 9am–8pm, Sat 9am–6pm | Kreuzberg | Prinzenstr. 85 | www.modulor.de | U 8 Moritzplatz*

ZAUBERKÖNIG (161 F5) *(🗺 M8)*
Welcome to the world of magic: a wide range of magic props, tricks as well as carnival and dressing-up costumes – not just fun for children. *Tue–Sat 11am–7pm | Neukölln | Hermannstr. 84–90 | www.zauberkoenig-berlin.de | U 8 Leinestraße*

FLEA MARKETS

AM MAUERPARK (146 C3–4) *(🗺 L1–2)*
Berlin's largest flea market not only offers any amount of second-hard goods and more-or-less valuable antiques and retro furniture, some young designers also sell their first collections here – usually printed T-shirts, jewellery and fashionable handbags. The clientele is hip and also spends a lot of time in the various beach bars on the site. *Sun 9am–6pm | Prenzlauer Berg | Eberswalder Str. | U 2 Eberswalder Straße*

BOXHAGENER PLATZ (154 C1) *(🗺 O5)*
A small square in the eastern part of Friedrichshain with a quiet flea market, relatively low prices and a public of young

people and students from the neighbourhood. The nearby cafés are ideal places to sit and watch the dealers and bargain-hunters. *Sun 10am–6pm | Friedrichshain | Boxhagener Platz | U5 Samariterstraße*

prices. But here bartering is the order of the day. The second-hand dealers are in the upper section towards the Siegessäule and the arts and crafts people in the other direction near Ernst-Reuter-Platz.

Berlin's flea markets offer all kinds of useful and unusual second-hand articles

NOWKOELLN
(153 E–F6) *(🗺 M6)*
The "in" flea market on Maybachufer with chic T-shirts by Berlin designers, retro second-hand stuff and other knick-knacks the hip people who live here need in their lofts. Live music and grilled sausages. *April–Nov 1st and 3rd Sun in the month 10am–6pm | Neukölln | Maybachufer | www.nowkoelln.de | U8 Schönleinstraße*

FLEA MARKET AM 17. JUNI ★
(150 A–B 3–4) *(🗺 F–G4)*
The most famous flea market in the west of the city. The many professional antique, clothing, jewellery, and record and CD dealers sometimes demand excessive

Sat/Sun 10am–5pm | Charlottenburg | Straße des 17. Juni | www.berlinertroedelmarkt.com | S Tiergarten

DEPARTMENT STORES

BIKINI BERLIN ●
(139 E4) *(🗺 G5)*
In the new factory-style shopping centre opposite the Gedächtniskirche, you can find creative accessories by Berlin designers, tableware or fashion from Carhartt or Gant. Splendid roof terrace with view onto the monkeys in the zoo. *Mon–Sat 10am–8pm | Charlottenburg | Budapester Str. 38–50 | www.bikiniberlin.de | U/S Zoologischer Garten*

DUSSMANN ● (140 C3) *(📖 K4)*
This so-called "cultural department store" boasts four floors of CDs, DVDs, videos, books, games and software. The many special offers will whet your appetite. You can listen to all of the CDs and other sound media in the music department. Helpful and professional advice. The INSIDER TIP hanging garden with 6,000 tropical plants by Patric Blanc is a feast for the eyes. *Mon–Fri 9am–midnight, Sat 9am–11:30pm | Mitte | Friedrichstr. 90 | www.kulturkaufhausde | U/S Friedrichstraße*

GALERIES LAFAYETTE (140 C4) *(📖 K4)*
An eldorado for shoppers with a wonderful delicatessen department, international fashion and sensational architecture. *Mon–Sat 10am–8pm | Mitte | Friedrichstr. 76–78 | U 6 Französische Straße*

KADEWE ★ (139 F5) *(📖 G5)*
It is worth visiting the KaDeWe just to go to the delicatessen department: they have (almost) everything from artichokes to zabaglione. The selection of high-fashion labels on the clothing floors is also overwhelming. *Mon–Fri 10am–9pm, Sat 9:30–9pm | Schöneberg | Tauentzienstr. 21–24 | U 1, 2, 3 Wittenbergplatz*

Even those who don't buy anything cannot help but admire the domed round building of the Galeries Lafayette

FASHION

CACHE CŒUR (147 D5) *(📖 L2)*
This is where vintage fashion by renowned Berlin designers is sold directly to men and women of the world. This is also where you can find unused fashion from times gone by including the 1960s; but this all has its price. Givenchy shoes, a dress by Alexander McQueen or fur caps and de-

signer telephones – here, trends become history. *Tue–Fri 2pm–8pm, Sat noon–6pm | Prenzlauer Berg | Schönhauser Allee 174 | www.cachecoeur.de | U2 Senefelderplatz*

NIX (141 D2) *(✉ K3)*
Discrete colours, robust materials and simple cuts are the secrets of Barbara Gebhardt's success. A Nix coat or skirt is just as suited for everyday wear as it is for visiting the opera. *Mon–Sat 11am–7pm | Mitte | Oranienburger Str. 32 | www.nix.de | S1, 2, 25 Oranienburger Straße*

QUARTIER 206 ★ (140 C5) *(✉ K4)*
Elegant designer shop with fashion by Cerruti, Yves Saint-Laurent, Strenesse, Gucci and others. There are bargains in the "Department-Store". *Mon–Fri 10:30am–7:30pm, Sat 10am–6pm | Mitte | Friedrichstr. 71 | U6 Französische Straße*

SUPERMARCHÉ (153 F6) *(✉ M6)*
Sustainably produced and inexpensive T-shirts, jeans and dresses. The store invites you to delve into fair trade fashion. Shop with a good conscience and without the alternative touch. *Mon–Fri 11am–7pm, Sat 11am–6pm | Kreuzberg | Wiener Str. 16 | www.supermarche-berlin.de | U 1 Görlitzer Bhf.*

THATCHERS (146 C4) *(✉ L2)*
Black-and-white transparent fabrics and grey tones are the ingredients of these classical fashions that offer unexpected revelations. The highlights are the evening and cocktail dresses: seductive, original! There is another branch in the Hackesche Höfe in Mitte. *Mon–Sat 11am–7pm | Prenzlauer Berg | Kastanienallee 21 | www.thatchers.de | U2 Eberswalder Straße*

THE CORNER (141 D4) *(✉ K4)*
Haute couture meets street wear and luxurious accessories. The huge shop will tempt you to stroll through its departments and gaze in awe at the jackets and dresses by Balenciaga, Chloé, YSL and Givenchy. There is a branch in *Charlottenburg (Knesebeckstr. 32). Mon–Fri 10:30am–7:30pm, Sat 10am–7pm | Mitte | Französische Str. 40/corner of Markgrafenstr. | www.thecornerberlin.de | U 6 Französische Straße*

WERTVOLL (147 E5) *(✉ M2)*
Organic cotton, recycled materials and pine fibres are the basic ingredients for fashionable underwear, blouses and dresses. Labels such as People Tree, Do You Green and format guarantee fair production conditions and part of the profits are donated to charitable organisations. *Mon–Fri 10am–8pm, Sat 10am–6pm | Prenzlauer Berg | Marienburger Str. 39 | www.wertvoll-berlin.com | tram M 2 Marienburger Straße*

14 OZ. ★ (141 E2) *(✉ L3)*
Mixture of fashionable brands and eco-streetwear. The shop is run by Karl-Heinz Müller, the initiator of the „Bread & Butter" fashion fair. You can make your purchases in the private atmosphere of a living room in some rooms on the first floor set up especially for this purpose. Branch at *Kurfürstendamm 194,* outlet store 500 m (1,640 ft) further on at *Memhardtstr. 7* near Alexanderplatz. *Mon–Sat 11am–8pm | Mitte | Neue Schönhauser Str. 13 | www.14oz.net | U 8 Weinmeisterstraße*

SHOES

INSIDER TIP JÜNEMANNS PANTOFFEL-ECK (147 D6) *(✉ L3)*
Felt slippers like grandma used to wear are stacked to the ceiling of this small workroom-cum-shop. The products of the more than 100-year-old family business have developed a cult status of their own. *Mon–Fri 9am–6pm | Mitte | Torstr. 39 | www.pantoffeleck.de | U2 Rosa-Luxemburg-Platz*

Trippen in the Hackesche Höfe displays its shoes as if they were works of art

LUCCICO (141 E1) *(📖 L3)*
Unusual design, fine workmanship and good value for money – all this leads to the house in the "shopping Bermuda triangle" being full all the time. Other branches are located at Oranienburger Str. 23 (Mitte, outlet) and Bergmannstr. 8 (Kreuzberg). *Mon–Fri noon–8pm, Sat 11am–8pm | Mitte | Weinmeisterstr. 12 | www.luccico.de | U 8 Weinmeisterstraße*

TRIPPEN ★ (141 E2) *(📖 L3)*
Absolutely first-rate, designer wood and leather shoes that have created a furore throughout the world. The showroom with the models displayed under spotlights in individual niches is more reminiscent of a gallery than a shop. The company's motto is "ecologically honest and anatomically sensible". *Mon–Fri 11am–8pm, Sat 10am–8pm | Mitte | Rosenthaler Str. 40/41 | Hackesche Höfe IV & VI | www.trippen.com | S Hackescher Markt*

ZEHA (147 E4) *(📖 M2)*
Berlin label with cult status with classic shoes made of calf leather and sneakers and court shoes of the highest quality. There are branches in Schöneberg *(Belziger Str. 21)* and Kreuzberg *(Friesenstr. 7). Mon–Fri noon–8pm, Sat 10am–6pm | Prenzlauer Berg | Prenzlauer Allee 213 | www-zeha-berlin.de | tram M2 Marienburger Straße*

SECOND HAND

COLOURS BERLIN (160 B2) *(📖 K7)*
Tucked away in an inner courtyard building, experimental fashionistas have tons of second-hand clothes to choose from on one vast floor. Clothes are assorted into styles and colours. 30% discount on all clothes on Tuesdays between 11am and 3pm. *Mon–Fri 11am–7pm, Sat noon–7pm | Kreuzberg | Bergmannstr. 102 | www.kleidermarkt.de | U 6, 7 Mehringdamm*

MADONNA (138 A5) *(📖 E5)*
A wide selection of exquisite designer and brand names. All of the Versace coats, Jil Sander pullovers and Chanel costumes seem to be new but are actually second hand. Bad buys on the part of their first owners? There is a branch with designer fashion for men at Mommsenstr. 43.

Mon–Fri noon–7pm Sat noon–4pm | Charlottenburg | Mommsenstr. 57 | S Charlottenburg

MEMORY (147 D5) *(🗺 L2)*
At first glance, this seems to be a chaotic mess of used suitcases, clothes and shoes. If you look closer, the goods reveal themselves as high-quality originals from times gone by: Prada costumes from the 1980s or elegant 1970s checked dresses. With a café. *Mon–Sat 9am–6pm | Prenzlauer Berg | Schwedter Str. 2 | U2 Senefelderplatz*

WEEKLY MARKETS

INSIDER TIP KARL-AUGUST-PLATZ
(149 E4–5) *(🗺 E5)*
Specialities from all over Europe make this market a real delicatessen paradise. Cheese from the Alps and organic carrots, fresh noodles, jam, high-quality fruit and much more not only attract gourmets from Charlottenburg. *Wed 7am–1:30pm, Sat 7am–2:30pm | Charlottenburg | Karl-August-Platz | U 7 Wilmersdorfer Straße*

KOLLWITZMARKT
(147 D4–5) *(🗺 M2)*
For a sophisticated clientele. Many local residents buy here; young families stock up on organic vegetables and meat and delicatessen from regional producers. Thu: organic food only; Sat: a wider selection. *Thu noon–7pm, Sat 9am–4pm | Prenzlauer Berg | Kollwitzplatz | U2 Senefelderplatz*

MARKT AM MAYBACHUFER ★
(153 E–F6) *(🗺 M6)*
Everything the large Anatolian family needs can be bought at the "Turkish market". Grapes, tomatoes and aubergines are sold by the crate. The young German smart set from Kreuzberg are more attracted to antipasti and organic cheese. *Tue, Fri 11am–6:30pm | Neukölln | Maybachufer | U 8 Schönleinstraße*

WINTERFELDTMARKT
(159 D1) *(🗺 H6)*
Visiting this weekly market is an absolute must in the Schöneberg gay and academic scene. And afterwards just watch the world go by from one of the cafés. *Wed 8am–2pm, Sat 8am–4pm | Schöneberg | Winterfeldtplatz | 1, 2 Nollendorfplatz*

LOW BUDGET

For fans of retro: *kultur propaganda* **(161 F2)** ***(🗺 M7)*** *(Tue–Fri afternoons, Sat irregular opening times | Reuterstr. 62 | www.kultur-propaganda.de | U 7 Hermannplatz)* in the Neukölln district offers everything from radios to eggcups from the 1930s to 1970s.

The *Marc-O'Polo-Outlet* **(148 C4)** ***(🗺 D4)*** *(Mon–Fri 10am–7pm, Sat 10am–6pm | Kaiserdamm 7 | U 2 Sophie-Charlotte-Platz)* is a haven for bargain hunters.

Discounts of up to 70 percent on high-street fashion brands at the *Zalando Outlet* **(154 A2)** ***(🗺 N5)*** *(Mon–Sat 11am–8pm | Kreuzberg | Köpenicker Str. 20 | www.zalando-outlet.de/berlin | U 1 Schlesisches Tor)*.

New and used CDs and records; indie, pop, rock, hip-hop are offered at *Logo An- und Verkauf* **(160 B2)** ***(🗺 K7)*** *(Mon noon–6:30pm, Tue–Fri noon–7pm, Sat 11am–3pm | Kreuzberg | Bergmannstr. 10 | U7 Gneisenaustraße)*.

ENTERTAINMENT

CITY WHERE TO START?
If you want to have a good time and not spend much money, the Neukölln district around **Weserstraße** is the place to go *(U7, 8 Hermannstraße)*. You will find many popular bars and clubs (including Riva Bar and House of Weekend Club) in Mitte between **Alexanderplatz** and **Hackescher Markt** or around the **Oberbaumbrücke** that connects Kreuzberg and Friedrichshain. At Watergate, you can dance with a view of the Spree. Nearby at the Ostbahnhof, the queues in front of Berghain show you that this is one of the best clubs in the world.

In Berlin, nights are not only for sleeping: dance to the early hours, sit as long as you like with your beer at the bar, visit concerts or theatre performances, go to the cinema – that gets you in the right mood.
Hardly anywhere else in the world is there a larger number of clubs, bars and cultural venues than in Berlin. Almost 300 clubs, 30 cabarets and variety theatres, more than 130 cinemas and countless pubs and bars all compete with each other. The council offices in Mitte district are not very generous about granting licences in some streets so that the locals can have some peace at night. And every summer there are disputes between people living above a pub and its guests about the excessive noise that comes from nocturnal chatter outside in the open. So far, however, pub-owners have usually

Photo: Club Watergate at Oberbaumbrücke

First stop, a theatre performance and then on to a bar and later dancing until dawn

managed to defend their interests. Even those who want to sleep will wake up sooner or later – and then it's off for a quick beer round the corner.

BARS

BILLY WILDER'S (151 F4) *(🗺 J5)*
The selection of 85 different vodkas is unique and, supposedly, unequalled in Berlin. But, the (120 different!) cocktails are also exceptional. Chic surroundings with art-deco elements. Ideal after you have visited one of the nearby cinemas or musical theatres. *Daily from 11am | Tiergarten | Potsdamer Str. 2 | tel. 030 26 55 48 60 | www.billywilders.de | U/S Potsdamer Platz*

CSA (165 D3) *(🗺 N4)*
Top address for design fans where Russian architecture meets modern minimalism. With a perfectly mixed Mai Tai in your hand, you can watch what is happening on the magnificent boulevard or sink into one of the deep leather chairs in the lounge area.

You can chill or dance the evening away at the Strandbar Mitte

Daily from 7pm | Friedrichshain | Karl-Marx-Allee 96 | tel. 030 29 04 47 41 | www.csa-bar.de | U 5 Weberwiese

GAINSBOURG (138 C4) *(🕮 F5)*
This American-style bar is a location from home for Charlottenburg's bohemians where they sip first-rate cocktails and listen to music by the French namegiver. *Daily from 4pm, in winter from 5pm | Charlottenburg | Jeanne-Mammen-Bogen 567–577 | tel. 030 3 13 74 64 | www.gainsbourg.de | S Savignyplatz*

KUSCHLOWSKI (161 F2) *(🕮 M7)*
Small living-room bar with a fireplace. One of the owners is a Russian woman who ensures that the vodka flows, served in a variety of different ways. *Daily from 8pm | Neukölln | Weserstr. 202 | tel. 0176 24 38 97 01 | www.kuschlowski.de | U 7, 8 Hermannplatz*

MONKEY BAR (139 F4) *(🕮 G5)*
TExcellent view of the monkeys in the zoo, best drinks and friendly guests. This mixture is attracting Berliners back to the city's west with the shopping centre Bikini Berlin and the *25hours Hotel* where this bar is located. *Sun–Thu noon–1am, Fri/Sat noon–2am | Charlottenburg | Budapester Str. 40/10th floor | www.25hours-hotels.com | U 1, 2, 3 Wittenbergplatz*

NEWTON (140 C5) *(🕮 K4)*
The nude photographs by the late Helmut Newton might distract you from your oysters, champagne and well-mixed cocktails. There is a cigar lounge on the first floor for those so inclined. *Sun–Wed 10am–3am, Thu–Sat 10am–4am | Mitte | Charlottenstr. 57 | tel. 030 20 29 54 21 | www.newton-bar.de | U 6 Französische Straße*

RIVA (141 E2) *(🕮 L3)*
Guests sit at oval tables under a railway arch; the bottle rack in the centre is modelled on the *Titanic*. This is the place for aesthetes with a fondness for cultivated cocktails. *Daily from 6pm | Mitte | Dircksenstr. 142 | tel. 030 24 72 26 88 | www.riva-berlin.de |S Hackescher Markt*

SOLAR ★ (152 A5) *(Ⓜ J5)*
It's great fun to sip your cocktails on the 16th floor and look down on the city. Especially after the trip in a glass lift up the façade of the building has given you your first thrill! By the way, you can also enjoy a Mediterranean meal here. *Daily from 6pm | Kreuzberg | Stresemannstr. 76 | tel. 0163 7 65 27 00 | www.solarberlin.com | S 1, 25 Anhalter Bahnhof*

STRANDBAR MITTE ●
(141 D2) *(Ⓜ K3)*
This is where young and old meet on the banks of the Spree in summer to order their cocktails, coffee or beer from the self-service bar and relax in the deckchairs with a view towards the Museumsinsel. Also has a dancefllor for tango dancing. *May–Sept daily from 10am | Mitte | Monbijoustr. 3 | www.strandbar-mitte.de | S1, 25 Oranienburger Straße*

WEINBAR RUTZ ★ (140 B–C1) *(Ⓜ K3)*
1,001 different wines lie waiting for you in the racks of this carefully-styled bar. The wine list is enormous but a sommelier will help you make your choice: in addition, exquisite cooking. *Tue–Sat from 6:30pm | Mitte | Chausseestr. 8 | tel. 030 24 62 87 60 | www.rutz-weinbar.de | U6 Oranienburger Tor*

CLUBS

ADAGIO (140 A6) *(Ⓜ J5)*
Gigantic nightclub underneath the Theater am Potsdamer Platz. It is impossible to be bored in these cheerful Baroque-style surroundings which include five bars and a large dance floor. *Fri/Sat from 10pm | admission 12 euros | Tiergarten | Marlene-Dietrich-Platz 1 | tel. 030 258 98 90 | www.adagio.de | U/S Potsdamer Platz*

A TRANE (138 C4) *(Ⓜ F5)*
The unpretentiously-styled modern jazz club has live performances – every day! The concerts are always well-attended, also because of reasonable entrance fees. *Daily from 8pm | Charlottenburg | Bleibtreustr. 1/*

MARCO POLO HIGHLIGHTS

★ **Weinbar Rutz**
Best wine bar in Berlin with over 1000 wines and gourmet cuisine → p. 89

★ **Solar**
Club on the 16th floor with spectacular view over Berlin → p. 89

★ **Berghain**
Internationally popular bar in a disused heating plant → p. 90

★ **Tausend**
Cool interior design; great drinks and DJs → p. 91

★ **Bar jeder Vernunft**
Shows, variety performances and top cuisine in the mirror tent → p. 91

★ **Friedrichstadt-Palast**
Glitz and glamour: the world's largest show stage with fabulous dancers → p. 94

★ **Philharmonie**
A must for classic fans: magnificent acoustics and top orchestras → p. 95

★ **Deutsches Theater**
As in its best days: top-quality classics → p. 97

corner of Pestalozzistr. | tel. 030 3 13 25 50 | www.a-trane.de | S Savignyplatz

BERGHAIN ★
(154 B1) *(🗺 N5)*
Techno-electro club that has fans from all over the world. Night-owls between 20 and 40 have fun on the two floors of this disused heating plant with 18 m (60 ft) high ceilings and refuel at one of the four bars. All this with art on the walls and a laid-back atmosphere. *Fri, Sat from midnight | admission 12 euros | Friedrichshain | Am Wriezener Bahnhof | S Ostbahnhof*

GRETCHEN (152 B6) *(🗺 J6)*
Set on two floors in the former stables of a Prussian regiment, this club attracts a mixed crowd of all ages. Music from electro to dubstep, indie to jazz. *Fri/Sat from 11:30pm, otherwise depending on the event | Kreuzberg | Obentrautstr. 19–21 | tel. 030 25 92 27 02 | www.gretchen-club.de | U 6, 7 Mehringdamm*

INSIDER TIP **HAFENBAR** (146 A6) *(🗺 J3)*
Fun interior with ships' ropes and portholes. Dance freaks between the ages of 20 and 50 cavort at ABBA parties, hit-parade and rock-'n-roll events. *Only Fri (German pop from 9pm) and Sat (9pm–midnight karaoke, then dancing) | admission 5–8 euros | Mitte | Chausseestr. 20 | tel. 030 2 82 85 93 | www.hafenbar-berlin.de | U 6 Naturkundemuseum*

HOUSE OF WEEKEND
(141 F2) *(🗺 L–M3)*
Dancing on the 12th floor of the former "Haus des Reisens" East German travel organisation. Fans of house music between the ages of 20 and 40 amuse themselves high up above Alexanderplatz. The terrace and bar on the 15th floor are only open in summer – and then, the view is magnificent. *Tue, Thu–Sat from midnight | admission 10–15 euros | Mitte | Alexanderplatz 5 | www.houseofweekend.berlin | U-/S Alexanderplatz*

PURO (139 E–F4) *(🗺 G5)*
Sky-lounge on the 20th floor of the Europa Center with a dance floor and Japanese-inspired interior for those over 20. Great view over the city! *Wed–Sat from 8pm | admission 8–12 euros | Charlottenburg | Tauentzienstr. 9–12 | tel. 030 26 36 78 75 | www.puro-berlin.de | U 1, 2, 3 Wittenbergplatz*

QUASIMODO (139 D4) *(🗺 F5)*
Traditional jazz club with concerts by well-known musicians. Almost all of the world-famous funk, soul and jazz stars – from Defunkt to Jasper van't Hof – have played

LOW BUDGET

The free concerts of the students from the *Hanns Eisler Music College* at *Charlottenstr. 55* **(140 C5)** ***(🗺 K4)*** *(U 2, 6 Stadtmitte)* and *Schlossplatz 7* **(141 E4)** ***(🗺 L4)*** *(U 2 Hausvogtei-platz)* locations present the virtuosos of the future. *Tickets: tel. 030 2 03 09 21 01 | www.hfm-berlin.de*

The ● *Sageclub* **(153 D3–4)** ***(🗺 M5)*** *(Kreuzberg | Köpenicker Str. 76 | www.sage-club.de | U 8 Heinrich-Heine-Straße)* presents "Rock at Sage" *(Thu 7pm–10pm)* – free of charge.

The *frannz-Club* **(147 D4)** ***(🗺 L2)*** *(Prenzlauer Berg | Schönhauser Allee 36 | www.frannz.de | U 2 Eberswalder Straße)* presents pop/rock for 3 euros on Sat before midnight for everyone older than 35 (otherwise 6 euros).

here. *Daily from 9pm | admission 15–22 euros | Charlottenburg | Kantstr. 12a | tel. 030 3 12 80 86 | www.quasimodo.de | U/S Zoologischer Garten*

SPINDLER & KLATT IN DER HEERESBÄCKEREI (154 A2) *(🕮 N5)*
Club restaurant with lounge atmosphere and a touch of Asia in an old warehouse. You eat lying down and this can sometimes mean that you will hear the crashed out night-owl on the sofa next to you snoring. Lovely terrace on the Spree. *Dinner Thu–Sat, in the summer daily from 8pm, club Fri, Sat from 11pm, closed Sun–Thu in the winter | admission 10 euros | Kreuzberg | Köpenicker Str. 16-17 | tel. 030 3 19 88 18 60 | www.spindlerklatt.com | U 1 Schlesisches Tor*

TAUSEND ★ (140 B3) *(🕮 J4)*
Perfectly mixed drinks and a discreet, elegant interior straight out of a James Bond film, along with a wall installation in the form of a gigantic eye. DJs from the dub and electro scene take care of the background sound. *Tue–Sat from 7:30pm | admission 7–15 euros | Mitte | Schiffbauerdamm 11 | tel. 030 27 58 20 70 | www.tausendberlin.com | U/S Friedrichstraße*

TRESOR (153 E3) *(🕮 M5)*
International techno DJs sit at the turntables in this former heating plant. A 30 m (110 ft) long tunnel leads to the dance floor in the cellar. Rough industrial atmosphere and the noise level is nothing for sensitive souls. The young crowd is international. *Mon, Wed, Fri, Sat from midnight | admission 7–15 euros | Mitte | Köpenicker Str. 70 | tel. 030 62 90 87 50 | www.tresorberlin.de | U 8 Heinrich-Heine-Straße*

WATERGATE
(154 B2–3) *(🕮 N5–6)*
The last dancing stop before the Spree. A great view of the water and Oberbaumbrücke makes this a popular place for well-heeled 25 to 40-year-olds to amuse themselves with drum-'n-bass and soul rhythms in carefully-styled modern surroundings. *Wed, Fri, Sat from midnight | admission 10–15 euros | Kreuzberg | Falckensteinstr. 49 | tel. 030 61 28 03 94 | www.water-gate.de | U1 Schlesisches Tor*

Live music at the Quasimodo

SHOWS & CABARET

BAR JEDER VERNUNFT ★
(139 E6) *(🕮 F6)*
It is worth visiting this cabaret just to see the extravagant Art Nouveau mirror tent. But, the innovative programme with stars

from the chanson and comedy world such as Max Raabe and the Geschwister Pfister also have a lot going for them. You can eat and drink while you enjoy the performance. *Box office Mon–Sat noon–6:30pm, Sun 3–5:30pm, door from 6:30pm | tickets 19–75 euros | Wilmersdorf | Schaperstr. 24 | tel. 030 8 83 15 82 | www.bar-jeder-vernunft.de | U 1, 9 Spichernstraße*

DIE STACHELSCHWEINE
(139 E–F4) *(⚲ G5)*
This political cabaret full of wit and verve is an institution in West Berlin. *Tickets 19–31 euros | Charlottenburg| Tauentzienstr. 9 | Europa Center | tel. 030 2 61 47 95 | www.diestachelschweine.de | U 9, 15 Kurfürstendamm*

DISTEL (140 C3) *(⚲ K3–4)*
This establishment has been in existence for more than 50 years and while the Wall was still standing its performers were complete masters at covertly criticising the East German system. Today, capitalism is the target of their irony . *Box office Mon–Fri 11am–6pm, Sat/Sun 11am–5pm | tickets 15–31 euros | Mitte | Friedrichstr. 101 | tel. 030 2 04 47 04 | U/S Friedrichstraße*

TIPI AM KANZLERAMT (151 E2) *(⚲ H4)*
Well-known entertainment stars such as Georgette Dee and Tim Fischer appear here as do up-and-coming a-cappella-ensembles and virtuoso African drummers. Rustic atmosphere in a marquee next to the Federal Chancellery. Tickets 24.50–29.50 euros. *Tiergarten | Große Querallee | ticket tel. 030 39 06 65 50 | www.tipi-am-kanzleramt.de | U/S Brandenburger Tor*

INSIDER TIP UFA-FABRIK
(165 D4) *(⚲ J10)*
The whole universe of off-culture on the former premises of the UFA film company: a circus for children to take part in, caba-

An atmospheric setting for cabaret, music and variety performances: Tipi am Kanzleramt

ret, variety shows. *Tempelhof | Viktoriastr. 10–18 | tel. 030 75 50 30 | www.ufafabrik.de | U6 Ullsteinstraße*

CINEMAS

The approximately 300 cinemas of all sizes and categories attract their audiences with their diversified programmes. You can find a list of what is showing in the individual cinemas (along with their addresses) in the Berlin events magazines *Zitty* and *tip*.

PUBS

DIENER – TATTERSALL (138 C4) *(🗺 F5)*
Many of the former and current guests, from Billy Wilder to Helmut Newton, have been immortalised in photographs. This is still a popular place for actors and bohemians to drop by for a glass of beer or for a plate of meatballs with mustard. But, of course less famous guests are also welcome. *Daily from 6pm | Charlottenburg | Grolmanstr. 47 | tel. 030 8 81 53 29 | www.diener-tattersall.de | S Savignyplatz*

INSIDER TIP KACHELLOUNGE
(165 D4) *(🗺 N7)*
One of the cosiest pubs in Berlin is decorated with old stove tiles and furnished with armchairs and sofas. Its mainly young guests reward this by coming regularly and it is usually crowded by midnight at the latest. *Mon–Thu 7pm–1am, Fri/Sat 7pm–5:30am | Neukölln | Weichselstr. 54 | U7 Rathaus Neukölln*

LEMKE (141 E2) *(🗺 L3)*
The rustic brewery in railway arch number 143 offers a lot of different beers and hearty food from the grill. Beer garden in summer. *Daily from noon, Mon–Fri lunch buffet noon–3pm | Mitte | S-Bahnbogen 143 | tel. 030 24 72 87 27 | www.brauhaus-lemke.de | S Hackescher Markt*

MÖBEL OLFE (153 E5) *(🗺 M6)*
At night, things really start to happen at one of the ugliest places in town, the run-down centre of Kreuzberg at Kottbusser Tor. The later it gets, the more Polish beer and vodka flows down the guests' parched throats. Mixed hetero and gay clientele. *Tue–Sun from 6pm | Kreuzberg | Reichenberger Str. 177 | tel. 030 23 27 46 90 | www.moebel-olfe.de | U1, 8 Kottbusser Tor*

RESTAURATION SOPHIEN 11
(141 E1) *(🗺 L3)*
Comfy pub with an inner courtyard next to the Hackesche Höfe where you can relax over reasonably-priced meatballs and beer. *Sun–Tue 4pm–midnight, Wed–Sat noon–midnight | Mitte | Sophienstr. 11 | tel. 030 2 83 21 36 | www.restauration-sophien11.de | S Hackescher Markt*

ROCK-'N'-ROLL-HERBERGE
(154 A2) *(🗺 M5)*
Even if you do not stay in this home-away-from home for musicians, you will be welcome to drink a beer and play billiards or tabletop football in the foyer. Maybe you'll meet one of tomorrow's rock stars. And, if you can't make it home, just book a room for the night. *Daily from 10am | Kreuzberg | Muskauer Str. 11 | tel. 030 61 62 36 00 | www.rnrherberge.de | U1 Görlitzer Bahnhof*

STÄNDIGE VERTRETUNG
(140 B3) *(🗺 K3–4)*
When the government moved to Berlin, many people from the Rhineland came with it. This is where lively exiled Bonners get together for a glass of Kölsch beer and celebrate carnival the way they did it back home. *Daily from 9am | Mitte |*

Schiffbauerdamm 8 | tel. 030 2 82 39 65 | U/S Friedrichstraße

YORCKSCHLÖSSCHEN ● (160 A1) *(🗺 J6)*
A bit run-down but still cosy is how regulars swigging their beer or listening to a live concert feel about this place. Lovely beer garden in summer. One of the oldest and most-popular jazz pubs in the city. *Mon–Sat 5pm–3am, Sun from 10am | Kreuzberg | Yorckstr. 15 | tel. 030 20 15 80 70 | www.yorckschloesschen.de | U 6, 7 Mehringdamm*

CONCERTS, MUSICALS, DANCE & OPERA

ADMIRALPALAST (140 C3) *(🗺 K3–4)*
New life has been breathed into the former entertainment palace from 1911: plays, musicals and theatre sport brighten up the stage near Friedrichstraße Station. *Mitte | Friedrichstr. 101 | tel. 030 47 99 74 99 | U/S Friedrichstraße*

DEUTSCHE OPER (138 A2) *(🗺 E4)*
Once the West's answer to the Staatsoper in the East. Today, a house with a unconventional interpretations. *Charlottenburg | Bismarckstr. 35 | tel. 030 34 38 43 43 | www.deutscheoperberlin.de | U 2 Deutsche Oper*

FRIEDRICHSTADT-PALAST ★
(140 C2) *(🗺 K3)*
Germany's only – and the world's largest – revue theatre with plenty of high-kicking dancing girls. *Mitte | Friedrichstr. 107 | tel. 030 23 26 23 26 | www.palast-berlin.eu | U 6 Oranienburger Tor*

GRIPS THEATER (139 F1) *(🗺 G4)*
A Berlin institution that shows socio-critical musicals for the city's youth and adults who have remained young. Volker Ludwig's musical set in the underground "Linie 1" has been playing for 25 years and its successor "Linie 2 – der Alptraum"

BOOKS & FILMS

Berlin Blues – Author and musician Sven Regener (Element of Crime) captured the zeitgeist in West Berlin just before the Wall fell in this novel

Russian Disco – Wladimir Kaminer, from whom the "Russian Disco" in Kaffee Burger originates, demonstrates his keen observation of everyday life in East Berlin in the 1990s in this and other books

Berlin Alexanderplatz – This classic novel by Alfred Döblin (1929) is still highly recommended reading. The story of an ordinary person attempting to get back on track after being released from prison is just as pertinent today – Rainer Werner Fassbinder's film has become a legend

Good Bye Lenin! – Wolfgang Becker's prize-winning film (2003) about life in an East Berlin flat at the time of reunification – told with humour and a sense of tragedy

Oh Boy – Black and white film (2012) depicting drop-out student life in Berlin. A young man from an affluent background is struggling to make an existence, but this he does with charm – and he's in love, too... Director: Jan Ole Gerster, leading role: Tom Schilling

Excellent acoustics: concert hall of the Philharmonic Orchestra

fills up the house as well. *Moabit | Altonaer Str. 22 / in the Hansaplatz underground station | tel. 030 3 97 47 40 | www.grips-theater.de | U 9 Hansaplatz*

HEBBEL AM UFER (152 B6) *(🗺 K6)*
Experimental concept focussing mainly on dance on three stages. *Kreuzberg | HAU 1 (Stresemannstr. 29) | HAU 2 (Hallesches Ufer 32), HAU 3 (Tempelhofer Ufer 10) | tel. 030 25 90 04 27 | www.hebbel-am-ufer.de | U 1, 6 Hallesches Tor*

KONZERTHAUS AM GENDARMENMARKT (141 D5) *(🗺 K4)*
Today, the Berlin Symphony Orchestra is the main performer in what was originally a theatre built by Schinkel between 1818 and 1821. One drawback, however, the acoustics are not ideal everywhere. *Advance sales Mon–Sat noon–7pm, Sun noon–4pm | Mitte | Am Gendarmenmarkt 2 | tel. 030 2 03 09 21 01 | www.konzerthaus.de | U 2, 6 Stadtmitte*

INSIDER TIP **NEUKÖLLNER OPER** (165 D4) *(🗺 N8)*
Comparatively small theatre with amusing performances and unconventional interpretations of light operas and musical plays. A real off-opera! *Neukölln | Karl-Marx-Str. 131–133 | tel. 030 68 89 07 77 | www.neukoellneroper.de | U 7 Karl-Marx-Straße*

PHILHARMONIE ★ (151 E4) *(🗺 J5)*
This is the home of the Berlin Philharmonic Orchestra and its conductor Sir Simon Rattle. The acoustics in the building designed by Hans Scharoun are first-rate. ●
INSIDER TIP Free concerts at 1pm on Tuesdays from September to June! *Advance sales Mon–Fri 3–6pm, Sat/Sun 11am–2pm |*

Tiergarten | Herbert-von-Karajan-Str. 1 | tel. 030 25 48 89 99 | www.berliner-philharmoniker.de | U/S Potsdamer Platz

STAATSOPER UNTER DEN LINDEN
(141 D4) *(🗺 K4)*
Berlin's oldest opera will be renovated until at least the end of 2016. Until then, performances under the house's musical director Daniel Barenboim will be given in the *Schillertheater (Charlottenburg | Bismarckstr. 110). Mitte | Unter den Linden 7 | tel. 030 20 35 45 55 | www.staatsoperberlin.de | U 6 Französische Straße*

THEATER DES WESTENS
(139 D4) *(🗺 F5)*
Musical theatre. The house opened in the 19th century and many stars, including Josephine Baker and Hildegard Knef, have performed here. *Charlottenburg | Kantstr. 12 | ticket hotline tel. 01805 44 44 (*) | www.stage-entertainment.de | U/S Zoologischer Garten*

THEATER AM POTSDAMER PLATZ
(140 A6) *(🗺 J5)*
Popular musical theatre. Currently, "Hinterm Horizont" (Beyond the Horizon) with hits by Udo Lindenberg is being performed. The play about an East-West love affair was developed by veteran rocker Udo himself with the help of author Thomas Brussig and director Ulrich Waller. *Tiergarten | Marlene-Dietrich-Platz 1 | tel. 01805 44 44 (*) | www.stage-entertainment.de | U/S Potsdamer Platz*

DANCE

GRÜNER SALON
(141 F1) *(🗺 L3)*
Thursday night is salsa time in a side wing of the Volksbühne theatre with open classes (8–9pm), after that it's party time. Concerts Thu, Sat. *Mitte | Rosa-Luxemburg-Platz 2 | tel. 030 6 88 33 23 90 | www.gruener-salon.de | U 2 Rosa-Luxemburg-Platz*

SPORTING FEVER

Football fans head for the *Olympiastadium* that was renovated for the 2006 World Championship (see p. 55). This is where the professionals from *Hertha BSC* play. There are fan shops in all major department stores in Berlin. Tickets online or from *tel. 030 3 00 92 8 18 92*. The main office is in the Olympiastadium **(164 C3)** *(🗺 A4) (Charlottenburg | Hanns-Braun-Str. | Friesenhaus II | tel. 030 30 68 81 00 (*) | www.herthabsc.de)*. The second-league team *FC Union (www.fc-union-berlin.de)* plays in the *An der Alten Försterei* stadium **(165 E4)** *(🗺 O)* out in the Wuhlheide park in Köpenick. Tickets can be purchased at most booking offices as well as online. The national-league basketball team *Alba Berlin (www.albaberlin.de)* is a must if you are interested in the sport. Home games are played in the *Mercedes Benz Arena* **(154 B2)** *(🗺 N5) (Mühlenstr. 12–30)* in Friedrichshain. Tickets under *tel. 01805 57 00 11 (*)* and in the *Max-Schmeling-Halle* **(146 C3)** *(🗺 L1) (Mon–Fri 10am–7pm, Sat noon–5pm | Mitte | Am Falkplatz | ticket tel. 030 44 30 44 30)*. Ice hockey fans won't want to miss a game by the *Polar Bears Berlin (www.eisbaeren.de)*. Tickets for DEL games: *tel: 01806 57 00 11 (*)* or online. Their home stadium is also the *Mercedes Benz Arena* at Ostbahnhof.

HAVANNA (159 D3) *(🗺 H7)*
There are separate areas for salsa, meringue, bachata and black music; so you can change your rhythm whenever you feel like it. *Wed (only salsa, from 9pm) and Fri/Sat from 10pm, Sun from 9pm | Schöneberg | Hauptstr. 30 | tel. 030 784 85 65 | www.havanna-berlin.de | U 7 Kleistpark*

THEATRE

Berlin has a great reputation as an important theatre city. Stage personalities who make it here have reached the pinnacle of the German theatre world.

BERLINER ENSEMBLE
(140 B–C2) *(🗺 J–K3)*
This is where Bertolt Brecht used to work. His plays are still a staple of its repertoire but other playwrights are also performed. Popular; often sold out. *Mitte | Bertolt-Brecht-Platz 1 | tel. 030 28 40 81 55 | www.berliner-ensemble.de | U/S Friedrichstraße*

DEUTSCHES THEATER ★
(140 B2) *(🗺 J3)*
This was Germany's most famous theatre 100 years ago when Max Reinhardt was its director. Today, the threads of a glorious past are being picked up. Many classical plays in the repertoire. *Mitte | Schumannstr. 13a | tel. 030 28 44 12 25 | www.deutschestheater.de | U 6 Oranienburger Tor*

MAXIM GORKI THEATER
(141 D3) *(🗺 K4)*
Ambitious plays by young authors as well as classics. *Mitte | Am Festungsgraben 2 | tel. 030 20 22 11 15 | www.gorki.de | S Hackescher Markt*

SCHAUBÜHNE (149 D6) *(🗺 E6)*
Today, the ensemble of the legendary Schaubühne, which achieved cult status when Peter Stein was its director, competes with the Volksbühne with its performances of socio-critical, unconventional plays. *Wilmersdorf | Kurfürstendamm 153 | tel. 030 89 00 23 | www.schaubuehne.de | U7 Adenauerplatz*

Sophisticated plays at the Maxim Gorki theater

INSIDER TIP **SOPHIENSAELE**
(141 E1) *(🗺 L3)*
The equipment is rather basic but the creative spirit is all the more productive. It is amazing to see how it is possible to produce dramas that really get under your skin with such limited resources. *Mitte | Sophienstr. 18 | tel. 030 2 83 52 66 | www.sophiensaele.com | S Hackescher Markt*

VOLKSBÜHNE (141 F1) *(🗺 L3)*
Cult stage director Frank Castorf tries to be provocative with his unconventional productions.After the end of his contract in 2017, new concepts are planned for the theatre. *Mitte | Rosa-Luxemburg-Platz 2 | tel. 030 24 06 57 77 | www.volksbuehne-berlin.de | U 2 Rosa-Luxemburg-Platz*

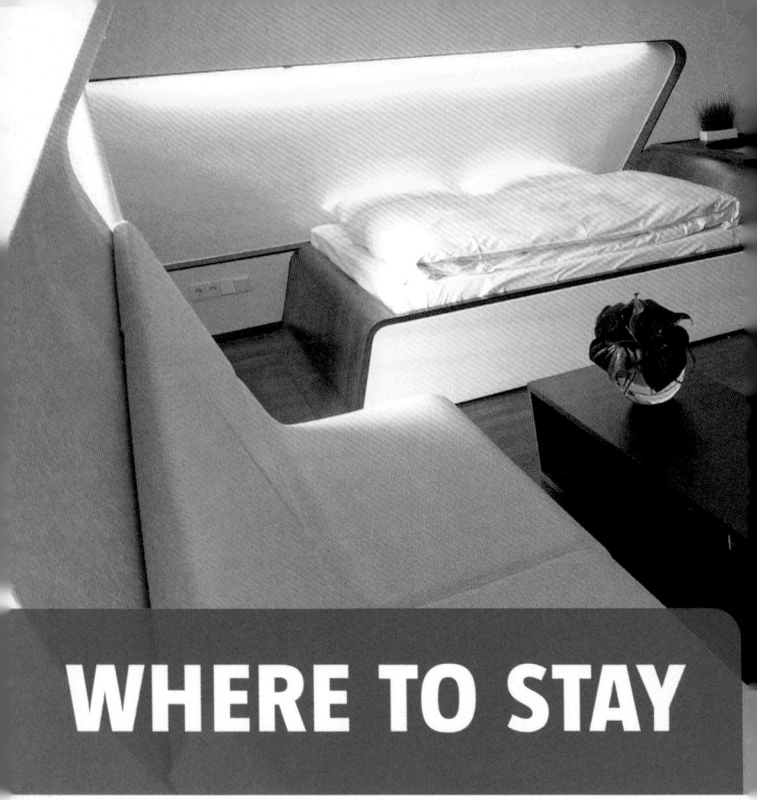

WHERE TO STAY

If there is one branch in Berlin that is really booming, it is tourism. Even while the Wall was still standing there were hardly ever as many guests in the city as there have been in recent years. Hotels are springing up everywhere.
Berlin has more than 135,000 beds waiting for its guests! And, some of the architecture is also quite impressive. Designer hotels such as the *Q!* or the *Grand Hyatt* with its spa high above the roofs of the city on Potsdamer Platz set new standards in architecture and interior design. The *Radisson Blu* opposite Berliner Dom is another highlight. The lobby is crowned by a six-storey aquarium visitors of the adjacent *Sealife Aquarium* can pass through in a lift. The many small guesthouses in the city don't need these kinds of frills; they have an advantage that cannot be bought – personal atmosphere! Many guests appreciate seeing the host or hostess standing at the stove in the morning preparing breakfast more than the most luxurious buffet.
The enormous choice of hostels, private rooms and flats means that it is cheaper to stay in Berlin than in most other cities. Chains like *Motel One* have branches located throughout the city but the small, privately-run hotels and guesthouses are also popular. Even if you have limited resources, you will be able to spend the night in comfort.
Hotel information: *tel. 030 25 00 23 23 | www.visitberlin.de.*

Photo: Hotel Q!

Berlin's hotels try to outdo each other when it comes to luxury and service, but the smaller establishments are also prospering

HOTELS: EXPENSIVE

ACKSELHAUS ★
(147 D5) *(🗺 M2)*
Beautifully themed rooms and apartments, a Balinese courtyard garden and a goldfish pond. To reach the rooms on the ground floor, you cross over water using stepping stones. Delightful accommodation! *35 rooms | Prenzlauer Berg | Belforter Str. 21 | tel. 030 44 33 76 33 | www.ackselhaus.de | U 2 Senefelderplatz*

BRISTOL HOTEL KEMPINSKI BERLIN
(139 D5) *(🗺 F5)*
The classic on Kurfürstendamm. After a stroll through the city, its guests can relax in great comfort. It also has Berlin's largest Presidential Suite on two floors. *301 rooms and suites | Charlottenburg | Kurfürstendamm 27 | tel. 030 88 43 40 | www.kempinski-berlin.de | U 1 Uhlandstraße*

ELLINGTON **(139 E5)** *(🗺 G5)*
Informally elegant, comfortable hotel that welcomes families with its idyllic

Ready for an elevator ride in an aquarium? Go to the Radisson Blue

summer garden in the inner courtyard. One child under the age of five may stay in the room of two full-paying adults free of charge; there is a charge of 15 euros for older children. *285 rooms and suites | Schöneberg | Nürnberger Str. 50–55 | tel. 030 68 3150 | www.ellington-hotel.com | U 1, 2, 3 Wittenbergplatz*

NHOW ★ (154 B–C2) *(Ⓜ N–O5)*
Many creative guests are attracted by Karim Rashid's cool design and the fact that sound studios can be rented. The retro-futuristic interior of the hotel's *Fabrics* restaurant on the banks of the Spree reminds one of a mixture between Alice in Wonderland and Star Trek. *304 rooms | Friedrichshain | Stralauer Allee 3 | tel. 030 2 90 29 90 | www.nh-hotels.de | U/S Warschauer Straße*

Q! (138 C5) *(Ⓜ L3)*
Sweeping lounge design – even the reception looks like a cocktail bar. Award-winning and widely acclaimed. *72 rooms, 4 studios, 1 penthouse | Charlottenburg | Knesebeckstr. 67 | tel. 030 8 10 06 60 | www.loock-hotels.com/qhotel | U 1 Uhlandstraße*

RADISSON BLU ★
(141 E3) *(Ⓜ L4)*
The five-star hotel is located on the banks of the Spree directly opposite Berliner Dom. The largest cylindrical aquarium in the world with a million litres of water is located in the lobby. A lift from the SeaLife Aquarium passes through the underwater world up to the sixth floor. *427 rooms | Mitte | Karl-Liebknecht-Str. 3 | tel. 030 23 82 80 | www.berlin.radissonblu.com | S Hackescher Markt*

25HOURS BERLIN ★
(139 F4) *(Ⓜ G5)*
Creatively styled rooms, free bike and mini hire, excellent bar on the 10th floor and the excellent *Neni* restaurant. The new attraction in the city's west is not only popular with hotel guests. *149 rooms | Charlottenburg | Budapester Str. 40 | tel. 030 3 01 20 22 10 | www.25hours-hotels.com | U 1, 2, 3 Wittenbergplatz*

THE WEINMEISTER
(156 C1) *(Ⓜ K3)*
Cool designer hotel with beauty spa on the 6th floor and roof terrace.

Each room has its own PC and docking stations for iPhones. 24-hr service. *84 rooms | Mitte | Weinmeisterstr. 2 | tel. 030 755 66 70 | www.the-weinmeister.com | U 8 Weinmeisterstraße*

HOTELS: MODERATE

AMANO ★

(152 C1) *(Ⓜ L3)*

Central location, roof terrace, brightly furnished rooms with soundproof windows – stay in style between the Hackesche Markt and Rosenthaler Platz. Tip: the *Amano Bar* diagonally opposite. *117 rooms | Mitte | Auguststr. 43 | tel. 030 8 09 41 50 | www.amanogroup.de | U 8 Rosenthaler Platz*

ARTE LUISE KUNSTHOTEL

(140 A–B 2–3) *(Ⓜ J3)*

Each room has been individually decorated by a different artist. But comfort and homeliness also get their due. Not only artists stay here – it is also popular with "normal" visitors to Berlin. *50 rooms | Mitte | Luisenstr. 19 | tel. 030 28 44 80 | www.luise-berlin.com | U/S Friedrichstraße*

GARDEN LIVING ★

(140 A1) *(Ⓜ J3)*

Live like in a Roman palazzo; its inner courtyard blossoms in summer with a fountain, palm trees, orange bushes and veranda to enjoy a leisurely breakfast. The rooms are furnished in wood and warm colours – in pleasant contrast to the grey skies over Berlin. *27 rooms/apartments | Mitte | Invalidenstr. 101 | tel. 030 2 84 45 59 00 | www.gardenliving.de | U 6 Naturkundemuseum*

IBIS BERLIN CITY OST

(153 F4) *(Ⓜ M4)*

Central location on the banks of the Spree; good value for money, non-smoking floors. *242 rooms | Friedrichshain | An der Schillingbrücke 2 | tel. 030 25 76 00 | www.ibishotel.com | S Ostbahnhof*

MARCO POLO HIGHLIGHTS

★ Amano
Best location at the Hackescher Markt. The roof terrace attracts guests in summer → p. 101

★ Radisson Blu
A gigantic aquarium soars up from the lobby to the 6th floor → p. 100

★ Nhow
Top designer hotel with interiors by Karim Rashid → p. 100

★ Heart of Gold Hostel
The Berlin Mitte party scene is not far away; light and quiet rooms for the not-so-well-off → p. 104

★ 25hours Berlin
Creatively furnished hotel, designed as a big city jungle – the zoo is right next door → S. 100

★ Ackselhaus
Exotic: flats with a goldfish pond and Balinese garden → p. 99

★ Miniloft Mitte
Spectacular architecture, friendly service → p. 105

★ Garden Living
Lovingly furnished boutique hotel with beautiful atrium and personal service → S. 101

INSIDER TIP DAS LITERATURHOTEL
(158 C5) *(Ⓜ G8)*
Books decorate the walls of the breakfast room furnished with antiques. This is also where readings are held. Personal atmosphere. *18 rooms | Friedenau | Fregestr. 68 | tel. 030 8 59 09 60 | www.literaturhotel-berlin.de | S1, 25 Friedenau*

PARK INN BERLIN ALEXANDERPLATZ
(153 D1) *(Ⓜ L3)*
The 40-storey hotel towers over Alexanderplatz. The rooms have various degrees of comfort. Guests are given vouchers for discounts at the Galeria Kaufhof department store next door. There is a INSIDER TIP viewing platform on the top floor *(in summer, from noon; in winter*

LUXURY HOTELS

Adlon Kempinski (140 B4) *(Ⓜ J7)*
Perfectly presented contemporary interpretation of the luxury hotel on the same site that was destroyed in the war. Impeccable service. *382 rooms, 78 suites | 224–16,000 euros | Mitte | Unter den Linden 77 | tel. 030 2 26 10 | www.hotel-adlon.de | S 1, 2, 25 Brandenburger Tor*

Grand Hyatt (151 F4) *(Ⓜ J5)*
The five star hotel at the Potsdamer Platz is characterized by its simple elegance and modern interior. Highlight is the wellness landscape on the top floor with a high grade steel pool and best view of the city. *342 rooms and suites | 170–3,470 euros | Tiergarten | Marlene-Dietrich-Platz 2 | tel. 030 25 53 12 34 | www.berlin.grand.hyatt.de | U/S Potsdamer Platz*

Waldorf Astoria (139 E4) *(Ⓜ F5)*
Highest standards of service in the new skyscraper at the Gedächtniskirche. With a Guerlain spa, the gourmet restaurant *Les Solistes, Romanisches Café* and *Peacock Gallery Bar. 152 rooms, 80 suites | 187–7780 euros | Charlottenburg | Hardenbergstr. 28 | tel. 030 8 14 00 00 | www.waldorfastoria.com | U /S Zoologischer Garten*

Hotel de Rome (141 D4) *(Ⓜ K4)*
Temple of luxury next to the Staatsoper on Bebelplatz. The rooms and suites are modern with a touch of traditional Berlin architecture. Beautiful rooftop terrace with bar. *146 rooms and suites | 430–4,630 euros | Mitte | Behrenstr. 37 | tel. 030 4 60 60 90 | www.hotelderome.com | U 6 Französische Straße*

The Ritz-Carlton Berlin (140 A6) *(Ⓜ J5)*
Top-class hotel, centrally-located at Potsdamer Platz: stately, large spa complex with indoor pool and luxury wherever you look. *303 rooms and suites | 250–14,500 euros | Mitte | Potsdamer Platz 3 | tel. 030 33 77 77 | www.ritzcarlton.com | U/S Potsdamer Platz*

Schlosshotel im Grunewald (156 B4) *(Ⓜ C7)*
Historical palace in a park near Kurfürstendamm. Spa facilities and gourmet restaurant. The interior was designed by Karl Lagerfeld. *53 rooms and suites | 239–5,000 euros | Wilmersdorf | Brahmsstr. 10 | tel. 030 89 58 40 | www.schlosshotelberlin.com | S 7, 9 Grunewald*

Revival of a traditional address at the Brandenburger Tor: Hotel Adlon

from 3pm | 3 euros). 1,012 rooms | Mitte | Alexanderplatz 7 | tel. 030 2 38 90 | www.parkinn-berlin.de | U/S Alexanderplatz

HOTELS: BUDGET

FABRIK
(154 B3) *(🗺 N6)*
Ideal for fans of the Kreuzberg nightlife, as they can fall into bed after a night out. Prices start at 18 euros, depending on the size of the room. *45 rooms | Kreuzberg | Schlesische Str. 18 | tel. 030 6 11 82 54 | www.diefabrik.com | U 1 Schlesisches Tor*

GASTEINER HOF
(158 A3) *(🗺 F7)*
Small hotel in the west of the city offering good value for money. Reasonably-priced en-suite doubles. *22 rooms | Wilmersdorf | Gasteiner Str. 8 | tel. 030 862 01 70 | www.gasteiner-hof.de | U 7 Blissestr.*

KARIBUNI (165 D4) *(🗺 N7)*
Family-run hotel in a typical old Berlin building with furniture and wall paintings inspired by Africa. In East Africa, *karibuni* means "welcome". *11 rooms, 1 flat | Neukölln | Neckarstr. 2/corner of Karl-Marx-Str. | tel. 030 6 87 15 17 | www.karibuni-hotel.de | U 7 Rathaus Neukölln*

MOTEL ONE (139 D4) *(🗺 F5)*
Designer hotel with reasonably-priced rooms. Other branches are located at the main railway station and on Alexanderplatz (Mitte), on Moritzplatz (Kreuzberg) and near Schloss Bellevue (Tiergarten). *250 rooms | Charlottenburg | Kantstr. 7–11a | tel. 030 31 51 73 60 | www.motel-one.com | S 7, 9, 75 Zoologischer Garten*

PETERS (138 C4) *(🗺 F5)*
Comfortable rooms for non-smokers – and also families – in one of Berlins typical old buildings near Savignyplatz. Many good restaurants in the vicinity. *34 rooms |*

Hüttenpalast: original accommodation in indoor caravans

Charlottenburg | Kantstr. 146 | tel. 030 3 12 22 78 | www.pension-peters-berlin.de | S Savignyplatz

HOSTELS

EASTERN COMFORT (154 B2) *(Ⓜ N5)*
Two small hotel ships along the Oberbaumbrücke offer you the opportunity to spend a night on the Spree, with a view through the bulls eyes included. (15–78 euros per night). *42 cabins | Friedrichshain | Mühlenstr. 73–77 | tel. 030 66 76 38 06 | www.eastern-comfort.com | U/S Warschauer Straße*

EASTSEVEN(147 D5) *(Ⓜ L2)*
Elected "Germany's best hostel" in 2009. The bedrooms are all decorated with murals and have their own bathrooms (14–39 euros/person in rooms for one to eight people). Quiet garden. *Prenzlauer Berg | Schwedter Str. 7 | tel. 030 93 62 22 40 | www.eastseven.de | U 2 Senefelderplatz*

GENERATOR(165 D3) *(Ⓜ O3)*
Germany's largest hostel with more than 900 beds soars into the sky near Landsberger Allee station. Overnight stays from 10 euros. *241 rooms | Prenzlauer Berg | Storkower Str. 160 | tel. 030 41 72 40 00 | www.generatorhostels.com | S 41, 42 Landsberger Allee*

HEART OF GOLD HOSTEL ★
(140 C2) *(Ⓜ K3)*
Guests from all over the world stay in bright, peaceful rooms near the Museumsinsel (from 9.90 euros). The lobby doubles up as a bar. *140 rooms | Mitte | Johannisstr. 11 | tel. 030 29 00 33 00 | www.heartofgold-hostel.de | U 6 Oranienburger Tor*

INSIDER TIP **HÜTTENPALAST**
(161 F 1–2) *(Ⓜ M7)*
Funny and convenient: camping in a factory hall in Neukölln. Let one of the three caravans or the three wooden huts harbour you. Nice café and garden terrace. Also a family room. *Neukölln | Ho-brechtstr. 65–66 | tel. 030 37 30 58 06 | www.huettenpalast.de | U 7, 8 Hermann-platz*

OSTEL (154 A–B1) *(Ⓜ N5)*
If you want to experience a bit of GDR feeling: hotel in a prefabricated house

with authentic East German furniture and the obligatory Honecker portrait in the foyer. Easily accessible location near the Ostbahnhof. The in-house restaurant *Volkskammer* serves original GDR cuisine. *79 rooms, 1 flat | Friedrichshain | Wriezener Karree 5 | tel. 030 25 76 86 60 | www.ostel.eu | S 7, 8, 9 Ostbahnhof*

INSIDER TIP PFEFFERBETT
(147 D5) *(✉ L2)*
Beautiful dormitories in a former Berlin brewery for two to eight people (from 12 euros). A double room with your own bathroom, TV and internet access costs approx. 60 euros. *43 beds, 3 flats | Prenzlauer Berg | Christinenstr. 18–19 | tel. 030 93 93 58 58 | www.pfefferbett.de | U 2 Senefelderplatz*

THREE LITTLE PIGS (152 A5) *(✉ J5)*
You can stay in two to eight-bed rooms in a converted monastery near Potsdamer Platz. Double room with bath: 32 euros/person. *80 rooms | Kreuzberg | Stresemannstr. 66 | tel. 030 26 39 58 80 | www.three-little-pigs.de | U/S Potsdamer Platz*

FLATS

LUX ELEVEN (141 F2) *(✉ L3)*
Modern-style apartment hotel: bright flats with fully-equipped kitchen including dishwasher and microwave. Ideal for lengthy stays. There is a restaurant with German-Mediterranean cuisine in the building. *72 flats | Mitte | Rosa-Luxemburg-Str. 9–13 | tel. 030 9 36 28 00 | www.lux-eleven.com | U 8 Weinmeisterstraße | Expensive*

MINILOFT MITTE ★
(140 B1) *(✉ J3)*
Prize-winning architecture with an impressive glass façade near the main station where you can choose between flats that are classically or extravagantly furnished. Personal, cordial service. Environmentally-friendly operation with eco-electricity and fair-trade products. *14 flats | Mitte | Hessische Str. 5 | tel. 030 8 47 10 90 | www.miniloft.com | U 6 Naturkundemuseum | Moderate*

PRIVATE ROOMS

Private rooms and apartments can be booked at *www.123berlinzimmer.de* and *www.airbnb.de*. There are also various agencies that can arrange shared accommodation including *Freiraum (Kreuzberg | Wiener Str. 14 | tel. 030 618 20 08 | www.freiraum-berlin.com)*.

LOW BUDGET

Staying with local hosts is an inexpensive way to travel. The Internet platform Couchsurfing *(www.couchsurfing.com)* helps travellers who don't want to spend money on their accommodation.

The Youth Hostel at Wannsee is a bit far out but idyllically located on the water and also has rooms for families. Overnight stays from 17 euros per person. *Nikolassee* **(164 C4)** *(✉ O) (Badeweg 1 | Tel. 030 803 20 34 | www.jh-wannsee.de | S 1, 7 Nikolassee)*

In the *Pension 11. Himmel* **(165 E3)** *(✉ O) (5 rooms | Wittenberger Str. 85 | tel. 030 93 77 20 52 | www.pension-11himmel.de | S 7 Ahrensfelde)* in a prefabricated concrete building in Marzahn, you can either sleep in a hammock or a prince's bed. One night with breakfast: 22 euros.

DISCOVERY TOURS

1 BERLIN AT A GLANCE

START: ① Reichstag building
END: ⑯ Riva bar

Distance:
➡ 26.5 km/16.5 miles, of which approx. 11 km/6.8 miles on foot

1 day
Walking time (without stops) approx. 2½ hours

COSTS: approx. 50 euros for a day ticket on the public transport network, Segway hire and snacks

IMPORTANT TIPS: Buy a one-day BVG ticket (6.90 euros) to travel for free on all buses, underground and district line trains.
Reserve a table in the Dachgartenrestaurant Käfer in advance.
Pre-book tickets online for the Fernsehturm on the ⑪ Alexanderplatz!

 Photo: Reichstag building

Cities have many faces. If you want to get behind the scenes to explore their unique charm and head off the beaten track or find your way to green oases, handpicked restaurants or the best local activities, then these tailored Discovery Tours are just the right thing. Choose the best route for the day and follow in the footsteps of the MARCO POLO authors – well-prepared to navigate your way to all the many highlights that await you along the tour.

This tour offers you a first insight into the capital's diversity: it takes you from the government quarters to the colourful Kreuzberg and from Brandenburger Tor onto the Fernsehturm (television tower). Although it requires endurance, you will be rewarded with having seen a lot of Berlin.

09:30am The best place to start the day is in **Dachgartenrestaurant Käfer** → p. 66 at the top of the **❶ Reichstag building** → p. 46 (advance reservation essential). From here, you will have a magnificent view over the inner city and can also follow the walkway up into the dome of the building. Hire

❶ Reichstag building

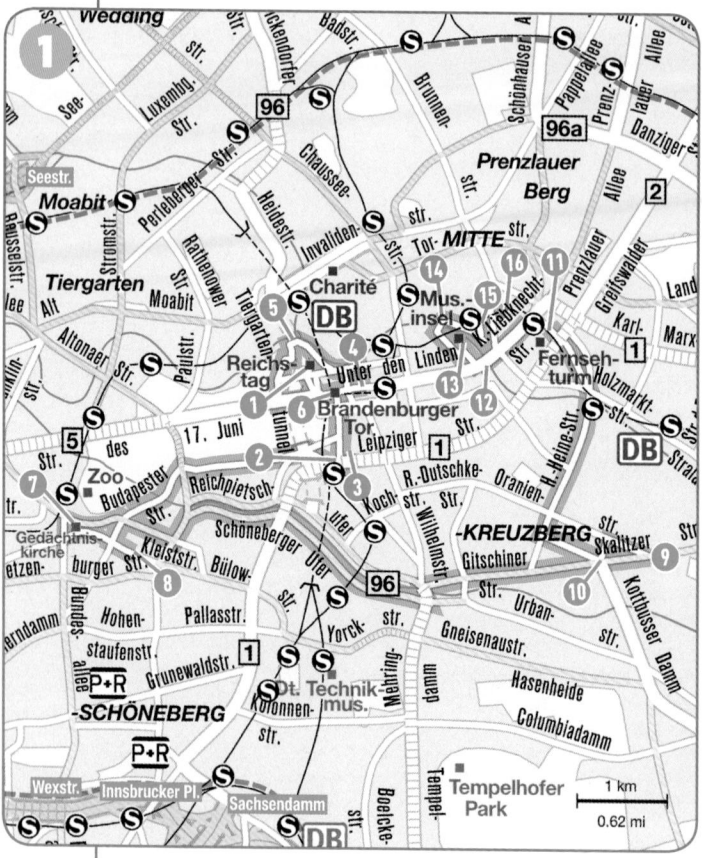

❷ Potsdamer Platz

❸ Leipziger Platz

❹ Unter den Linden

❺ Capital Beach bar

❻ Brandenburger Tor

a Segway at the nearby ❷ **Potsdamer Platz** → p. 45 and zoom around the centre of Berlin on one of these fun, electrically powered "personal transporters". The perfect route: ❸ **Leipziger Platz, then turn left into Wilhelmstraße, cross the boulevard** ❹ **Unter den Linden, and carry on just before reaching the Spree. Turn left there. Keep going passed the Reichstag on through the government quarters.** Feel like a coffee? Then drive in the direction of the main railway station to the Gustav Heinemann Bridge. Take the stairs that lead down to the Spree to the ❺ **Capital Beach bar** (don't forget to lock up the Segway!). After that, keep zooming in the direction of the ❻ **Brandenburger Tor** → p. 41 and you'll find yourself back on the Potsdamer Platz again.

11:30am **Bus no. 200 will take you past the diplomatic district to the Breitscheidplatz** with the ⑦ **Gedächtniskirche (memorial church)** → p. 53 and the Tauentzienstraße with its many shops. Here on the ⑧ **Wittenbergplatz** with its splendid weekly market *(Tue 8am–2pm, Fri 8am–4pm)* is the exclusive department store **KaDeWe** → p. 82. Take a lunchtime break on the INSIDER TIP gourmet floor and later take a closer look at the enormous selection in the delicatessen and clothing.

01:30pm How about a tour of Kreuzberg? **The bus M 29 will take you there right from KaDeWe.** Get off at ⑨ **Görlitzer Bahnhof** and take a stroll past the wild mixture of bars, boutiques and döner kebab stands between Oranienplatz and Wiener Straße. **From "Görli" work your way down Oranienstraße** where you will come across many shops selling fashion items by Berlin designers as well as Turkish bakeries.

03:00pm **At the** ⑩ **Kottbusser Tor get into the U8 that takes you from Kreuzberg to** ⑪ **Alexanderplatz** → p. 34. The "Alex" main attraction is the Berlin **Fernsehturm (TV tower)** → p. 34 with its 203 m (666 ft) high viewing platform. Take the express lift and let it catapult you up the tower in just 40 seconds. Book your tickets online in advance without any queuing time! **From the "Alex", it is just a stone's throw on foot west along the Karl-Liebknecht-Straße** to the ⑫ **Schlossplatz** with the almost finished **Humboldt-Forum** in the restored castle and to the ⑬ **Museumsinsel** → p. 38, the mecca within Berlin's museum landscape. Art-lovers will be fascinated by the enormous exhibition building with valuable art collections and archaeological treasures. You should definitely plan to visit the **Neuen Museum** which re-opened in 2009 with its famous Nefertiti. As it is now too late, come back another day. Due to the vast crowds of visitors, it is recommended to buy your ticket in advance – preferably online. During summer, treat yourself to a well-earned break **on the banks of the Spree opposite the Museumsinsel (at the Monbijou bridge)** at the ⑭ **Strandbar Mitte** → p. 89.

07:00pm In the ⑮ **Ampelmann-Restaurant** → p. 74 you can order pasta in East German "Ampelmännchen" (little traffic men) shapes as well as try some excellent international cuisine. Take a well-earned night cap at the ⑯ **Riva bar** → p. 88 located under the arches of the district line

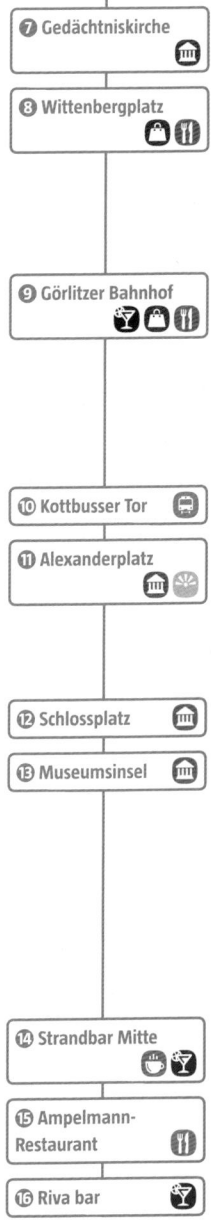

railway at the Hackescher Markt. The bar in the shape of the sunken luxury liner "Titanic" is unique and the drinks are also recommended.

2 WHERE THE WALL ONCE STOOD

START: ❶ Checkpoint Charlie
END: ⑬ Friedrichstraße

Distance:
➡ 5 km/3.1 miles

4 hours
Walking time
(without stops)
1¼ hours

COSTS: approx. 20 euros for café food and snacks

You will hardly notice that Berlin was once cut in two by a tremendous amount of cement, barbed wire and minefields. However, there are some places where you can still get an impression of how things were at the time when the city was divided. A walk along the old line of the Wall between Checkpoint Charlie and Friedrichstraße station is especially worthwhile.

❶ Checkpoint Charlie

10:00am The walk begins at the former ❶ **Checkpoint Charlie.** Only the small guard house and larger-than-life photographic portraits of Russian and American soldiers remain of what used to be the border crossing for visitors entering East Germany from the west. There is an impressive documentation of escape stories and conditions in the East and West in the **Haus am Checkpoint Charlie** → p. 52. Until Reunification, 254 people attempting to escape over the Wall were killed by East German border guards. **With the stacks of sand sacks behind you, turn left into Zimmerstraße** where the Wall originally blocked the view from one side of the street to the other. When you walk along Zimmerstraße you will pass by houses whose occupants used to be almost in the East if they just put their hand out of the window; the Wall was not the actual border, it was a "virtual" line 2.50 m (8 ft) in front of it! This means that people walking on Zimmerstraße were really in East Berlin.

Continue along Wilhelmstraße towards the Martin Gropius Building. Here, you will see the last remnants of the almost 4-m (13 ft) high ❷ **Wall** constructed of concrete slabs. However there are a lot of holes in this section because souvenir hunters have hacked out many chunks. The ❸ **Topographie des Terrors** → p. 53 exhibition centre is located to the left. This used to be the headquarters of the

❷ Wall

❸ Topographie des Terrors

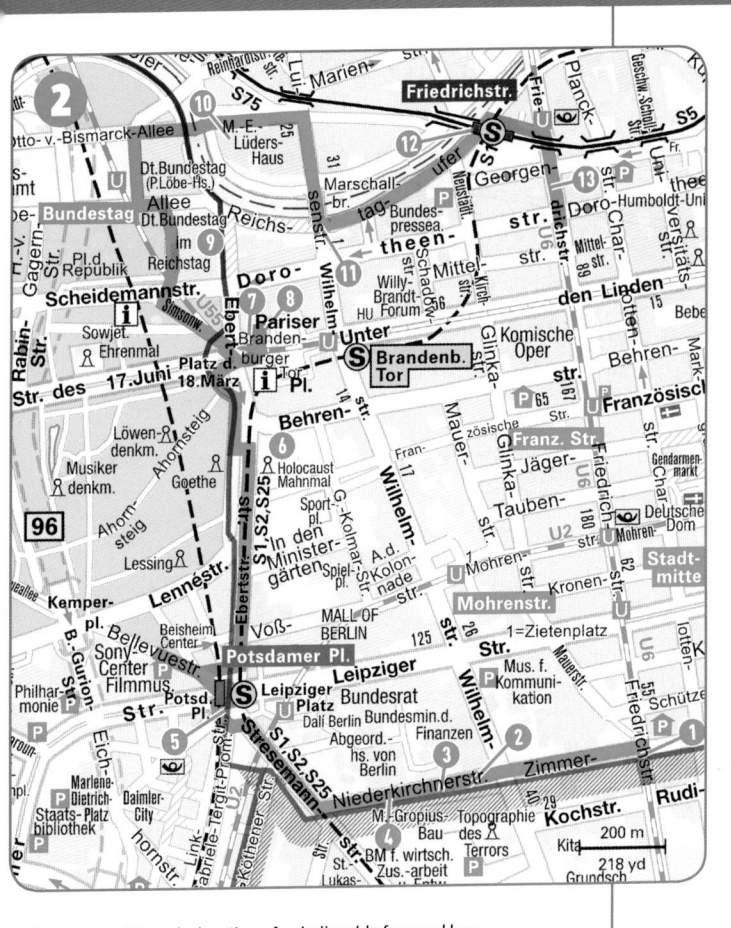

Gestapo and SS and a location of unbelievable fear and horror. There is hardly anywhere else on earth where so much terror, torture and murder was planned and carried out. A new documentation centre on the premises complements the open-air exhibition with 15 sections including one along the remains of the Wall that recalls the fate of the many victims as well as the buildings that once stood there.

Today, the ④ Martin-Gropius-Bau → p. 53, the former Museum of Applied Art that was opened in 1881 and severely damaged in World War II, shows temporary exhibitions. It is named after the architect who was a great-uncle of the famous Bauhaus architect Walter Gropius. The Wall made

④ Martin-Gropius-Bau

A labyrinth of columns at the Holocaust Memorial

it impossible to use the main entrance and visitors had to go in through the back door. The building in the style of the Italian High Renaissance opposite – on what used to be the east side of the Wall – has housed the **Berlin House of Representatives** since 1993. It was opened as the Prussian House of Representatives in 1892.

5 Potsdamer Platz

11:30am Take a look at the copper inserts in the ground; they mark the former course of the Wall. **From Stresemannstraße you can see 5 Potsdamer Platz** → p. 45 **on the right.** New buildings hide where the Wall used to be and only a copper band in the cobblestones along Stresemannstraße recalls the once-divided city. Where the skyscrapers of the German Federal Railways and Daimler Benz are today, there used to be an area of wasteland covering 480,000 square metres (more than 118 acres) when the Wall was still standing. Until the air-raids in World War II, Potsdamer Platz was the busiest place in Europe and was also the site of Berlin's first traffic lights that were installed in 1925. This is commemorated by a tower with a clock and horizontal set of lights at the entrance to the district line station. Looking for more of a view? Then take the fastest lift in Europe to the roof of the **Kollhoff Tower** → p. 45. From there you have a fantastic view of your surroundings. The gigantic tent roof of the **Sony Center** → p. 45 is flooded with coloured light emitted by thousands of LEDs after

night falls. Enjoy a hearty snack and try some fried chicken on the terrace of the **Lindenbräu brewery** *(Moderate)* with a fine view into the circle of this impressive building designed by Helmut Jahn.

01:00pm Continue along Ebertstraße towards Pariser Platz. The so-called Ministergärten (Minister Gardens) with the representations of numerous federal states lie on the right. This is adjacent to the Holocaust Memorial ❻ **Denkmal für die ermordeten Juden Europas** → p. 42 based on plans by the New York architect Peter Eisenman. When you reach ❼ **Brandenburger Tor** → p. 41, you should take a break and visit the INSIDER TIP **Raum der Stille** (Room of Silence). It is located in the northern column of the gate. It is hard to believe that only 27 years ago nobody was allowed to pass through the Brandenburger Tor because it was in no-man's land between East and West. The buildings to the north of Brandenburger Tor are new even though they do not look it. The best place to go if you feel like having a cup of coffee or something small to eat is the café ❽ **Theodor Tucher** → p. 69 offering authentic Brandenburg food. **After this well-earned break, head off to the** ❾ **Reichstag building** → p. 46, today the seat of the German Parliament. Visitors to its dome have a fantastic view over the centre of Berlin. The rays of sun flowing in through the glass dome are channelled downwards using mirrors to provide the parliament chamber beneath with natural light.

The Wall used to run behind the parliament building on the Spree side. The memorial site "Parliament of Trees against War and Violence" conceived by the Berlin environmental artist Ben Wargin in 1990, is located opposite the Reichstag in the ❿ **Marie-Elisabeth-Lüders-Haus**. Take the path along the riverbank past the ⓫ **ARD-Hauptstadtstudio** *(ARD television's capital studio | Mitte | Wilhelmstr. 67a | tel. 030 22 88 1110 | www.ard-hauptstadtstudio.de)*. If you are interested, take a free guided tour *(Wed, Sat 2pm)* through the studios and find out how news programmes are produced. It is now only a stone's throw to the ⓬ **Friedrichstraße Station; just walk along the Spree to the east and you will reach it in five minutes.** Maybe you'd like to do some shopping? There is plenty of choice on ⓭ **Friedrichstraße** with its many fashion and trendy shops and the **Dussmann** → p. 82 "culture department store".

3 THROUGH BERLIN'S HISTORY: THE SPANDAUER VORSTADT

START: ❶ Hackescher Markt
END: ❶ Hackescher Markt

Distance:
1.5 km/1 mile

2 hours
Walking time
(without stops)
30 minutes

COSTS: approx. 10 euros for café food

The name "Vorstadt" (outside the city) says it all: in the 18th century, new housing was needed and the city expanded into an area that became known as the Spandauer Vorstadt – "suburban Spandau", as the road to Spandau started outside the city gates. The Scheunenviertel ("barn district") is located to the north of the Hackescher Markt district line station. In the 18th century there was a row of barns here. The "golden 20s" saw culture and crafts flourish. Many Jews – mainly from Eastern Europe – lived in the eastern part of the quarter. Today this suburb is once again seeing a resurgence of this tradition as a centre of the theatre, arts and crafts, together with shops and cafés.

11:00am The ❶ **Hackescher Markt** district line station, where our walk begins, marks the former border of the city; regional and long-distance trains travel above the foundations of the old city wall between Jannowitzbrucke and Friedrichstraße. The district line station is named after the City Commandant von Hacke who had the swampland drained in the middle of the 18th century. The ❷ **Hackesche Höfe** → p. 37 opposite the square in front of the station are also named after him. The eight courtyards, one behind each other, form Europe's largest complex of this kind and now offer a great variety of fashion, culture, arts and crafts, and restaurants. **If you walk through all the courtyards you will reach** INSIDER TIP Sophienstraße, a spruced-up street that was renovated in the 1980s for the 750th anniversary of the city. **Going to the left, you will pass the old churchyard of the** ❸ **Sophienkirche** after 50 m (164 ft) with the oldest Baroque church tower in the city. The ❹ **Handwerksvereinshaus** (House of the Arts and Crafts Association) is on the right. This was built in 1844 as the gathering place of Berlin's first labour organisation. As many as 3,000 people held meetings and had discussions inside. In the 1920s in particular, Communists, Social Democrats and National Socialists held their party meetings here. A popular dance theatre with alternative-culture flair can be found at the **Sophiensaele** → p. 97.

A few yards further on, the route leads us through a gateway into the ❺ **Sophie-Gips-Höfe** where multimedia companies, galleries and gastronomic businesses have opened up. The American cakes in **Barcomi's** café are delicious and in summer you can sit in bliss on the courtyard terrace. **The rear exit of the courtyard ensemble leads to** ❻ **Gipsstraße** ("plaster street"). This is one of Spandauer Vorstadt's oldest streets. There used to be a lime kiln in the street for the production of plaster – hence the name. Today it is home to many beautiful shops and studios such as from the virtuous ceramic artist **Hinrich Kröger** *(Gipsstr. 13 | www.galerie-hinrich-kroeger.de)* for you to gaze in the shop windows. **Go along the street on the left to the end.** The 19th/early 20th century "Gründerzeit" houses have now been renovated and it is worth taking a look into the courtyards that often still have single-storey barns.

12:00pm **From Auguststraße after around 50 m (164 ft) turn left onto the** ❼ **Große Hamburger Straße**. In the 1920s it was famous as a place where Jews, Protestants

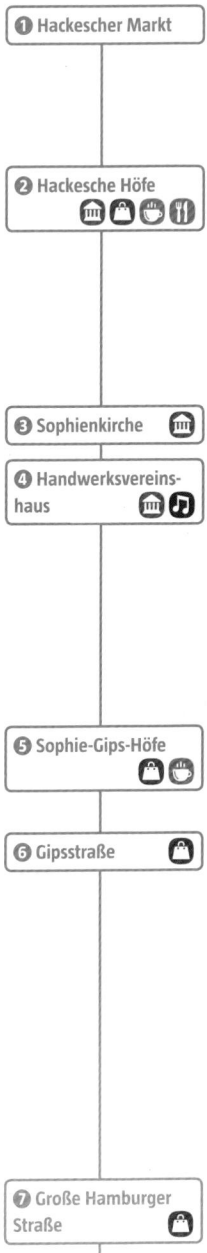

and Catholics lived together peacefully. There are also many shops waiting for customers. You will soon see the pretty clinker facade of ⑧ **St.-Hedwig-Krankenhaus** on your right. It was opened as a hospital for the old and infirm in 1888. Diagonally opposite the hospital, the Jewish community runs a ⑨ **school**. There used to be a Jewish cemetery next to the schoolyard but it was turned into a park for the former Jewish old people's home in 1827. The SS organised deportations to concentration camps from this home that no longer stands today. A memorial stone and sculpture remind us of the 56,000 Berlin Jews who were deported to Nazi death camps. **House No. 19a** opposite the former cemetery is thought to be the oldest in Spandauer Vorstadt. **Turn left onto Oranienburger Straße at the end of the street** where you can find a hive of trendy fashion stores and restaurants. Straight across from where the Große Hamburger Straße enters the Oranienburger Straße stands house number 86 A, home to ⑩ **Maskworld** *(www.maskworld.com)*; with its collection of 4,000 costumes and the wildest masks on 5 floors. **After a few steps you will once again see the ① Hackescher Markt, where our tour now ends.**

⑧ St.-Hedwig-Krankenhaus

⑨ school

⑩ Maskworld

① Hackescher Markt

4 BIKE TOUR INTO NATURE

START: ① Ahrensfelde district train station
END: ⑪ Forum Köpenick

District:
19 km/11.8 miles

4 hours
Cycling time (without stops)
1¾ hours

COSTS: around 10 euros for café food, 8–12 euros for bike hire, 4 euros for admission to the ⑤ Gärten der Welt
WHAT TO TAKE: hire bike (s. S. 129), climbing gear if required

The Wuhletalweg trail takes you around the city's eastern outskirts offering you both an escape into nature as well as interesting sights on both sides including Europe's largest prefabricated housing estate, the continent's largest Chinese gardens and a climbing tower built out of balustrades from demolished prefabricated buildings!

① Ahrensfelde district train station

11:00am It takes around half an hour on the S7 from Alexanderplatz to the end of the line at ① Ahrensfelde district train station. For just a small fee, you can take the bike you have hired in the city on to the train (a bike ticket costs

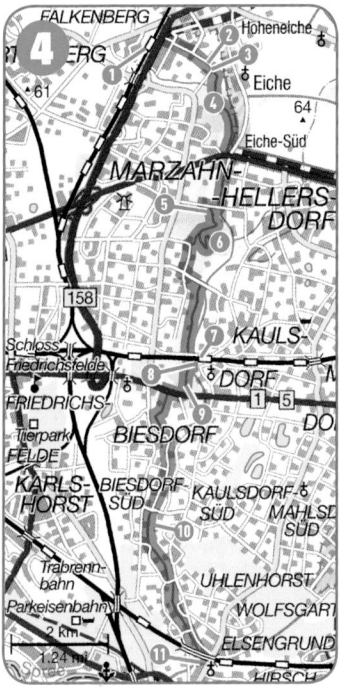

Gärten der Welt (Gardens of the World): China in Berlin

1.80 euros a journey). **Head south from the Ahrensfelde district line station along the Havemannstraße to the Wuhletal (Wuhle valley).** Shortly after the district line station you will notice brightly orange-painted three-storey buildings on your left. Hard to believe that these were once as high as the depressing eleven-storey prefabricated buildings on the opposite side of the road. At the start of the 2000s, architects were assigned with the task of transforming some of the city's high-rises into residential villas. The transformation has attracted worldwide interest. After approx. 1 km (0.6 mile), you'll welcome the green landscape of the ❷ **Wuhletal**, a floodplain marking the city's border. **Follow the signposted Wuhletalweg in a southerly direction.** Shortly after setting off you'll spot a INSIDER TIP climbing rock on the right-hand side, the so-called ❸ **Wuhletalwächter**. It was built using 550 concrete slabs taken from balconies of demolished prefab buildings from the area around and stands an impressive 17.50 m (57 ft) high. Whoever likes climbing and has the right gear with them can choose between several climbs varying

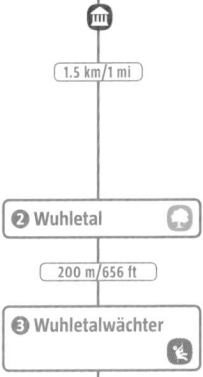

500 m/1,640 ft

4 Ahrensfelder Berge

3.5 km/2.2 mi

5 Gärten der Welt

2 km/1.2 mi

6 Kienberg

4 km/2.5 mi

in difficulty; anyone can use the facility (at their own risk!). **100 m (320 ft) to the south of the rock** is a herd of Scottish highland cattle which have been grazing there since 2011 to keep the meadows short. In stark contrast to this are the prefabricated high-rises of Marzahn on the skyline. **After approximately 1 km (0.6 mile), the path leads you around the 4 Ahrensfelder Berge**, but if you're feeling sporty, why not try the ascent (leave the bike at the bottom or push it up) to be rewarded with an amazing view over the fields to the east and Europe's largest prefabricated housing estate to the west in Marzahn. These hills (114 and 101 m (374 ft and 331 ft) high) are higher now than they used to be (69 m (226 ft)); they were used as landfill sites up until the start of the 1990s for building rubble due to the many new prefabricated buildings built in those days.

12:00pm **The trail takes you past the wetlands of Fasanenpfuhl to the Landsberger Allee.** This is a relatively tricky section as some of the signposts directing you along the Wuhletalweg are difficult to spot. **Your route now continues on the left parallel to the Landsberger Allee. Cross the Eichener Chaussee, then the Landsberger Allee and follow the Zossener Straße for a short distance.** To the right follows another idyllic green section of your journey. **Continue along the Wuhletalweg and after approximately 1 km (0.6 mile) you'll reach the congested Eisenacher Straße.** Here is the main entrance (approx. 200 m (656 ft) on your right) to the **5 Gärten der Welt** → p. 56, the "Gardens of the world", with Europe's largest **Chinesischer Garten**. Here you can enjoy a bite to eat: The Chinese snack-bar pavilion sells drinks, salads, noodle soups and tea from the Land of the Rising Sun.

01:00pm After taking in the garden's splendid flowers, **continue on the Wuhletalweg towards 6 Kienberg**, where preparations are already well underway for the 2017 International Garden Show (IGA). The latest attraction in planning is a cable railway linking the Neue Grottkauer Straße underground station to the Gärten der Welt. From the viewing platform on the 102 m (335 ft) high Kienberg, you have an excellent view over the IGA site and the Marzahn pre-fabricated building skyline in the distance. From up here you can also see the Marzahn Flower Tower (Allee der Kosmonauten 145), a high-rise building decorated with jungle, alpine and Mediterranean landscapes as well as Chinese flowers – Europe's highest facade artwork. **Continue** south along **the trail for 2 km (1.2 miles) past allotments and meadows**

to the ⑦ Wuhletal station and another 7 km (4.3 miles) to the Köpenick district line station. Behind the subway to the district line and underground station, ⑧ **Kaulsdorf** can soon be seen on the left, a village which has retained its rural charm with its church and historical buildings.

02:00pm **After 3 km (1.8 miles) along the ⑨ Biesdorfer Höhe** (82 m/269 ft) – offering splendid views of the area around – and through a new housing estate and butterfly meadows, you will reach a splendid location to take a break at the ⑩ **Wuhlesee** a lake surrounded by old trees and reeds. You can't swim here but it is an idyllic spot to take a picnic. **Head back to the Köpenick district line station (3 km (1.8 miles)) along the Wuhle** through nature and urban development. The tour ends at the shopping centre ⑪ **Forum Köpenick** with a vast selection of snack bars and cafés to choose from. **The S3 line takes you back to the city centre in 25 minutes.**

5 CRUISE THROUGH THE CITY BY SHIP

START: ① Alt-Tegel
END: ⑧ Pfaueninsel

Distance:
➡ 35 km/22 miles, of which 4 km/2.5 miles on foot

6 hours
Cruising time (without stops) 2 hours, walking time (without stops) 1 hour

COSTS: 18 euros for ship ticket, approx. 20 euros for food, 6.90 euros for the BVG one-day ticket
WHAT TO PACK: do not forget sun protection and head gear!
IMPORTANT TIP: The ship leaves from ① Alt-Tegel at 10:20 am in summer; tickets available online: *www.sternundkreis.de*

Berlin is a city on water with the Havel river flowing from Tegel to the Wannsee and Pfaueninsel past forest scenery, Spandau Old Town and other idyllic spots. Take the ship service along this route and disembark at points to discover the nearby sights.

10:00am The tour starts at the jetty in ① **Alt-Tegel**. **You can get there in 30 minutes by taking the U6 underground line from the Friedrichstraße station.** On your way from the underground station to the jetty (signposted), you pass through a pretty historic centre with shops and fruit and vegetable stalls where you can pick up your food supplies for the day. At the ② **Greenwich promenade**

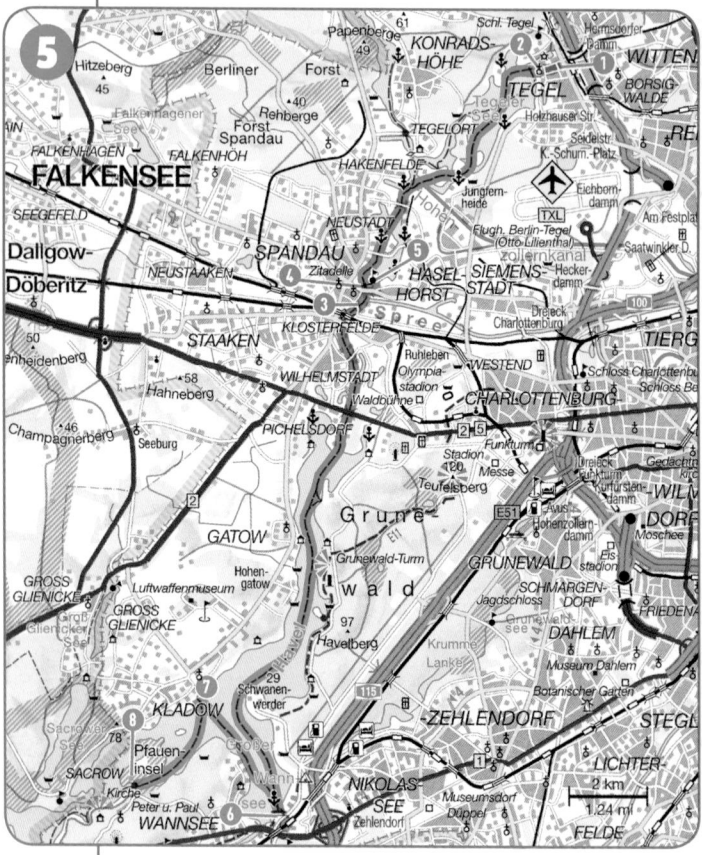

(named after the London district twinned with Reinickendorf), you'll see many docked ships. **The ship belonging to the "Stern-und Kreisschifffahrt" shipping line leaves in summer at 10:20 am to take you to Wannsee.** The first attraction on your cruise is the **Villa Borsig** on your right at the harbour where the Foreign Office houses its guests as well as an academy. The ship chugs quickly along the Tegeler See (Lake Tegel), direction Spandau, sailing in between the small islands. One of these, the **Scharfenberg island**, is home to Berlin's only state-run boarding school.

11:00am **After approx. 40 min. the ship docks at the jetty in ③ Spandau,** a pretty old town close to the harbour

③ Spandau

with historical timbered houses inviting you to take a stroll around. Until 1920, Spandau (approx. 800 years old) was a city in its own right. It is now home to 200,000 Berliners who still prefer to call themselves Spandauers. The old part of the town has many shops and pubs with beer gardens. The ④ **Brauhaus Spandau** *(Neuendorfer Str. 1 | www.brauhaus-spandau.de | Budget–Moderate)* close to the jetty (8 minutes on foot), produces the traditional Berlin speciality "Fassbrause" (non-alcoholic drink made from fruit and malt extract). The city district is famous for its ⑤ **Spandau citadel** *(www.zitadelle-spandau.de)*, one of the best retained renaissance fortresses in Europe with real moat and even bats.

White fleet: ships and swans on the Havel River

01:00pm Now take the next ship heading to Wannsee. On your left, you will soon spot the **Grunewaldturm**. The tower was built between 1897–99 in remembrance of the 100th birthday of Kaiser Wilhelm I. The Havel now widens and the east bank is covered in thick grass until you reach the **Wannsee Lido** with its 1.2 km (0.75 miles) of sandy beach. From the ship, you will notice its grand layout. Thousands of Berliners have been coming here every summer since 1907 to enjoy the next best thing to a Baltic Sea holiday. The ship will soon reach the ⑥ **Ronneby promenade** jetty. If you've had enough for today, disembark now and take the district line back to the city; the station is directly at the jetty.

④ Brauhaus Spandau

⑤ Spandau citadel

⑥ Ronneby promenade

02:00pm After a short stay, the ship chugs on further along the opposite bank of the Havel to ⑦ Kladow. This small Berlin suburb attracts many day tourists. The Italian restaurant INSIDER TIP **La Riviera** *(Moderate)* at the jetty with pizza baked in a wood-fired oven and delicious pasta is recommended. Get off the ship and enjoy a break while soaking up the fantastic views of the Havel River. **The next ship takes around 15 minutes to reach the ⑧ Pfaueninsel** → p. 58. It's worth taking a stroll around "Peacock island" with its fairytale castle, real peacocks and beautiful landscape. **Take the ferry across to the mainland and then the bus 218 back to the Wannsee station.**

⑦ Kladow

⑧ Pfaueninsel

TRAVEL WITH KIDS

INSIDER TIP BONBONMACHEREI
(140–141 C–D2) *(🗺 K3)*
How are sweets made? Kids can see how the mixture is prepared and also try them while still warm. Of course, you can also buy the drops packed up in little bags. Yummy! *Wed–Sat noon–8pm, closed July/August and over Christmas/New Year | admission free | Mitte | Oranienburger Str. 32 | tel. 030 44 05 52 43 | www.bonbonmacherei.de | S 1, 2, 25 Oranienburger Straße*

INSIDER TIP BVG CABRIOTOUR
(141 F2) *(🗺 L3)*
A "ghost train" ride in the underground: during the summer season, a roofless carriage races through 35 km (22 miles) of dark tunnels in the underground system. Ready, set , helmets on – for the two hour tour starting at Alexanderplatz. *April–Oct Fri 7 and 10:20pm | tickets 40 euros, children 25 euros | tel. 030 25 62 52 56 | www.bvg.de | U/S Alexanderplatz*

KINDERBAD MONBIJOU
(141 D2) *(🗺 K3)*
A lovely pool only for children with their parents or accompanying adult. The water is not deeper than 1.30 m (4 ft 3 in.) and parents quickly make contact with others at the water's edge. Nobody over the age of 15 is allowed in unless they are accompanied by a child. *June–Sept Mon–Fri 11am–7pm, Sat/Sun 10am–7pm | admission 5.50 euros | Mitte | Oranienburger Str. 78 | tel. 030 2 82 86 52 | www.berlinerbaederbetriebe.de | S 1, 2, 25 Oranienburger Straße*

KOLLE 37
(147 D5) *(🗺 L2)*
Exciting adventure playground very close to the Kollwitzplatz. Here children can run around wild, hammer on the workbench or stroke the rabbits while adults can stroll around the district. *Mid-April–mid-Oct Mon–Fri noon–7pm, Sat 1–6pm, in winter Mon–Fri 11:30am– 6pm, Sat 1–6pm | admission free | Prenzlauer Berg | Kollwitzstr. 37 | www.kolle37.de | U 2 Senefelderplatz*

KULTURPROJEKTE BERLIN
Most of the state museums have regular guided tours for children and workshops on the art on display. Just one example; in the Music Instrument Museum, the way instruments function is investigated playfully using the work "Peter and the Wolf" by Sergei Prokofiev. The staff have all studied art history or are trained

Children love big cities because there is so much to discover. And there is a great deal waiting for them in Berlin. Enjoy yourselves!

teachers and have no difficulties in making young people really enthusiastic about museums. You can find out details of current events by phone. *Office: Mon–Fri 9am–4pm, Sat/Sun 9am–1pm | Mitte | Klosterstr. 68 | tel. 030 24 74 98 88 | www.kulturprojekte-berlin.de | U 2 Klosterstraße*

LOXX
(153 D2) *(🗺 L4)*
One of the world's largest digitally-controlled model railways will make children's hearts beat faster. Intercity expresses, regional and local trains travel over 4 km (2.5 miles) of tracks through a quaint Berlin-style cityscape with the Brandenburger Tor, an airport and a sea of houses. *Daily 10am–8pm | admission 12.90 euros; concessions 8 euros, children under 1m (3,28 ftft) tall get in free | Mitte | Grunerstr. 20 in the Alexa Shopping Centre, 3rd floor | www.loxx-berlin.de | U/S Alexanderplatz*

MACH MIT! MUSEUM
(147 E4) *(🗺 M2)*
Shelves you can climb on, soap shops, a crawling area – there are a lot of experiences in the Museum for children. There are workshops for handicrafts, pottery and acting. Exhibitions are also shown – on salt, for example. You can park your parents in the Family Café while you have fun! *Tue–Sun 10am–6pm | admission 5.50 euros; concessions 3.50 euros | Prenzlauer Berg | Senefelderstr. 5 | tel. 030 74 77 82 00 | www.machmitmuseum.de | S 41: Prenzlauer Allee*

THEATER AN DER PARKAUE
(165 E3) *(🗺 P4)*
State theatre for children and youngsters. "Peter and the Wolf" after Sergei Prokofiev is a hit with children from the age of five. "The Children's Transport – Berlin Kids on the Way to London" has even won prizes. *Lichtenberg | Parkaue 29 | tel. 030 5 57 75 20 | www.parkaue.de | S 41, 42 Frankfurter Allee*

FESTIVALS & EVENTS

Numerous events are real crowd-pullers. These include the "Long Night of the Museums" that is held twice a year and gets thousands up and about. Shuttle buses transport visitors from one museum to the next and – in spite of all the crowding – everyone has a good time. In any case, the people of Berlin like to do things in big groups. Whether it's the Carnival of Cultures or Christopher Street Day, the motto is always "the more, the merrier"!

SPECIAL EVENTS

JANUARY/FEBRUARY

Sechstagerennen (Six-day race): High-spirited bicycle race in the Velodrom; *Prenzlauer Berg | Landsberger Allee | tel. 030 44 30 44 30 | www.sechstagerennen-berlin.de*

Grüne Woche: Delicatessen specialities from all over the world at the Funkturm (Radio Tower); *Charlottenburg | info tel. 030 3 03 80 | www.gruenewoche.de*

FEBRUARY

★ ***Berlinale:*** International film festival; ten days of razzmatazz with German and international film stars and new cinema productions; *info tel. 030 25 92 00 | www.berlinale.de*

MARCH

Internationale Tourismusbörse (ITB): International Tourism Fair at the Funkturm; *Charlottenburg | tel. 030 3 03 80 | www.itb-berlin.de*

MAY/JUNE

Theatertreffen Significant productions from Germany, Austria and Switzerland performed on Berlin's stages; *info tel. 030 25 48 90 | www.berlinerfestspiele.de/theatertreffen*

Internationale Luft- und Raumfahrtausstellung: Every two years, Schönefeld Airport is the place to be for all aviation enthusiasts 2016, 2018); *www.ila-berlin.de*

DFB Cup Final: Football festival in the Olympiastadium; *Charlottenburg | info tel. 030 8 96 99 40*

Lange Nacht der Wissenschaften: Presentation of work at research institutions; *www.langenachtderwissenschaften.de*

Karneval der Kulturen: Colourful, intercultural carnival procession on Whit Sunday; *www.karneval-der-kulturen.de*

JUNE/JULY

Christopher Street Day: Top event for gays and lesbians with a great parade from

Not only in summer is Berlin a city where people like to have a good time – the calendar is full of festivals of all kinds

Kreuzberg to Brandenburger Tor; *www.csd-berlin.de*

Classic Open Air on Gendarmenmarkt: Festive setting, catchy tunes; *Mitte | tel. 01805 9 69 00 06 06 (*) | www.classicopenair.de*

AUGUST

Long Night of the Museums: A visit to van Gogh & Co. in the evening; *info tel. 030 24 74 98 88 | www.lange-nacht-der-museen.de*

SEPTEMBER

Jüdische Kulturtage (Jewish Culture Days): Theatre performances, concerts and readings; *www.juedische-kulturtage.org*

Berlin Festival: Pop, electro and techno at Tempelhof Airport; *www.berlinfestival.de*

Internationale Funkausstellung: Entertainment/electronics fair at the Funkturm; *Charlottenburg | b2c.ifa-berlin.de*

Berlin Marathon: More than 40,000 participants from all over the world start at Brandenburger Tor; *info tel. 030 30 12 88 10 | www.berlin-marathon.com*

Musikfest Berlin: three wekks of classical music of the highest standard; *www.berlinerfestspiele.de*

SEPTEMBER/OCTOBER

Internationales Literaturfestival: readings and more; *www.literaturfestival.com*

Festival of Lights: After nightfall, installations cast many of Berlin's sights in a new light for ten days; *festival-of-lights.de*

NOVEMBER

Jazzfest Berlin: An institution with international stars; *info tel. 030 25 48 91 00 | www.berlinerfestspiele.de/jazzfest*

DECEMBER

Weihnachtsmarkt am Gendarmenmarkt: the most beautiful – offering artisan craftwork and concerts

LINKS, BLOGS, APPS & MORE

LINKS & BLOGS

www.berlin.de/international is Berlin's official internet site that offers comprehensive listings for hotels, entertainment, tickets for local events well as practical information about local authorities and online maps

www.visitberlin.de is an informative site with interesting offers for tourists to Berlin; including a list of events and travel tips for various age groups along with some useful listings for special interest groups like for example the environmentally aware

90erberlin.tumblr.com On this fascinating site, Michael Lange shows his black and white photos of Berlin in the 90s when it was full of empty spaces and construction sites – often directly next to a picture of the same place 20 years later

www.needleberlin.com Popular Berlin blog by Berlin writer Jseph Pearson. He writes about things like "How to get into the Berghain", but more often about serious, political topics.

www.exberliner.com Berlin's online English language magazine which includes listings for cultural events, reviews, general interest articles and a large classified section. The title is a play on expat

www.thewednesdaychef.com/berlin_on_a_platter/ an excellent and informative foodie blog written by the cookbook editor and award winning blogger Luisa Weiss. She writes about her "favourite bakeries and snack stands, hidden gems, gustatory wonders" and new restaurant discoveries

www.digitalinberlin.de is a site that is perfect for 'music lovers, adventures and individualists' with listings for music, movies, literature, interviews and free downloads

www.toytowngermany.com is the best online forum for expats in Germany and the topics of discussion include lo-

Regardless of whether you are still preparing your trip or already in Berlin: these addresses will provide you with more information, videos and networks to make your holiday even more enjoyable.

cal news, reviews, relocation issues as well as legal and financial advice. The forum also organises a number of live social events via the site

www.iheartberlin.de Exciting Berlin blog with a calendar of upcoming events, a city guide and lots of interesting posts, e.g. about fashion or the inspiring people of Berlin

kreuzberged.com Beautiful blog with small, contemplative, often historical vignettes about Berlin, updated almost every day. From nostalgic pictures via poetic musings about trees to David Bowie's Berlin... it's all here.

VIDEOS & MUSIC

www.myvideo.de/Videos_A-Z?search Word=berlin if you search for 'Berlin' on MyVideo you will not only find many TV series but also documentaries and whimsical short films

www.art-in-berlin.de/video.php Video documentary reports about current exhibitions and the corresponding artists

https://itunes.apple.com/us/podcast/berlin-stories-podcast/id302399493?mt=2 These podcasts are from the bi-weekly English radio broadcasts of 104.1 fm NPR Berlin. American and British writers read their reflections on Berlin and there also special editions with readings of passages from historical novels about B

APPS

Fahrinfo Berlin Important accompaniment when travelling on Berlin's public transport: with a planner that shows you the fastest route from A to B. With the BVG smartphone app, you can buy a ticket (and the WelcomeCard, but no four-journey tickets) for all public transport (see also p. 130). The VBB app (from the Berlin-Brandenburg transport association) on the other hand offers four-journey tickets, but no WelcomeCard

Kultur Berlin Information about all types of concerts, theatres, exhibitions and cultural events. With admission prices, opening times and map of the event location

My Taxi Free app that connects to a taxi nearby; extremely reliable especially within the city centre. Only available for iPhones

TRAVEL TIPS

ARRIVAL

Most planes land and take off from *Tegel Airport* (142 C2) *(D1)* in the north-west of the city. You can reach Bahnhof Zoo, the centre of the western part of the city, in about 20 min by taking the buses X9 and 109. To reach Alexanderplatz (in about 30 min, via Unter den Linden) take the express bus TXL. From *Schönefeld Airport (www.berlin-airport.de)* take the S 9 to Alexanderplatz (35 min) or to Bahnhof Zoo (50 min). A faster alternative is the airport express, a regional train that departs for the airport every half an hour. A taxi ride from Tegel to Bahnhof Zoo costs around 19 euros, to the Alexanderplatz approx. 25 euros. A taxi driver will take you from Schönefeld into the city centre for approx. 35–40 euros. *Airport information (tel. 030 60 91 11 50)*

The most convenient way to travel is by railway. There are fast train connections from major European stations to Berlin-Spandau, Hauptbahnhof (main station) and Ostbahnhof. *Information: tel. 0800 150 70 90 | www.bahn.de*

The motorways to and from Berlin are good. However, there are often traffic jams on the A10 ring road. The centre within the inner district line ring is a "green zone"; only cars with a green sticker are allowed to drive here. *www.umwelt-plakette.de*

There are regular bus services several times a week from all German and many foreign towns to Berlin. It usually takes longer than by train.. Berlin's Central Bus Station is located in Charlottenburg opposite the Funkturm. *Zentraler Omnibusbahnhof (ZOB)* (148 B5) *(C5) (info tel. 030 3 51 95 20 | www.iob-berlin.de)*

RESPONSIBLE TRAVEL

While traveling you can influence a lot. Don't just keep track of your carbon footprint *(www.myclimate.org)* by planning an ecologically harmless route. Also think about how you can protect nature and culture abroad *(www.ecotrans.org)*. It is all the more important that as a tourist you take into consideration aspects such as the conservation of nature *(www.wwf.org)*, regional products, minimal use of cars, saving water and many more things. For more information on ecological Tourism look at *www.ecotourism.org*.

ADVANCE SALES

HEKticket (Hardenbergstr. 29d | tel. 030 2 30 99 30 | www.hekticket.de) sells remaining tickets at half-price until shortly before performances begin. INSIDER TIP Tickets for museums are also available at reduced prices. *Showtime (tel. 030 80 60 29 29 | www.showtimetickets.de)* sell tickets in the KaDeWe department store; box office inside Friedrichstraße station: *Mon–Fri 8am–8pm, Sat 10am–6pm | Georgenstr. 14–18 | www.ber-ticket.de*

BANKS

Normal opening hours are 10am to 5pm on weekdays; some banks however are open until 2pm on Saturdays.

From arrival to weather

Holiday from start to finish: the most important addresses and information for your Berlin trip

BICYCLES, VELOTAXIS & SEGWAY

You can rent a bicycle from many bike shops and hotels in the city centre. The German Railway's (DB) "Call a Bike" *(www.callabike-interaktiv.de)* is very practical. The conspicuous DB bikes can be found at 150 different places in the heart of Berlin. They can be rented directly at a terminal, by telephone or app using your bank card or credit card. New clients have to register first. Fees are 8 cents/minute rising to a maximum of 15 euros/day.

You can also rent a *Biketaxi (tel. 030 93 95 83 46 | www.biketaxi.de)* from March to Oct and have somebody else do the hard work. A 60-minute tour with an individual route costs 45 euros. Or just stop an empty rickshaw on the street. The first kilometre costs 6 euros; after that, there is an hourly rate.

Yoove (tel. 030 6 52 15 73 97 | www.yoove.com) hires out Segways for 19.90 euros an hour; they can be collected at three different hire stations. Tours on Segways are also organised. You need a moped license and be at least 16 years old.

CITY TOURS

Bus no. 100 is terrific for those who like to get an overview on their own. It runs from Bahnhof Zoo to Alexanderplatz and is ideal for sightseeing – you pass most of the important attractions in the centre.

BEROLINA SIGHTSEEING

City-Circle-Tour with 18 stops to hop on or off (daily 10am–6pm, in winter until 5pm, every 10 minutes in summer.) Day ticket 20 euros; two days 24 euros; start: Kurfürstendamm/Meinekestraße. *Info tel. 030 88 56 80 30 | www.berolina-berlin.com*

NEW BERLINERS BIKE TOURS

Free guided tours by bike for new Berliners, run by the ADFC *(German Bike Club, tel. 030 4 48 47 24 | www.adfc-berlin.de)*. Berlin visitors can also take part if they bring their own bike. You can rent one cheaply beforehand, e.g. at NextBike *(www.nextbike.de, various rental points)*.

INSIDER TIP ROUTE 44

Migrant women guide visitors through the Neukölln district around Richardplatz. Those taking part find out how the women and girls live here. Incl. visit to a mosque. *Kulturbewegt e.V. | 5 euros | tel. 030 70 22 20 23 | www.route44-neukoelln.de*

SEGWAY-TOUR

Glide along the pavement and discover the city on two wheels. *Yoove* organises guided Segway tours starting from Potsdamer

BUDGETING

Coffee	2–3 euros *for a cup of coffee*
Ice cream	2 euros *for two scoops of ice cream*
Döner	2.50–3.50 euros *for a döner kebab*
Museum	4–12 euros *state-run museums*
Bus	2.70 euros *for a one-way bus ticket*
Swimming pool	from 3.50 euros *admission*

Platz for approx. 50 euros / person. *Tel. 030 6 52 15 73 97 | www.yoove.com*

SOLAR BOAT TOUR

With the four-hour circular tour on the quiet solar boat you will see many places and buildings and save energy at the same time. Starting and finishing point: Urbanhafen in Kreuzberg. *Tel. 0151 54 22 80 44 | www.solarpolis.de*

INSIDER TIP TOURS OF THE WALL BY TAXI

Two-hour personal tour with stops at historically-important sites. 60 euros per person; 10 euros for each additional passenger. *Tel. 0160 95 32 80 52 | www.taxi-wall-fahrten.de*

CURRENCY CONVERTER

£	€	€	£
1	1.40	1	0.72
3	4.17	3	2.15
5	6.96	5	3.59
13	18.08	13	9.34
40	55.65	40	28.75
75	104	75	53.89
120	167	120	86
250	348	250	180
500	696	500	359

$	€	€	$
1	0.92	1	1.09
3	2.75	3	3.27
5	4.58	5	5.45
13	11.92	13	14.18
40	36.67	40	43.64
75	69	75	81.82
120	110	120	131
250	229	250	273
500	458	500	545

For current exchange rates see www.xe.com

CUSTOMS

EU citizens may import and export goods for their personal use tax-free. Duty-free for non-EU citizens are: 50g perfume, 2 l of wine, 1 l of spirits and 200 cigarettes.

EMBASSIES & CONSULATES

BRITISH EMBASSY

Wilhelmstr. 70/71 | 10117 Berlin | tel. 030 20457 0 | www.ukingermany.fco.gov.uk

EMBASSY OF THE UNITED STATES

Clayallee 170 | 14191 Berlin | tel. 030 83 05 0 | www.germany.usembassy.gov

EMBASSY OF CANADA

Leipziger Platz 17 | 10117 Berlin | tel. 030 20 312 0 | travel.gc.ca/assistance/embassies-consulates/germany

EMERGENCY SERVICES

On-call medical service: 030 31 00 31 | Fire brigade: tel. 112 | Police: tel. 110 | childrens' emergency service: tel. 030 61 00 61 | veterinarian emergency service: tel. 030 4 37 46 63 34 | on-call dentist: tel. 030 89 00 43 33

IMMIGRATION

No visa is necessary for EU citizens to travel to or work in Germany. Non-EU citizens require a visa (valid up to 90 days) – or a residence or settlement permit. More detailed, up-to-date information online, e.g. *www.workpermit.com/germany/employer1.htm*.

INFORMATION

BERLIN TOURISMUS & KONGRESS GMBH

Karlsbad 11 | 10785 Berlin | tel. 030 25 00 25 | www.visitberlin.de | hotline Mon–Fri 9am–7pm, Sat 10am–6pm, Sun 10am–2pm. Branches:

- *Mitte (Pariser Platz | Brandenburger Tor, south wing | April–Oct daily 9:30am–7pm, Nov–March until 6pm)*
- *Mitte (Panoramastr. 1a | in the TV tower | daily 10am–6pm, Nov–March until 4pm)*
- *Mitte (Europaplatz 1 | main railway station | daily 8am–10pm)*
- *Charlottenburg (Kranzler-Eck (Kurfürstendamm Passage) | Mon–Sat 9:30am–8pm)*
- *Tegel Airport (Terminal A, main hall | daily 8am–9pm)*
- *Schönefeld Airport (Terminal A, main hall | daily 7am–10pm)*

PHONE & MOBILE PHONE

The dialling code for Germany is 0049, the area code for Berlin is (0)30. Dial 0044 for Great Britain followed by the area code without "0" and 001 for USA and Canada.

PUBLIC TRANSPORT

Most underground lines run around the clock on Fri and Sat. If there is no underground to where you are staying, night buses will bring you back to your accommodation. The district line usually runs until around 1am. There are three fare zones for suburban services. A and B cover the whole city; C also covers the surrounding area including Potsdam. Currently, a single ticket (A) costs 2.70 euros (concessions: 1.60 euros); day ticket 6.90 euros. *BVG Information: tel. 030 194 49 | www.bvg.de*. Families can travel economically with the *WelcomeCard*: For just 27 euros, the *WelcomeCard* voucher booklet allows you to discover Berlin and Potsdam three days long on the Berlin-Brandenburg public network. A max. of three children (under 15 years old) can travel on an adult ticket. The card is available under *www.visitberlin.de*, where tickets for the district line, BVG, and DB Regio are sold, as well as at the information centres run by Berlin Tourismus Marketing and in many hotels.

WEATHER IN BERLIN

	Jan	Feb	March	April	May	June	July	Aug	Sept	Oct	Nov	Dec
Daytime temperatures in °C/°F	2/36	3/37	8/46	13/55	19/66	22/72	24/75	23/73	19/66	13/55	7/45	3/37
Nighttime temperatures in °C/°F	–3/27	–3/27	0/32	4/39	8/46	12/54	14/57	13/55	10/50	6/43	2/36	–1/30
Sunshine hours/day	2	3	5	6	8	8	8	7	6	4	2	1
Precipitation days/month	11	9	8	9	9	9	11	9	8	9	10	9

Sunshine hours/day Precipitation days/month

USEFUL PHRASES GERMAN

PRONUNCIATION

We have provided a simple pronunciation aid for the german words (see the square brackets). Note the following:

ch usually like ch in Scottish "loch", shown here as [kh]
g hard as in "get"
ß is a double s
ä like the vowel in "fair" or "bear"
ö a little like er as in "her"
ü is spoken as ee with rounded lips, like the French "tu"
ie is ee as in "fee", but ei is like "height", shown here as [ei]
' stress on the following syllable

IN BRIEF

Yes/No/Maybe	Ja [yah]/Nein [nein]/Vielleicht [fee'leikht]
Please/Thank you	Bitte ['bi-te]/Danke ['dan-ke]
Sorry	Entschuldige [ent'shul-di-ge]
Excuse me, please	Entschuldigen Sie [ent'shul-di-gen zee]
May I...?/ Pardon?	Darf ich...? [darf ikh]/Wie bitte? [vee 'bi-te]
I would like to.../ have you got...?	Ich möchte... [ikh 'merkh-te]/ Haben Sie...? ['hab-en zee]
How much is...?	Wie viel kostet...? [vee-feel 'koss-tet]
I (don't) like this	Das gefällt mir/nicht [das ge-'felt meer/nikht]
good/bad	gut/schlecht [goot/shlekht]
broken/doesn't work	kaputt [ka-'put]/funktioniert nicht/ funk-tsion-'eert nikht]
too much/much/little	(zu) viel/wenig [tsoo feel/'vay-nikh]
Help!/Attention!/ Caution!	Hilfe! ['hil-fe]/Achtung! [akh-'tung]/ Vorsicht! ['for-sikht]
ambulance	Krankenwagen ['kran-ken-vaa-gen]/ Notarzt ['note-aatst]
police/fire brigade	Polizei [pol-i-'tsei]/Feuerwehr ['foy-er-vayr]
danger/dangerous	Gefahr [ge-'far]/gefährlich [ge-'fair-likh]

GREETINGS, FAREWELL

Good morning!/after-noon!/evening!/night!	Gute(n) Morgen ['goo-ten 'mor-gen]/Tag [taag]/ Abend ['aa-bent]/Nacht [nakht]
Hello!/Goodbye!	Hallo ['ha-llo]/Auf Wiedersehen [owf 'vee-der-zayn]

Sprechen Sie Deutsch?

"Do you speak German?" This guide will help you to say the basic words and phrases in German.

See you!	Tschüss [chüss]
My name is...	Ich heiße... [ikh 'hei-sse]
What's your name?	Wie heißt Du [vee heist doo]/ heißen Sie? ['heiss-en zee]
I'm from...	Ich komme aus... [ikh 'ko-mme ows]

DATE & TIME

Monday/Tuesday	Montag ['moan-tag]/Dienstag ['deens-tag]
Wednesday/Thursday	Mittwoch ['mit-vokh]/Donnerstag ['don-ers-tag]
Friday/Saturday	Freitag ['frei-tag]/Samstag ['zams-tag]
Sunday/holiday	Sonntag ['zon-tag]/Feiertag ['fire-tag]
today/tomorrow/ yesterday	heute ['hoy-te]/morgen ['mor-gen]/ gestern ['gess-tern]
hour/minute	Stunde ['shtun-de]/Minute [min-'oo-te]
day/night/week	Tag [tag]/Nacht [nakht]/Woche ['vo-khe]
What time is it?	Wie viel Uhr ist es? ['vee-feel oor ist es]
It's three o'clock	Es ist drei Uhr [ez ist drei oor]

TRAVEL

open/closed	offen ['off-en]/geschlossen [ge-'shloss-en]
entrance (vehicles)	Zufahrt ['tsoo-faat]
entrance/exit	Eingang ['ein-gang]/Ausgang ['ows-gang]
arrival/arrival (flight)	Ankunft ['an-kunft]/Abflug ['ap-floog]
toilets/restrooms / ladies/gentlemen	Toiletten [twa-'let-en]/ Damen ['daa-men]/Herren ['her-en]
(no) drinking water	(kein) Trinkwasser [(kein) 'trink-vass-er]
Where is...?/Where are...?	Wo ist...? [vo ist]/Wo sind...? [vo zint]
left/right	links [links]/rechts [rekhts]
straight ahead/back	geradeaus [ge-raa-de-'ows]/zurück [tsoo-'rük]
close/far	nah [naa]/weit [veit]
taxi/cab	Taxi ['tak-si]
bus stop/ cab stand	Bushaltestelle [bus-hal-te-'shtell-e]/ Taxistand ['tak-si- shtant]
parking lot/parking garage	Parkplatz ['park-plats]/Parkhaus ['park-hows]
street map/map	Stadtplan ['shtat-plan]/Landkarte ['lant-kaa-te]
airport/ train station	Flughafen ['floog-ha-fen]/ Bahnhof ['baan-hoaf]
schedule/ticket	Fahrplan ['faa-plan]/Fahrschein ['faa-shein]
I would like to rent...	Ich möchte... mieten [ikh 'mer-khte... 'mee-ten]
a car/a bicycle	ein Auto [ein 'ow-to]/ein Fahrrad [ein 'faa-raat]
a motorhome/RV	ein Wohnmobil [ein 'vone-mo-beel]
a boat	ein Boot [ein 'boat]

petrol/gas station	Tankstelle ['tank-shtell-e]
petrol/gas / diesel	Benzin [ben-'tseen]/Diesel ['dee-zel]
breakdown/repair shop	Panne ['pan-e]/Werkstatt ['verk-shtat]

FOOD & DRINK

Could you please book a table for tonight for four?	Reservieren Sie uns bitte für heute Abend einen Tisch für vier Personen [rez-er-'vee-ren zee uns 'bi-te für 'hoy-te 'aa-bent 'ein-en tish für feer pair-'zo-nen]
The menu, please	Die Speisekarte, bitte [dee 'shpei-ze-kaa-te 'bi-te]
Could I please have...?	Könnte ich... haben? ['kern-te ihk... 'haa-ben]
with/without ice/ sparkling	mit [mit]/ohne Eis ['oh-ne eis]/ Kohlensäure ['koh-len-zoy-re]
vegetarian/allergy	Vegetarier(in) [veg-e-'taa-ree-er]/Allergie [al-air-'gee]
May I have the bill, lease?	Ich möchte zahlen, bitte [ikh 'merkh-te 'tsaa-len 'bi-te]

SHOPPING

Where can I find...?	Wo finde ich...? [vo 'fin-de ikh]
I'd like.../I'm looking for...	Ich möchte... [ikh 'merkh-te]/Ich suche... [ikh 'zoo-khe]
pharmacy/chemist	Apotheke [a-po-'tay-ke]/Drogerie [dro-ge-'ree]
shopping centre	Einkaufszentrum [ein-kowfs-'tsen-trum]
expensive/cheap/price	teuer ['toy-er]/billig ['bil-ig]/Preis [preis]
more/less	mehr [mayr]/weniger ['vay-ni-ger]
organically grown	aus biologischem Anbau [ows bee-o-'lo-gish-em 'an-bow]

WHERE TO STAY

I have booked a room	Ich habe ein Zimmer reserviert [ikh 'haa-be ein 'tsi-me rez-erv-'eert]
Do you have any... left?	Haben Sie noch ein... ['haa-ben zee nokh]
single room	Einzelzimmer ['ein-tsel-tsi-mer]
double room	Doppelzimmer ['dop-el-tsi-mer]
breakfast/half board	Frühstück ['frü-shtük]/Halbpension ['halp-pen-si-ohn]
full board	Vollpension ['foll-pen-si-ohn]
shower/sit-down bath	Dusche ['doo-she]/Bad [baat]
balcony/terrace	Balkon [bal-'kohn]/Terrasse [te-'rass-e]
key/room card	Schlüssel ['shlü-sel]/Zimmerkarte ['tsi-mer-kaa-te]
luggage/suitcase	Gepäck [ge-'pek]/Koffer ['koff-er]/Tasche ['ta-she]

BANKS, MONEY & CREDIT CARDS

bank/ATM	Bank/Geldautomat [bank/'gelt-ow-to-maat]
pin code	Geheimzahl [ge-'heim-tsaal]
I'd like to change... euros	Ich möchte... Euro wechseln [ikh 'merkh-te... ' oy-ro 'vek-seln]

cash/credit card	bar [bar]/Kreditkarte [kre-'dit-kaa-te]
bill/coin	Banknote ['bank-noh-te]/Münze ['mün-tse]

HEALTH

doctor/dentist/ paediatrician	Arzt [aatst]/Zahnarzt ['tsaan-aatst]/ Kinderarzt ['kin-der-aatst]
hospital/ emergency clinic	Krankenhaus ['kran-ken-hows]/ Notfallpraxis ['note-fal-prak-sis]
fever/pain	Fieber ['fee-ber]/Schmerzen ['shmer-tsen]
diarrhoea/nausea	Durchfall ['doorkh-fal]/Übelkeit ['ü-bel-keit]
inflamed/injured	entzündet [ent-'tsün-det]/verletzt [fer-'letst]
prescription	Rezept [re-'tsept]
pain reliever/tablet	Schmerzmittel ['shmerts-mit-el]/Tablette [ta-'blet-e]

POST, TELECOMMUNICATIONS & MEDIA

stamp/letter	Briefmarke ['brief-maa-ke]/Brief [brief]
postcard	Postkarte ['posst-kaa-te]
I'm looking for a prepaid card for my mobile	Ich suche eine Prepaid-Karte für mein Handy [ikh 'zoo-khe 'ei-ne 'pre-paid-kaa-te für mein 'hen-dee]
Do I need a special area code?	Brauche ich eine spezielle Vorwahl? ['brow-khe ikh 'ei-ne shpets-ee-'ell-e 'fore-vaal]
Where can I find internet access?	Wo finde ich einen Internetzugang? [vo 'fin-de ikh 'ei-nen 'in-ter-net-tsoo-gang]
socket/adapter/ charger/wi-fi	Steckdose ['shtek-doh-ze]/Adapter [a-'dap-te]/ Ladegerät ['laa-de-ge-rayt]/WLAN ['vay-laan]

LEISURE, SPORTS & BEACH

bike/scooter rental	Fahrrad-['faa-raat]/Mofa-Verleih ['mo-fa fer-lei]
rental shop	Vermietladen [fer-'meet-laa-den]
lesson	Übungsstunde ['ü-bungs-shtun-de]

NUMBERS

0 null [null]	10 zehn [tsayn]	20 zwanzig ['tsvantsikh]
1 eins [eins]	11 elf [elf]	50 Fünfzig ['fünf-tsikh]
2 zwei [tsvei]	12 zwölf [tsvölf]	100 (ein) Hundert ['hun-dert]
3 drei [drei]	13 dreizehn [' dreitsayn]	200 Zwei Hundert [tsvei 'hun-dert]
4 vier [feer]	14 vierzehn ['feertsayn]	1000 (ein) Tausend ['tow-zent]
5 fünf [fünf]	15 fünfzehn ['fünftsayn]	2000 Zwei Tausend [tsvei 'tow-zent]
6 sechs [zex]	16 sechzehn ['zekhtsayn]	10 000 Zehn Tausend [tsayn 'tow-zent]
7 sieben ['zeeben]	17 siebzehn ['zeebtsayn]	
8 acht [akht]	18 achtzehn ['akhtsayn]	½ ein halb [ein halp]
9 neun [noyn]	19 neunzehn ['noyntsayn]	¼ ein viertel [ein 'feer-tel]

STREET ATLAS

The green line indicates the Discovery Tour "Berlin at a glance"
The ble line indicates the other Discovery Tours
All tours are also marked in the pull-out map

 Photo: Berlin Mitte with TV Tower

Exploring Berlin

The map on the back cover shows how the area has been sub-divided

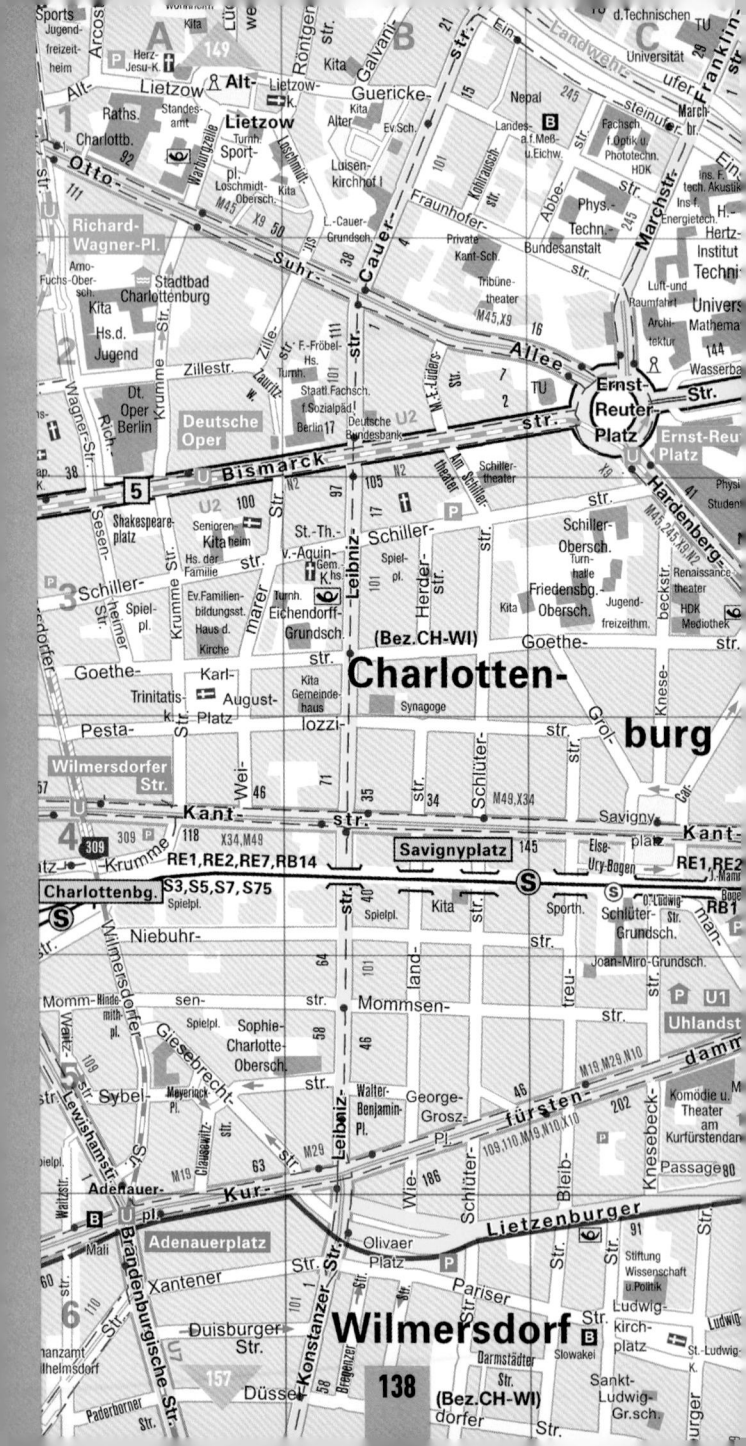
Charlotten-
burg
(Bez.CH-WI)
Wilmersdorf
(Bez.CH-WI)
Ernst-Reuter-Platz
Savignyplatz
Adenauerplatz
Uhlandst
Charlottenbg.
Wilmersdorfer Str.
Richard-Wagner-Pl.
Deutsche Oper
Bismarck-str.
Kant-str.
Kurfürstendamm
Lietzenburger str.
Otto-str.
Suhr-str.
Cauer-str.
Leibniz-str.
Schlüter-str.
Knesebeck-str.
Hardenberg-str.
Marchstr.
Fasanenstr.
Kantstr.
Krumme str.
Zillestr.
Wilmersdorfer str.
Brandenburgische str.
Konstanzer str.
Xantener str.
Duisburger str.
Düsseldorfer str.
Paderborner str.
Pariser str.
Olivaer Platz
Mommsen-str.
Niebuhr-str.
Goethe-str.
Pestalozzi-str.
Schiller-str.
Schillerdamm
Hardenbergstr.
Fasanenstr.
Joachimsthaler str.
Kurfürstendamm
Lietzenburger str.
Uhlandstr.
Savignyplatz
Charlottenbg.
Wilmersdorfer str.
Adenauerplatz
Olivaer Platz
Wilmersdorf
Charlotten-
burg
138

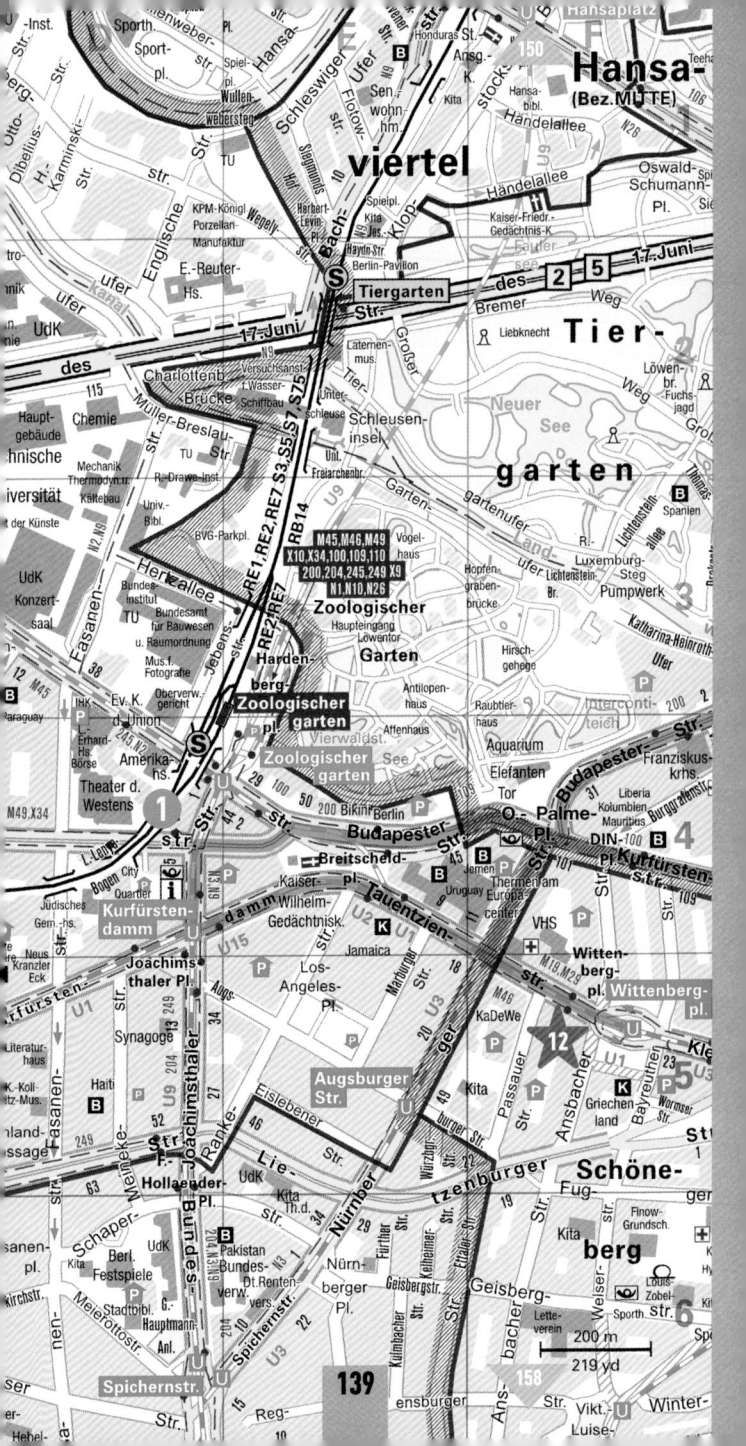
Hansa-
(Bez.MITTE)
viertel
Tiergarten
Tier-
garten
Zoologischer
Garten
Zoologischer
garten
Zoologischer
garten
Hansaplatz
Hansa-
bibl.
Händelallee
Oswald-
Schumann-
Pl.
Kaiser-Friedr.-
Gedächtnis-K
Bremer
Weg
Liebknecht
Laternen-
mus.
Schleusen-
insel
Neuer
See
Löwen-
br.
Fuchs-
jagd
Spanien
Luxemburg-
Steg
Pumpwerk
Hirsch-
gehege
Antilopen-
haus
Raubtier-
haus
Aquarium
Elefanten
Tor
Interconti-
teich
Affenhaus
Vogel-
haus
Hopfen-
graben-
brücke
Lichtenstein-
allee
Lichtenstein-
Br.
Katharina-Heinroth-
Ufer
Franziskus-
krhs.
Budapester
Str.
O.-Palme-
Pl.
DIN-
Pl.
Kurfürsten-
Str.
Tauentzien-
Str.
Kaiser-
Wilhelm-
Gedächtnisk.
Los-
Angeles-
Pl.
Jamaica
Thermen am
Europa-
center
VHS
Wittenberg-
pl.
Wittenberg-
pl.
KaDeWe
Kita
Augsburger
Str.
Fislebener
Str.
Ansbacher
Str.
Passauer
Str.
Griechen-
land
Bayreuther
Str.
Wormser
Str.
Schöne-
berg
Finow-
Grundsch.
Kita
Lette-
verein
Sporth.
Geisberg-
str.
Weiser-
str.
Fug-
str.
Nürn-
berger
Pl.
Geisbergstr.
Fürther
Str.
Kulmbacher
Str.
Würzburger
Str.
Nürnberger
Str.
Pakistan
Bundes-
Dt.Renten-
vers.
Spichernstr.
Spichernstr.
Hollaender-
Pl.
Joachimsthaler
Pl.
Joachimsthaler
Str.
Ranke-
Str.
Meineke-
Str.
Fasanen-
Str.
Schaper-
Str.
Berl.
Festspiele
Stadtbibl.
Hauptmann-
Anl.
Meierottostr.
Bundes-
Str.
Kurfürsten-
damm
Joachims-
thaler Pl.
Synagoge
Haiti
Literatur-
haus
Neus
Kranzler
Eck
Bogen City
Quartier
Jüdisches
Gem.-hs.
Amerika-
hs.
Theater d.
Westens
Ev. K.
d. Union
Oberverw.
gericht
Bundesamt
für Bauwesen
u. Raumordnung
Bundesinstitut
Mus.f.
Fotografie
Harden-
berg-
pl.
Hardenbergstr.
Fasanenstr.
Hertzallee
Jebensstr.
Englische
Str.
Kantstr.
Wegely
Porzellan-
Manufaktur
KPM-Königl.
E.-Reuter-
Hs.
Charlottenb.
Brücke
Muller-Breslau-
Str.
Chemie
Hauptgebäude
Mechanik
Thermodyn.
Kältebau
Univ.-
Bibl.
BVG-Parkpl.
Schleswiger
Ufer
Flotow-
str.
Siegmunds
Hof
Bachstr.
Klopstock-
str.
Herbert-
Levin-
Pl.
Haydn-Str.
Berlin-Pavillon
Kita
Jus.
Sen.
wohn.
hm.
Spielpl.
Wullen-
weberstieg
Sporth.
Sport-
pl.
Honduras St.
Ansg.
K.
Teeha
Oswald-
Schumann-
Pl.
Tiergarten
Str.
17.Juni
17.Juni
des
Großer
Tier-
Garten-
gartenufer
Land-
ufer
Luxemburg-
Steg
Pumpwerk
Katharina-Heinroth-
Ufer
Budapester
Str.
Franziskus-
krhs.
Liberia
Kolumbien
Mauritius
Burgrafenstr.
Kurfürsten

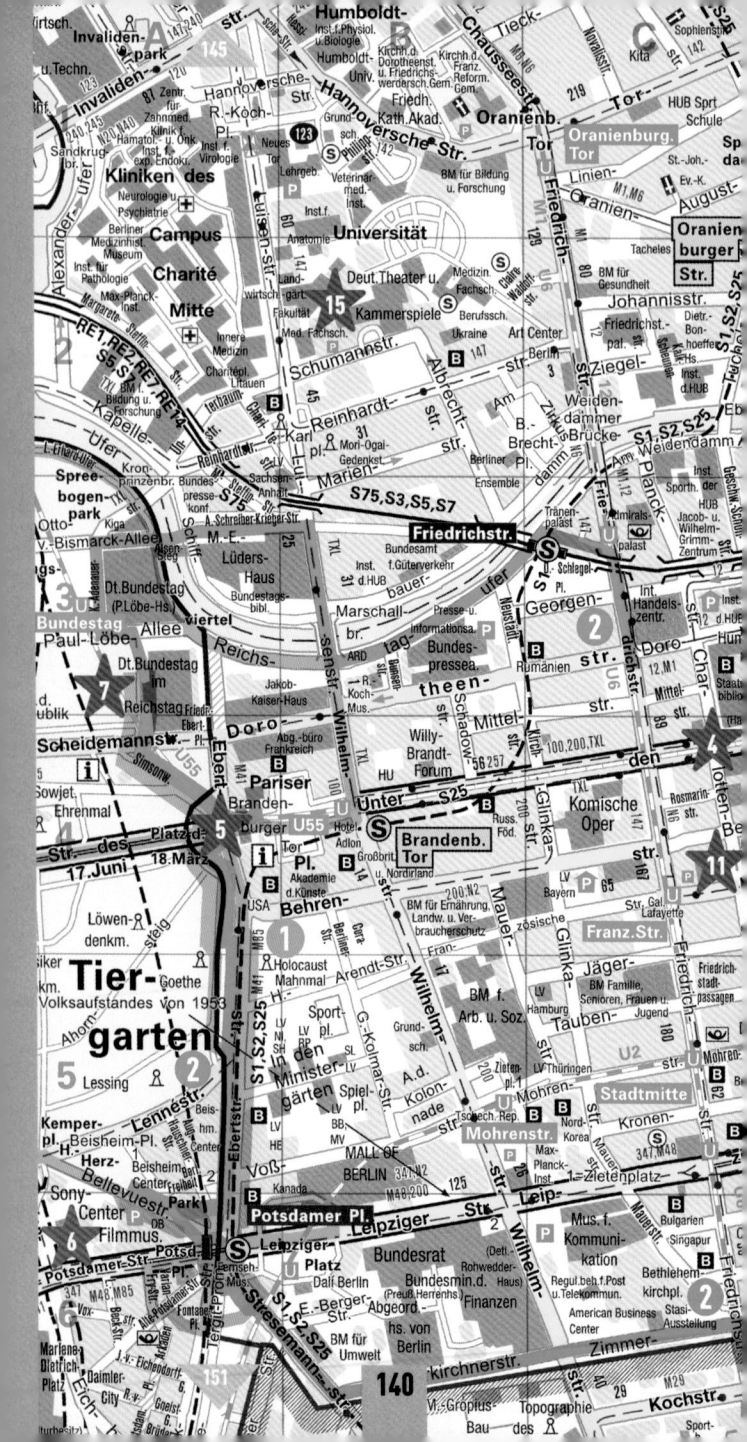
Humboldt-
Invaliden-park
Invaliden-
Hannoversche-
Hannoversche Str.
Oranienb.
Oranienburg. Tor
Oranienburger Str.
Kliniken des
Campus
Charité
Mitte
Universität
Deut.Theater u.
Kammerspiele
Friedrichstr.
Friedrich-
Johannisstr.
Schumannstr.
Albrecht-str.
Reinhardt-str.
Marien-
Ziegel-
Weidendamm
Brecht-
Brücke
Spree-bogen-park
Bismarck-Allee
Dt.Bundestag
Bundestag
Paul-Löbe-Allee
Dt.Bundestag im
Reichstag
Scheidemannstr.
Lüders-Haus
Bundesamt f.Güterverkehr
Marschall-br.
Georgen-
Bundes-pressea.
Rumänien
Doro-theen-str.
Mittel-str.
Willy-Brandt-Forum
Pariser Brandenburger Tor
Brandenb. Tor
Unter den Linden
Komische Oper
Glinka-str.
Mauer-str.
Behren-str.
Tier-garten
Holocaust Mahnmal
Arendt-str.
Wilhelm-str.
Minister-gärten
Jäger-str.
Tauben-str.
Franz.Str.
Friedrich-stadt-passagen
Stadtmitte
Mohrenstr.
Kronen-str.
Zietenplatz
Leipziger Str.
Potsdamer Pl.
Leipziger Platz
Bundesrat
Bundesmin.d. Finanzen
Stresemann-str.
Zimmer-str.
Kochstr.
Topographie des Terrors
Sony-Center
Filmmus.
Bellevuestr.
Lennéstr.
Beisheim-Pl.
Herz-
Kemper-pl.
Tiergarten
Lessing
Löwen-denkm.
17.Juni
18.März
Platz d.
Str. des
Ebertstr.
Sowjet. Ehrenmal
Simsonw.
Alexander-ufer
Spree-ufer
Kapelle-ufer
Reichs-tagsufer
Dorotheen-str.
Friedrichstr.
Georgen-str.
Chausseestr.
Tor-str.
Linien-str.
Oranien-str.
August-str.
Tacheles
Sophienstr.
Kita
HUB Sport Schule
Sandkrugbr.
Neues Tor
Lehrgeb.
Veterinärmed. Inst.
Anatomie
Inst.f.Physiol. u.Biologie
Humboldt-Univ.
Kirchn.d. Dorotheenst. u. Friedrichswerdersch. Gem.
Friedh.
Kath. Akad.
BM für Bildung u. Forschung
BM für Gesundheit
Friedrichst.-pal.
Dietr.-Bonhoeffer-Hs.
Inst. d.HUB
Berlin 3
Ukraine
Art Center
Berliner Ensemble
Mori-Ogai-Gedenkst.
Tränenpalast
Admiralpalast
Sporth. der HUB
Jacob- u. Wilhelm-Grimm-Zentrum
Int. Handelszentr.
Presse- u. Informationsa.
Russ. Fód.
Bulgarien
Singapur
Bethlehem-kirchpl.
American Business Center
Stasi-Ausstellung
Regul.beh.f.Post u.Telekommun.
Mus. f. Kommunikation
Rohwedder-Haus
Dall Berlin
Abgeordn. hs. von Berlin
BM für Umwelt
Holocaust Mahnmal
Sport-pl.
Spiel-pl.
Grund-sch.
Tschech. Rep.
Nord-Korea
Max-Planck-Inst.
Kanada
MALL OF BERLIN
Hotel Adlon
Akademie d.Künste
Großbrit. u. Nordirland
USA
BM für Ernährung, Landw. u. Verbraucherschutz
Bayern
Str. Gal. Lafayette
Hamburg
Thüringen
Russ. Fód.
Rumänien
Ukraine
Kaiser-Haus
Jakob-Kaiser-Haus
Abg.-büro Frankreich
Bundespresse-ball
Bundestagsbibl.
Chariteplatz
Innere Medizin
Med. Fachsch.
Landwirtsch. gart. Fakultät
Berufssch.
Fachsch.
Medizin
Berliner Medizinhist. Museum
Inst. für Pathologie
Max-Planck-Inst. für Bildung u. Forschung
Neurologie u. Psychiatrie
Inst. f. exp. Endokr.
Klinik u. Onk.
Hamatol.
Zentr. für Zahnmed.
Inst. f. Virologie
Sachsen-Anhalt
Kron-prinzenbr.
Kiga
Lützow-pl.
Tiergarten
Volksaufstandes von 1953
Goethe
Holocaust Mahnmal
Sport-pl.
Grund-sch.
Spiel-pl

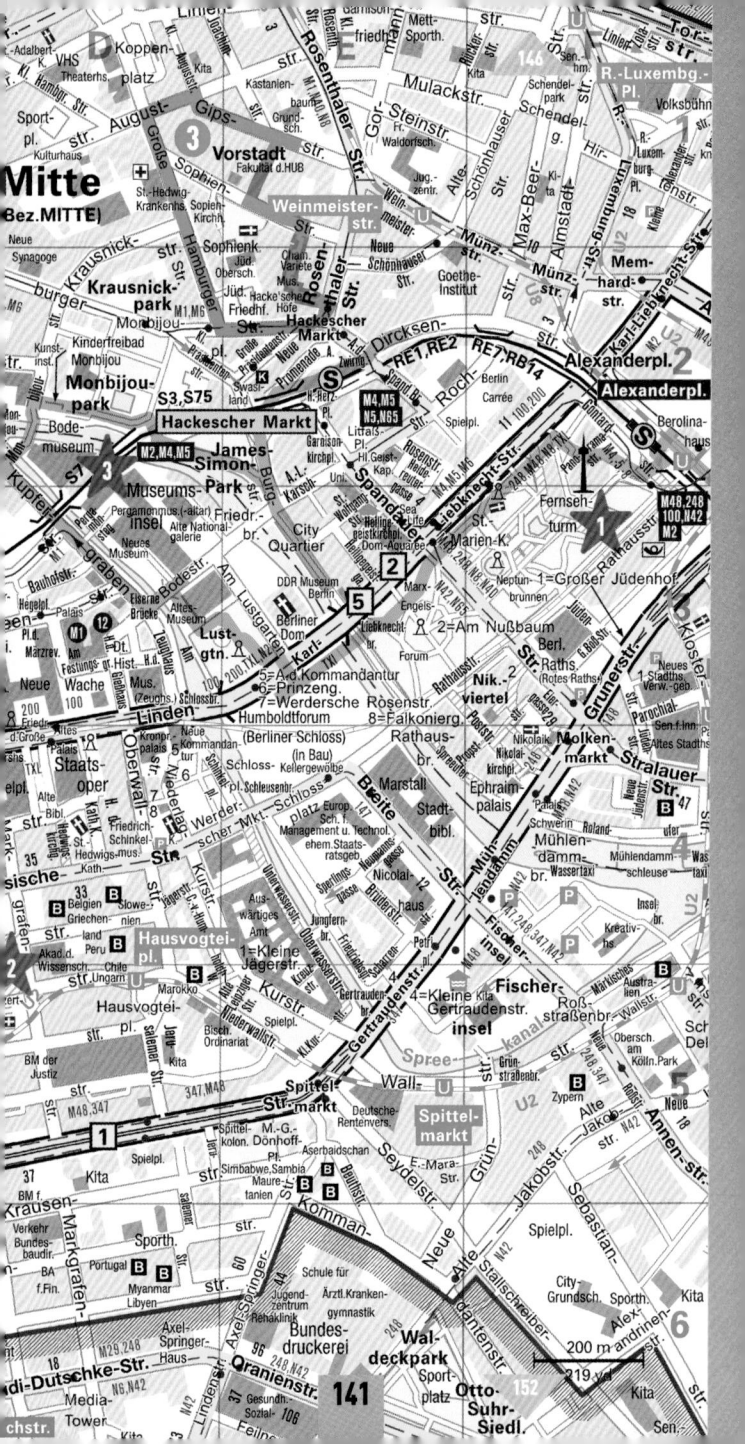
Mitte
Bez.MITTE)
Koppen-platz
Sport-pl.
Kulturhaus
August-
Gips-
Vorstadt
Fakultät d.HUB
Sophien-
St.-Hedwig-Krankenhs.
Sophien-Kirchh.
Weinmeister-str.
Mulackstr.
Gor-
Steinstr.
Rosenthaler Str.
Mett-mann
Sporth.
Garnison-friedhof
R.-Luxembg.-Pl.
Volksbühne
Schendel-park
Max-Beer-
Almstadt
Münz-str.
Memhard-str.
Karl-Liebknecht-Str.
Alexanderpl.
Neue Synagoge
Sophienk
Jüd. Obersch.
Chain Variete
Hackesche Höfe
Hackescher Markt
Neue Schönhauser Str.
Goethe-Institut
Krausnick-burger
Krausnick-park
Monbijou-
Kinderfreibad Monbijou
Monbijou-park
S3,S75
Hackescher Markt
Dircksen-
RE7,RE2
RE7,RB14
Berlin Carrée
Berolina-haus
Bode-museum
M2,M4,M5
James-Simon-Park
Museums-Insel
Pergamonmus.(-akad.)
Alte Nationalgalerie
Neues Museum
Friedr.-br.
City Quartier
Spandauer
Liebknecht-Str.
Fernseh-turm
M48,248 100,N42 M2
Bauhdstr.
Eiserne Brücke
Altes Museum
Lust-gtn.
DDR Museum Berlin
Berliner Dom
Neptun-brunnen
1=Großer Jüdenhof
2=Am Nußbaum
5=A.d.Kommandantur
6=Prinzeng.
7=Werdersche Rosenstr.
8=Falkonierg.
Humboldtforum
(Berliner Schloss)
(in Bau)
Linden
Oberwall-str.
Staats-oper
Neue Wache
Kronprinzenpalais
Neue Kommandantur
Schloss-br.
Schloßpl.
Schleusenbr.
Marstall
Breite Str.
Stadt-bibl.
Rathaus-br.
Nik.-viertel
Rathaus
Rathausstr.
Grunerstr.
Molkenmarkt
Stralauer Str.
Ephraimpalais
Mühlendamm-br.
Mühlendamm-schleuse
Hausvogtei-pl.
1=Kleine Jägerstr.
Kurstr.
Friedrichs-Schinkel-mus.
Akad.d. Wissensch.
Hausvogtei-pl.
Fischer-insel
4=Kleine Gertraudenstr.
Gertraudenstr.
Roßstraßenbr.
Spree-kanal
Wall-str.
Spittel-markt
Spittel-markt
Deutsche Rentenvers.
Annen-str.
Jakobstr.
Sebastian-str.
Krausen-str.
Markgraf-en-str.
Kommandant-str.
Neue Grünstr.
Alte Jakobstr.
Alte Stallschreiber-str.
Axel-Springer-Haus
Bundes-druckerei
Wald-deckpark
Sport-platz
Otto-Suhr-Siedl.
Oranienstr.
Media-Tower
141
200 m
219 yd

A
B
C
300m
328 yd
Flughafen
"Otto L
Berlin
Terminal
Empfangsgebäude
Terminal
Tower
Siedlung
Mäckeritzwiesen
Hangars
Kolonie
Luftfracht-
hof
Zoll-
amt
Beusselsche
Kol.
Neuland II
Kol.
Eigenland
Erben
Köppensche
Kol.
Erben
Kol.
Fabiansche
Albrechtsche
Erben
Erben
Kol.am Wasser-
Mäckeritz-
brücke
Kol.
Neuland I
Kol.
Vor d.Toren Feld 1
Vor
d. Toren
Feld 2
Hohl-
weg Am Kanal
Saatwinkler
Damm
Saatwinkler
General-
Ganeval-Br.
Tennis-
plätze
Baum-
schule
Landes-
leistungs-
zentr.
Rudern
1=Straße B
Sportplätze
Jungfernheide
Sport-
pl.
Anschlussstelle
Flughafen
Tegel
Volkspark
Wild-
gehege
Wasserturm
Spielwiese
Spielpl.
Erholungsanlage
Hinckeldey-
denkmal
Jungfernheide
Jungfern-
heideteich
Freibad
Jungfernheide
Wilhelm- von-
Siemens- Park
Schuckert-
pl.
G.-Böß-
Freilicht-
bühne
AS
Hecker-
damm
Hecker-
damm
R.-Reinick
Grundsch.
Alten- und Pflegeheim
MM Birkholz
Geißlerpfad
Getelsteig
Goebel-
str.
Goebelpl.
Sühne-
Christi- K.
Jugend-
club
Sportpl.
Hofacker-
zeile
Schumacher-
Halemweg
Popitz-
weg
Siemensdamm
Nonnenallee
Siemensd.
1 = Dahrendorfzeile
Jak.-Kaiser-Platz
Jakob-
Kaiser-
Pl.
Anschlussstelle
Siemensdamm
Siemens-
damm
Ohm-
str.
Kol.-Groß-
Weg
Landes-
branddirektion
Kol.
Bleibtreu-
Schleuse
Charlottenburg
Brücke
Dreieck
Charlottenburg
Spree-
Kol.
Schleusenland
142
148

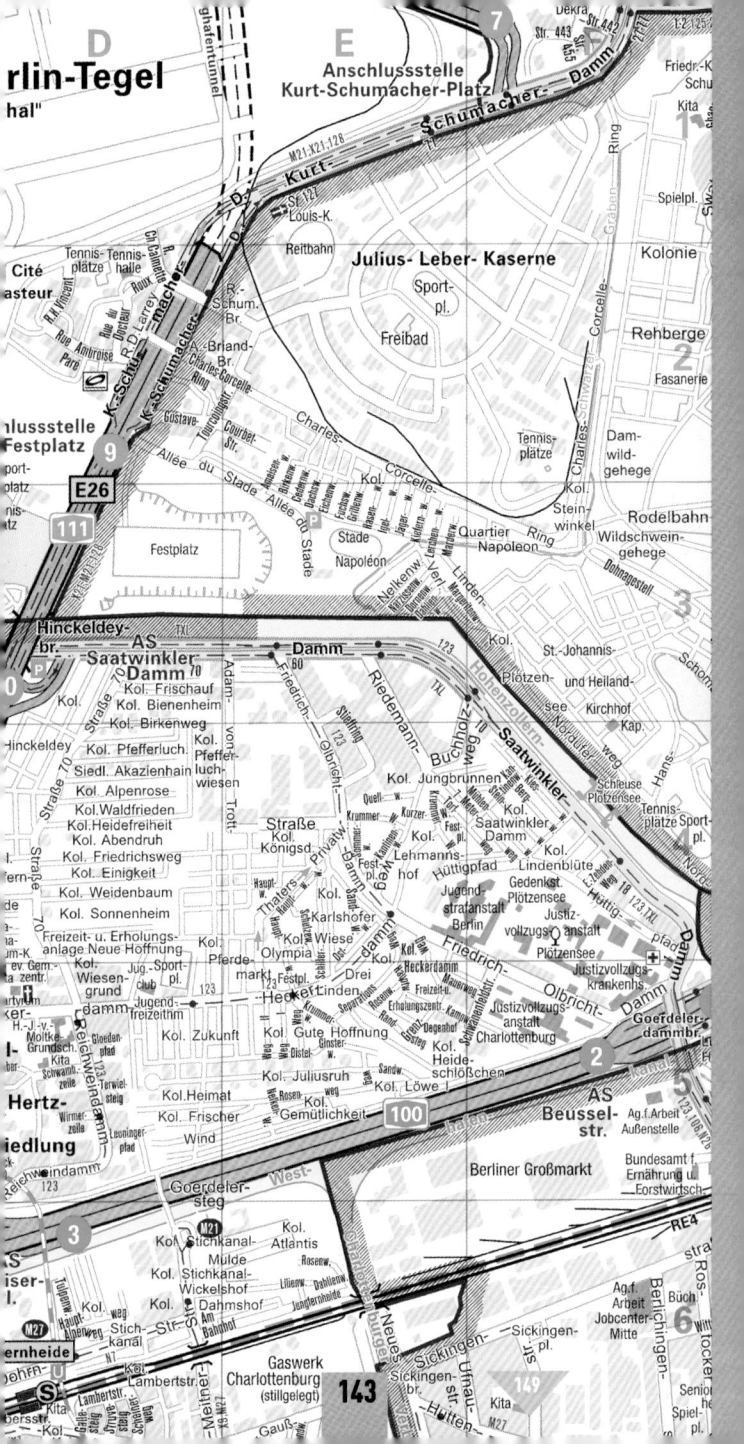
D
E
rlin-Tegel
hal"
Anschlussstelle
Kurt-Schumacher-Platz
Schumacher-Damm
Kurt-Schumacher-Damm
Julius- Leber- Kaserne
Reitbahn
Sport-pl.
Freibad
Kolonie
Rehberge
Fasanerie
Tennis-plätze
Tennis-halle
Cité
asteur
Festplatz
E26
111
Hinckeldey-br.
Saatwinkler Damm
Kol. Frischauf
Kol. Bienenheim
Kol. Birkenweg
Kol. Pfefferluch
Siedl. Akazienhain
Kol. Alpenrose
Kol. Waldfrieden
Kol. Heidefreiheit
Kol. Abendruh
Kol. Friedrichsweg
Kol. Einigkeit
Kol. Weidenbaum
Kol. Sonnenheim
Freizeit- u. Erholungsanlage Neue Hoffnung
Kol. Wiesengrund
Jug.-Sport-club pl.
Jugendfreizeitheim
Kol. Zukunft
Kol. Heimat
Kol. Frischer Wind
Kol. Pfeffer-luchwiesen
Kol. Pferdemarkt
Kol. Olympia
Kol. Wiese
Kol. Karlshofer
Kol. Drei Linden
Kol. Gute Hoffnung
Kol. Juliusruh
Kol. Gemütlichkeit
Kol. Löwe
Kol. Heideschlößchen
Kol. Heimat
Kol. Jungbrunnen
Kol. Saatwinkler Damm
Kol. Lindenblüte
Kol. Plötzensee
Kol. Stein-winkel
Kol. St.-Johannis- und Heiland-
Kol. Atlantis
Kol. Stichkanal-Mulde
Kol. Stichkanal-Wickelshof
Kol. Dahmshof
Quartier Napoleon
Napoléon
Stade
Allée du Stade
Charles-Corelle-Ring
Gustave-Roux-Str.
Courbet-Str.
Briand-Br.
R.-Schum.-Br.
Tennis-plätze
Dam-wild-gehege
Rodelbahn
Wildschwein-gehege
Kirchhof
Kap.
Schleuse Plötzensee
Tennis-platze
Sport-pl.
Lehmanns-hof
Hüttlingpfad
Jugend-strafanstalt Berlin
Justiz-vollzugs-anstalt Plötzensee
Justizvollzugs-krankenhs
Justizvollzugs-anstalt Charlottenburg
Gedenkst. Plötzensee
Heckerdamm
Friedrich-Olbricht-Damm
Riedemann-Damm
Buchholz-weg
Hohenzollern-Damm
Saatwinkler
Adam-von-Trott-Straße
Friedrich-Olbricht-Straße
Privatw.
Hauptweg
Krummer Weg
Kurzer Weg
Quell-weg
Festpl.
Hauptweg

Afrikanische Str.
300m
328 yd
Müller-
Ebert-
Togostr.
Siedl.
Nachtigalplatz
Kolonie
Rehberge
Volkspark
Rodelbahn
Rehberge
Fasanerie
Sport-pl.
Tennis-plätze
Stadion Rehberge
Tennis-plätze
Afrikanische
Sansibar-
Transvaal-
Guinea-
Togo-
Kon-go-
Kamerun
Kameruner
Wedding
(Bez.MITTE)
Seestr.
Schiller-park
Liverpoder Str.
Dubnes Str.
Luderitz-
Barfus-straße
Ungarn-straße
Lüderitzstr.
Brüsseler Str.
Ostender Str.
Limburger Str.
Luxemburger
Amrumer Str.
Fehrbelliner Str.
Buchstr.
Nordufer
Berlin-
Westhafen
Kraftwerk Moabit
Eppstein-
Quitzow-
Stephan-
Birkenstr.
Perleberger
Moabit
(Bez.MITTE)
144
Goethe-park
Dohnagestell
Schönburgk-
Transvaal-
Dohnaer
Friedhof am Plötzensee
Plötzen-see
Hans-
Freibad Plötzensee
Tennis-plätze
Sport-pl.
Spielpl.
Jugend-gästeh.
Kinderheim Frohsinn
Saalwinkler Damm
Hohenzollern-
Hafen
Brückenmeist.
Seestraßen-insel
Spennrath-br.
See-
H.-Maass-Br.
Südliche Seestraßenbr.
Anschlussst. Seestr.
Goerdeler-dammbr.
Ludw.-Hoffm.-Br.
Westhafen
Becken II
Becken I
Beusselstr.
Beussel-br.
Bebsselstraße
Ring-bahn
S41-S42
Samuel-
Erna-
RE4
Siemens-straße
Sickingen-straße
Berlichingen-straße
Ros-locker-straße
Beussel-straße
Wicle-f-straße
Wilhelmsaue
Bir-ken-straße
Stromstraße
Wilsnacker Str.
Drey
Sonntags-freude
Auto-busbeitr.-hof (BVG)
Dom-kirchhof II
Kornelusk.
Centre Francais
Lessing-Obersch.
Jug. club
Sport-pl.
Turnh.
Integr. Sch. am Schiller-park
Kita
Kirchhof
Jugend-wohnhm.
Senioren-wo
DSZ
Gesundh.
St. Aloysius-K.
Sport.
Kita
Kinder-zentr.
Grundsch. Mövensee
Sport.
Bibl.
Freilicht-bühne
Möwen-see
Kol. Klein-Afrika
Tanzpl.
Sen. freiz.
Kita.
Sport-platz
P. Gerhardt-Stift
U-Bahn Hauptwerkst.
Sport-platz
Anna-Lindh-
Grundsch.
Kita
Kol. Kame-run
Kapernaumk.
E.-Schering-Obersch.
Sen.-freizeitst.
Inst.f. Lebens-mitteltechn.
Anti-kriegs-mus.
Zucker-mus.
Kol. Lüttich
Kita
Tennis-pl.
Spielpl.
Spöttn.
St.-Paul-Kirch-hof.
Inst.f. Mikrobiologie Brauerei- u. Biotechnologie
Nazareth-Kap.
Kirchhof I
Inst.f. Getreidetechn.
Inst. f. Arzneimittel
Sch. in der Charité
Augusterpgr.
Dt. Herz-zentr. Pl.
Charité Campus Virchow-Klinikum
Zahnklinik
Robert-Koch-Inst.
Straßen- u. Grünflächen-amt
Jugend-freizeithm.
St.-Johannis-Kirchhof II
Eckern-förder-Pl.
Nördl. Seestraßenbr.
Staatsbibliothek zu Berlin (Zeitungsabt.)
Zentrale Westhafen
BEHALA
Friedr.-Bewag
Krause-Ufer
Ausländ.
Obdachl.-heim
Integr. Sek.-sch. i.d. Stephanstr.
Moabiter Stadtgarten
Sporthalle
Unionpl.
Unionstr.
Spielpl.
2.Gemein-schaftssch. in Mitte (Filiale)
Jugendclub
Mosambique
Verkehrs-garten
Bugenhagenstr.
Senioren-
Ag.f. Arbeit Außenstelle
Bundesamt f. Ernährung u. Forstwirtsch.
Reform.-
Wittstocker
Senioren-heim
Spielpl.
C.-Bolle
Walden-ser-str.
St.
Kigaz
Buch.
Sen.-hm.
Hl.-Geist-
Sen.-heim
Med. Klinik f. Vers.zentr.
Geriatrische Betr.
Tadschikistan
LA GeSo
Diakonie
St.-Laurentius-K.
Hs.d.

MITTE
Humboldthain
Wedding
Reinickendorfer Str.
Osloer Str.
Osloer Straße
Nauener Pl.
Pankstr.
Ringbahn
Naturkundemuseum
Logistikzentrum Nord
Schwartzkopffstr.
Heidestr.
Seestraße
Chaussee-Str.
Schönwalder Str.
Ravenestr.
Müllerstr.
Prinzenallee
Brunnenplatz
Amtsgericht Wedding
Amtsgericht Tiergarten
Bundesmin. f. Wirtsch. u. Techn.
Bundeswehr-Krankenhaus
Invalidenfriedhof
Sportplatz
Poststadion
Stadtbad Tiergarten
Schloß-Park
Geschichts-Park-Moabit
Nordhafen
Sellerbr.
Kieler Br.
Usbekistan
Sportplätze
Tennisplätze
Sportplatz
Friedhof
Kirche Maria-Regina
Kloster zum Guten Hirten
Jüdisches Krkhs.
Kol. Nordkap
Kol. St. Georg
Evangelisches Geriatriezentrum Berlin
Jerus.-Bibl.
Jugendwohnhm.
Jugendverkehrsch.
Kiga.
Integr. Sek.-sch. i.d. Pankstr.
Sommerbad Humboldthain
Humboldthain-Grundsch.
Musik-Kunst-u.
Dankesk. Wedding
Dorotheenstadt II
Kirchhof
Kirchh. d. Franz. Gem.
St.-Hedwigs-Gem.
Kirchh. d. Berl. Domgem.
Sebastian-K.
Inst. HUB
Erika-Heß-Eisstadion
Tennisplz.
Nordhafenbr.
Nordhafen
Fennbr.
Nordhafenbr.
Usbekistan
Sportplatz
Friedhof
Geschichts-Park-Moabit
Sportplatz
Poststadion
Stadtbad Tiergarten
Schloß-Park
Amtsgericht Tiergarten
Bundesmin. f. Wirtsch. u. Techn.
Bundeswehr-Krankenhaus
Invalidenfriedhof
Naturkundemuseum
Institute
Mus.f. der Naturkunde
Neuen Tor
Hannoversche Str.
R.-Koch-Pl.
Schwartzkopffstr.
BND (in Bau/2016)
Ringbahn
RE3,RE5,S41,S42
S1,S2,S25
Heidestr.
RE3,RE4,RE5
Ringbahn S41,S42
Reinickendorfer Str.
Osloer Straße
Osloer Str.
Nauener Pl.
Pankstr.
Humboldthain
Wedding
Wedding
Prinzenallee
Brunnenplatz
Amtsgericht Wedding
Amts-u. Finanzger.
Meldestelle
Sommerbad Humboldthain
Humboldtsteg
Wiesenbr.
Turnh.
Sport-pl.
Senioren-freizeitst.
Obersch. am Brunnenpl.
Sportpl.
Integr. Sek.-sch. i.d. Pankstr.
Kiga
Kita
Sportpl.
Pol.-dir.
Th.-Heuss-Obersch.
Sportpl.
Kiga
Kita
Kita
Kita

Gesundbrunnen
Gesundbrunnen
Humboldthain
Humboldt-höhe
Volkspark
Gesundbrunnen
(Bez.MITTE)
Voltastr.
Bernauer
Bernauer Str.
Bornholmer Str.
Prinzenallee
Osloer
Pankstr.
Bad-
Behm-
Mauer-
Eberswalder
Oderberger
Ernst-Reuter-
Siedl.
Nordbf.
Volkspark a. Weinbergsw.
Rosenth.Pl.
Naturkunde-museum
Institute der Humboldt-
Hannoversche-Str.
Oranienb. Tor
Chausseestr.
Invaliden-
Gartenstr.
Schönhauser
Esplanade
1=Aalesunder Straße
1=Kleine Behmstraße
2=Hanne-Sobek-Platz
3=Badstraßenbrücke
1=Am Nordbahnhof
Platz des 9. November 1989
300m
328 yd
146

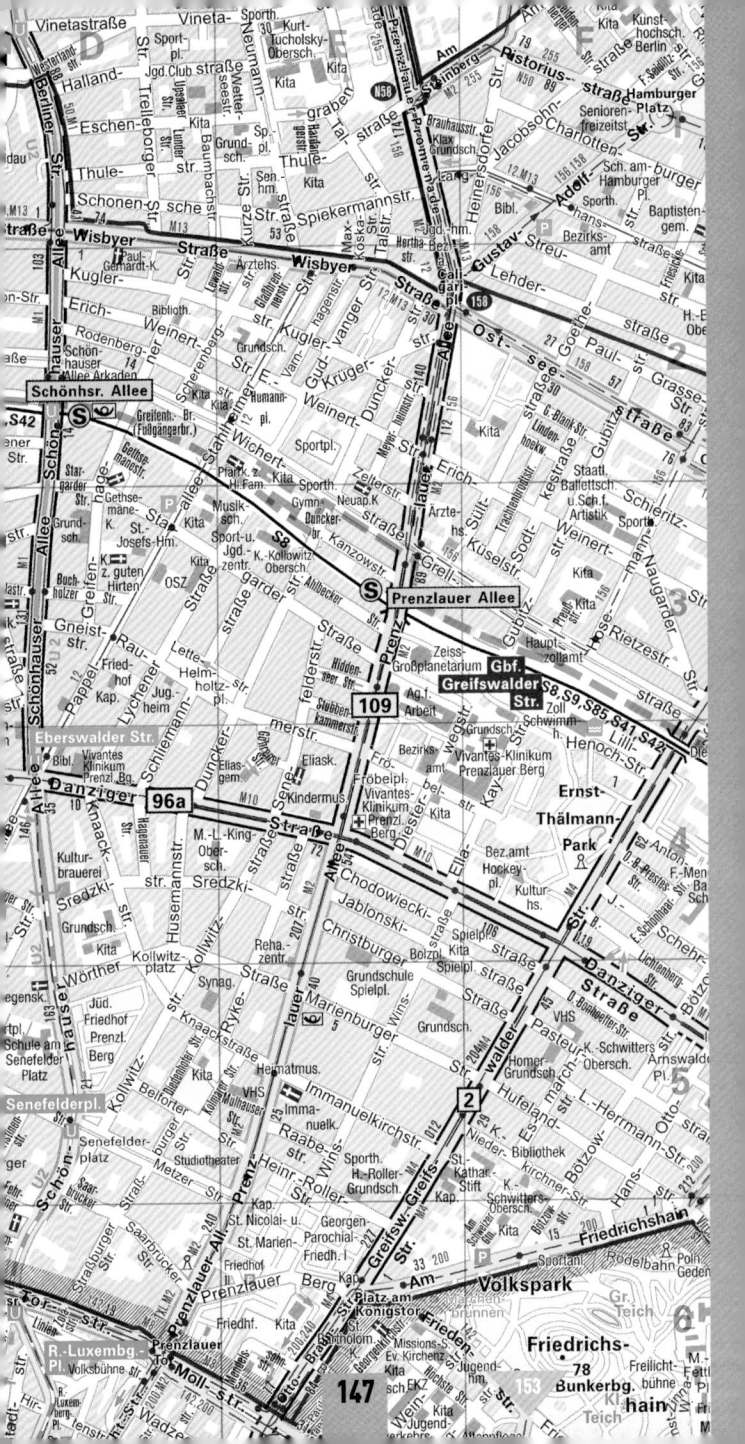
Vinetastraße
Schönhsr. Allee
Wisbyer Straße
Prenzlauer Allee
Eberswalder Str.
Danziger Straße
Senefelderpl.
Ernst-Thälmann-Park
Volkspark Friedrichshain
Friedrichs-hain
Bunkerbg.
R.-Luxemb.-Pl.
Mollstr.
Prenzlauer Berg
Ostsee
Greifswalder Str.
Gbf.
Ostseestraße
Schönhauser Allee
Danziger Straße
Kastanienallee
Prenzlauer Allee
Greifswalder Str.
Friedrichshain
Volkspark
Friedrichs-hain
Bunkerbg.
Mollstr.
R.-Luxemb.-Pl.
Prenzlauer Berg
Senefelderpl.
Eberswalder Str.
Danziger Straße
Schönhauser Allee
Wisbyer Straße
Prenzlauer Allee
Greifswalder Str.
Ostseestraße
Kastanienallee
Danziger Straße

300m
328 yd
Westend
Spandauer Damm
Kaiserdamm
Messe Nord ICC
Messe-Sommergelände
Westkreuz
Rastanl. Avus
CityCube
Funkturm
Schloss-garten
Charlottenburg
Spandauer Damm
Kaiserdamm
Kaiserd.-Süd
Messedamm
Knobelsdorffstr.
Heerstr.
Masurenallee
Neuer Kant-see
Jaffestr.
Rudolf-Wissell-Brücke
Spree
Kolonie Kaiserd.-Süd
Kolonie Spreewiesen
Kolonie Tiefer Grund
Kolonie Schlackenloch
Kolonie Schleusenland
Kolonie Tiefer Grund II
Kolonie Spreeufer
Kolonie Wasserturm
Kolonie Gesundheitspflege
Kolonie Birkenwäldchen
Kolonie Roßtrappe
Kolonie Bismarcksfelde
Kolonie Brauns-felde
Kolonie Luisenkirchhof III
Kolonie Neuer Fürstenbrunner Weg
Kolonie Fürstenbrunner Weg
Kolonie Kaiserd.-Süd
Kolonie Messedamm

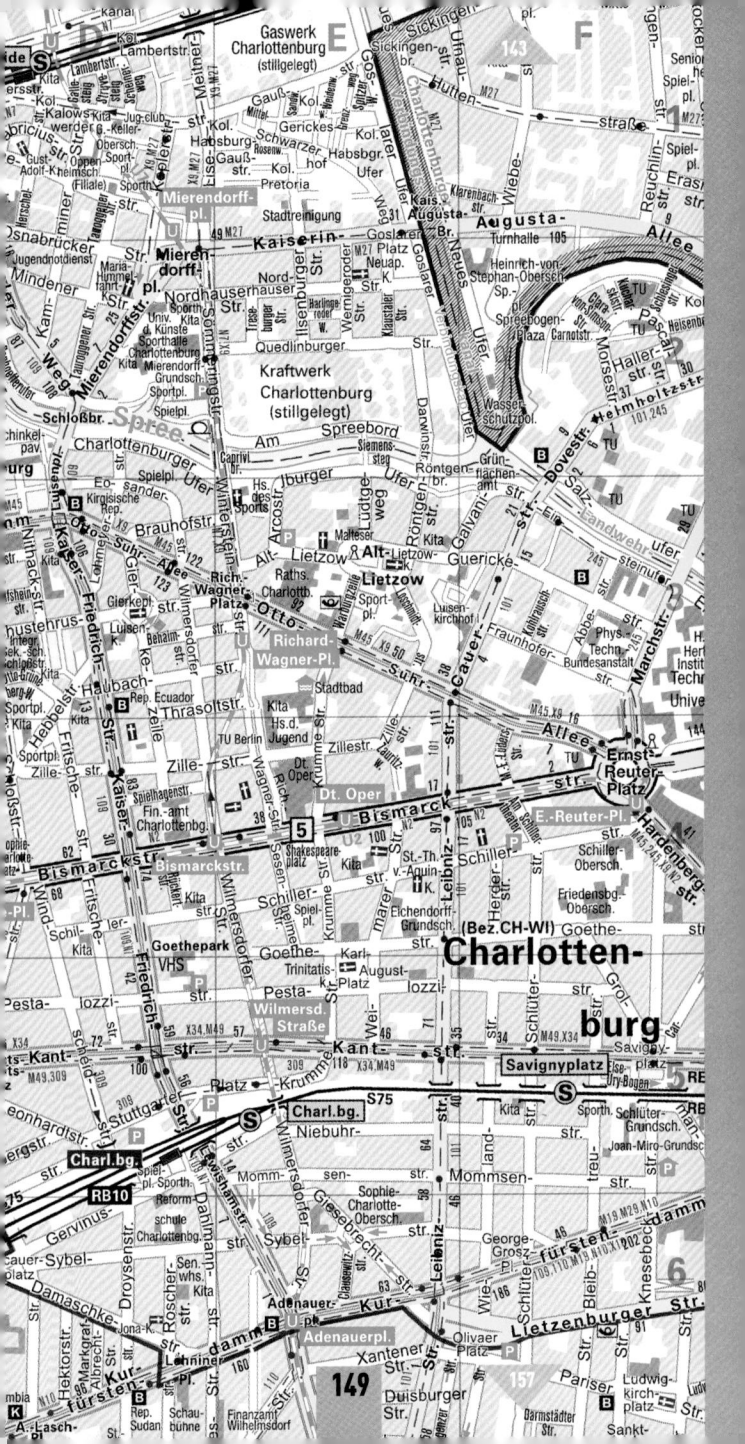
Charlotten-
burg
Kaiserin-
Augusta-
Allee
Mierendorff-
Pl.
Mierendorff-
str.
Nordhauser
Str.
Kraftwerk
Charlottenburg
(stillgelegt)
Gaswerk
Charlottenburg
(stillgelegt)
Spree
Schloßbr.
Charlottenburger
Ufer
Brauhofstr.
Suhr-
Str.
Rich.-
Wagner-
Platz
Richard-
Wagner-Pl.
Otto-
Suhr-
Allee
Lietzow
Alt-Lietzow
Guericke-
Str.
Galvani-
Str.
Röntgen-
Str.
Dovestr.
Str.
Helmholtzstr.
Haller-
Str.
Fraunhofer-
Str.
Marchstr.
Ernst-
Reuter-
Platz
E.-Reuter-Pl.
Hardenberg-
str.
Dt. Oper
Bismarck-
str.
Bismarckstr.
Kaiser-
Friedrich-
Str.
Wilmersdorfer
Str.
Schiller-
Str.
Leibniz-
str.
Goethe-
str.
Goethepark
Wilmersd.
Straße
Kant-
str.
Savignyplatz
Charl.bg.
Stuttgarter
Platz
Krumme
Str.
Mommsen-
str.
Sophie-
Charlotte-
Obersch.
Adenauer-
Pl.
Adenauerpl.
Olivaer
Platz
Lietzenburger
Str.
Kurfürsten-
damm
Xantener
Str.
Duisburger
Str.
Pariser
Str.
Ludwig-
kirch-
platz
Darmstädter
Str.
Sankt-
Augusta-
Str.
Kais.-
Str.
Sickingen-
Str.
Hutten-
straße
Str.
Charlottenburger
Str.
Ufer
Wiebe-
Str.
Reuchlin-
Str.
Heinrich-von-
Stephan-Obersch.
Spreebogen-
Plaza
Carnotstr.
Wasser-
schutzpol.
Str.
Morsestr.
Schwarzer
Hof
Gauß-
Str.
Kol.
Habsburg
Rosenw.
Pretoria
Gerickes-
Habsbgr.
Ufer
Klarenbach-
str.
Stadtreinigung
Goslarer
Br.
Turnhalle
Nord-
Str.
Ilsenburger
Str.
Wernigeroder
Str.
Neuap.
Harlingerode
Str.
Str.
Quedlinburger
Str.
Tresebur
Str.
Sommerfeldstr.
Wilmersdorfer
Str.
Caprivi-
br.
Am
Spreebord
Siemens-
steg
Röntgen-
br.
Ludwig-
weg
Arcostr.
Alt-
Str.
Malteser
Kita
Raths.
Charlottb.
Sport-
pl.
Lusen-
kirchhof
Gierkepf.
Str.
Lusen-
Str.
Behaim-
str.
Haubach-
str.
Rep. Ecuador
Thrasoltstr.
Heberstr.
Fritsche-
str.
Zille-
str.
Kita
Hs.d.
Jugend
TU Berlin
Dt.
Oper
Zillestr.
Zillestr.
Krumme
Str.
Spielhagenstr.
Fin.-amt
Charlottenbg.
Shakespeare-
platz
Kita
St.-Th.
v.-Aquin
K.
Schiller-
Obersch.
Friedensbg.
Obersch.
Eichendorff-
Grundsch.
(Bez.CH-WI)
Karl-
August-
Platz
Trinitatis-
Kr.
Pesta-
lozzi-
str.
Schlüter-
Grundsch.
Joan-Mirò-Grundsch.
Sporth.
Niebuhr-
str.
Momm-
sen-
str.
Sybel-
str.
Dahlmann-
str.
Droysenstr.
Roscher
str.
Sen.
whs.
Kita
Damaschke-
platz
Hektorstr.
Markgraf-
Albrecht-
Str.
Jona-K.
Lehniner
Pl.
Rep.
Sudan
Schau-
bühne
Finanzamt
Wilhelmsdorf
Gerwinus-
str.
Cauer-
Sybel-
platz
Kneseb
Bleib-
Str.
Wie
Schlüter
Str.
George-
Grosz-
Pl.
Claszweig-
Str.
Str.
br.
Str.
Galvani-
Str.
Str.
Landwehr-
ufer
Steinuf.
Str.
Kirgisische
Rep.
Sander-
Str.
Eo-
Str.
Kaiser-
Friedrich-
Str.
Nithack-
str.
damm
Lehniner
Str.
Kurfürsten-
damm
Kant-
str.
Stuttgarter
Str.
Charl.bg.
Spiel-
pl.
Sporth.
Reform-
schule
Charlottenbg.
Univ.
Sporth.
Univ.
Kita
Sporthalle
Charlottenburg
Mierendorff-
Grundsch.
Sportpl.
Spielpl.
Univ.
Kita
Jugendnotdienst
Maria-
Kirche
Mindener
Weg
Kam-
Str.
Osnabrücker
Str.
Kalows-
werder
Kita
Jug.club.
Keller-
Obersch.
Sport-
pl.
Sporth.
Gust.-
Adolf-Kheimsch.
(Filiale)
Opper-
Str.
Lambertstr.
Lambertstr.
Kita

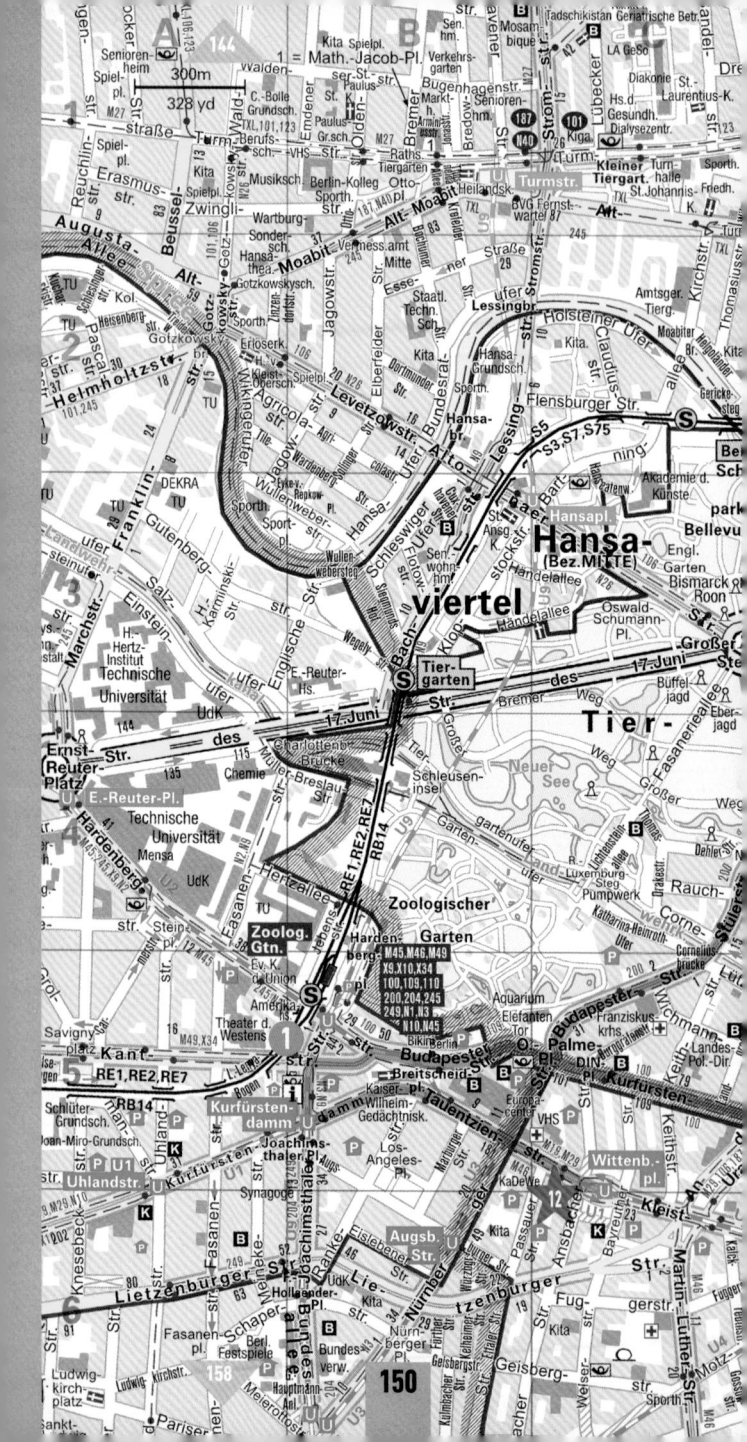
300m
328 yd
Hansa-viertel
(Bez. MITTE)
Tiergarten
Zoologischer Garten
Zoolog. Gtn.
Bellevu
Hansapl.
Kurfürstendamm
Kurfürsten
Lietzenburger
Augsb. Str.
Wittenb.
Kleist
Uhlandstr.
Joachimsthaler
Fasanen
Knesebeck
Savigny
Kant
Ernst-Reuter-Platz
E.-Reuter-Pl.
Technische Universität
Charlottenb. Brücke
Zwingli
Moabit
Alt-Moabit
Turmstr.
Lessingbr.
Hansa-br.
Bachstr.
Lessing-
Flensburger Str.
Bismarck
Roon
Großer
Tier-
17-Juni
Bremer
Weg
Fasanenallee
Hardenberg
Budapester
Palme-
Breitscheid-
Jaulentzien-
Nürnberger
Geisberg-
Martin-Luther-
Fugger
Motz-
Bayreuther
Ansbacher
Passauer
Meinekes
Pariser
Ludwig-kirch-platz
Sankt-
Hauptmann-
Meierotto-
Kurfürsten-
Joachimsthaler
Fasanen-
Schaper-
Berl. Festspiele
Bundesverw.
Nürnberger
Geisbergstr.
Kulmbacher
Weiser-
Sporth.
Kita
Kirchstr.
Thomasiusstr.
Kleist-
Fugger
Kalk-
Martin-Luther-
Motz-
Bayreuther
Ansbacher
Passauer
Nürnberger
Geisberg-

Tiergarten
Hauptbahnhof
Bundeskanzleramt
Bundestag
Potsdamer Pl.
Kulturforum
Philharmonie
Neue Nationalgalerie
Sigismundstr.
Staufenbergstr.
Reichpietschufer
Schöneberger Ufer
Kurfürstenstr.
Nollendorfpl.
Bülowstr.
Gleisdreieck
Mendelssohn-Bartholdy-Park
Kleiner Stern
Straße des 17. Juni
Platz der 18. März
Bellevueallee
Lützowplatz
Lützowstr.
Derfflingerstr.
Genthiner Str.
Potsdamer Str.
Rousseauinsel
Lortzing (Bez.MITTE)
Flora Rosengarten
Moabit
Alt-Moabit
Invalidenstr.
Kliniken des Campus Charité Mitte
Deut.Theater u. Kammerspiele
Dt.Bundestag (Pl.Leo-Ins.)
Pariser Platz
Brandenburger Tor
Holocaust Mahnmal
Musiker denkm.
Goethe
Lessing
Kemperpl.
Sony Center
Filmmuseum
Leipziger Platz
Mendelssohn-Bartholdy-Park
Kothener Br.
Schöneberger Br.
Tempelhofer Ufer
Nelly-Sachs-Park
Dennewitzpl.
Wasserturm
Technikmus.
Spektrum Berlin
Lok-schuppen
Park am Gleisdreieck
Bundesministerium des Inneren
Haus der Kulturen der Welt (Kongresshalle)
Moltkebrücke
Otto-v.-Bismarck-Allee
Tiergartentunnel
Washington Platz
Sowjet. Ehrenmal
Scheidemannstr.
Ebertstr.
Stresemannstr.
Hannoversche Str.
R.-Koch-Pl.
Alexanderufer
Kapelleufer
Friedhof Geschichtspark Moabit
Sport-platz
Senatsverw. f. Gesundh. u. Soziales
Ravene Obersch.
Carl-von-Ossietzky-Park
Grundsch.
Flemingstr.
Ingeborg-Drewitz-Allee
Jakob-Miersch-Steg
Paul-Löbe-Allee
Joachim-Karnatz-Allee
El Salvador
Guatemala
Nicaragua
Panama
Bellevueallee
Kleiner Stern
Bremer Weg
Straßen- u. Grünflächenamt
Querallee
Amazone
Löwenkenkmal
Ahornsteig
Lessingstr.
Kemperpl.
Beisheim Center
Potsdamer Pl.
Leipziger Platz
Tiergarten
Kulturforum
Philharmonie
Gemäldegal.
Neue Nationalgalerie
Marlene-Dietrich-Platz
Staats-bibliothek
Daimler-City
Bernburger
Kothener Br.
Schöneberger Br.
Tempelhofer Ufer
Nelly-Sachs-Park
Dennewitzpl.
Wasserturm
Park am Gleisdreieck
Technikmus.
Spektrum Berlin
Lok-schuppen
Gleisdreieck
Kurfürstenstr.
Nollendorfpl.
Bülowstr.
Bülowstr.
Potsdamer Str.
Lützowplatz
Lützowstr.
Derfflingerstr.
Genthiner Str.
Kluckstr.
Pohlstr.
Pohlstraße
Körnerstr.
Tempelhofer Ufer
Schöneberger Ufer
Reichpietschufer
Staufenbergstr.
Sigismundstr.
Stresemannstr.
Ebert

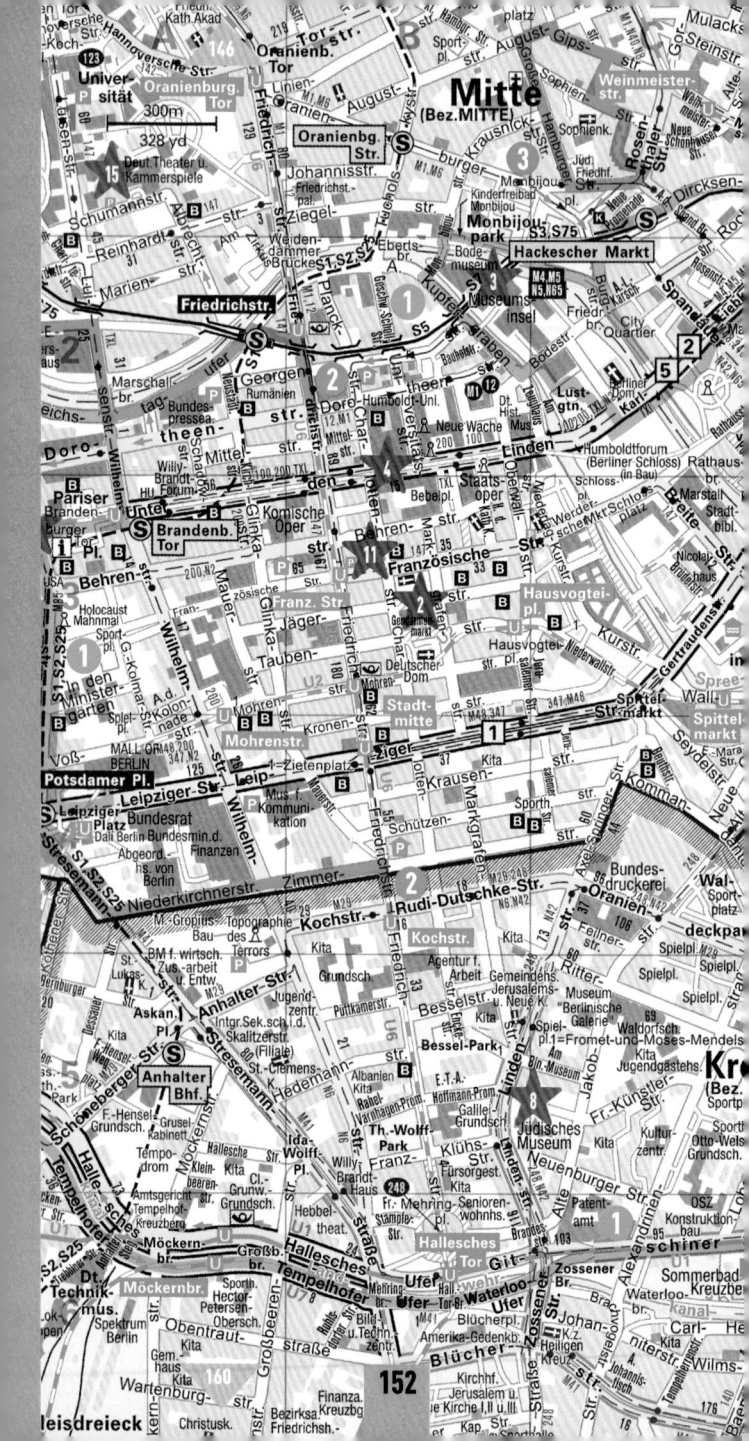
Mitte
(Bez.MITTE)
Oranienb. Tor
Oranienb. Str.
Oranienburg. Tor
Univer-sität
300m
328 yd
Deut.Theater u. Kammerspiele
Friedrichstr.
Hackescher Markt
Monbijou-park
Museums-insel
Lust-gtn.
Humboldtforum (Berliner Schloss) (im Bau)
Staats-oper
Französische
Hausvogtei-pl.
Gertrauden-str.
Spittel-markt
Stadt-mitte
Mohrenstr.
Potsdamer Pl.
Leipziger-Str.
Leipziger Platz
Bundesrat
Bundesmin.d. Finanzen
Niederkirchnerstr.
Kochstr.
Rudi-Dutschke-Str.
Anhalter-Str.
Anhalter Bhf.
Askan. Pl.
Bessel-Park
Th.-Wolff-Park
Ida-Wolff-Pl.
Möckern-br.
Tempelhofer Ufer
Hallesches Tor
Waterloo-Ufer
Blücher-
Zossener Br.
Sommerbad Kreuzberg
Wilms-
Wartenburg-
Obentraut-
Grobbeer-straße
Dt. Technik-mus.
Spektrum Berlin
Christusk.
Bezirksa. Friedrichsh.-
Finanza. Kreuzbg
Kirchhf. Jerusalem u. Kirche I,II u.III
Leisdreieck
152

FRIEDRICHS-
HAIN-
KREUZBERG
Alexanderplatz
Alexanderstr.
Karl-Marx-Str.
Schillingstr.
Allee
Strausberger Platz
Friedrichshain
Bunkerbg.
Jannowitzbr.
Ostbahnhof
Stralauer Str.
Holzmarktstr.
Lichtenberger Str.
Singer Str.
Grünerstr.
Klosterstr.
Spree
Märk. Mus.
Brückenstr.
Heinrichstr.
Heinrichplatz
Moritzplatz
Oranienplatz
Oranienstr.
Dresdener Str.
Adalbertstr.
Bethanien
Mariannenplatz
Skalitzer Str.
Görlitzer Bhf.
Kottbusser Tor
Kottbusser Br.
Wassertorstr.
Gitschiner Str.
Böckler-park
Urbanhafen
Planufer
Fraenkelufer
Paul-Lincke-Ufer
Maybachufer
Hobrecht-br.
Bürknerstr.
Sonnenallee
Hermannstr.
Mehlbeerenweg
RE1, RE2
RE7, RB14
S3, S5, S7
S75
U1
U2
U3
U4
U5
U6
U7
U8
U9
153

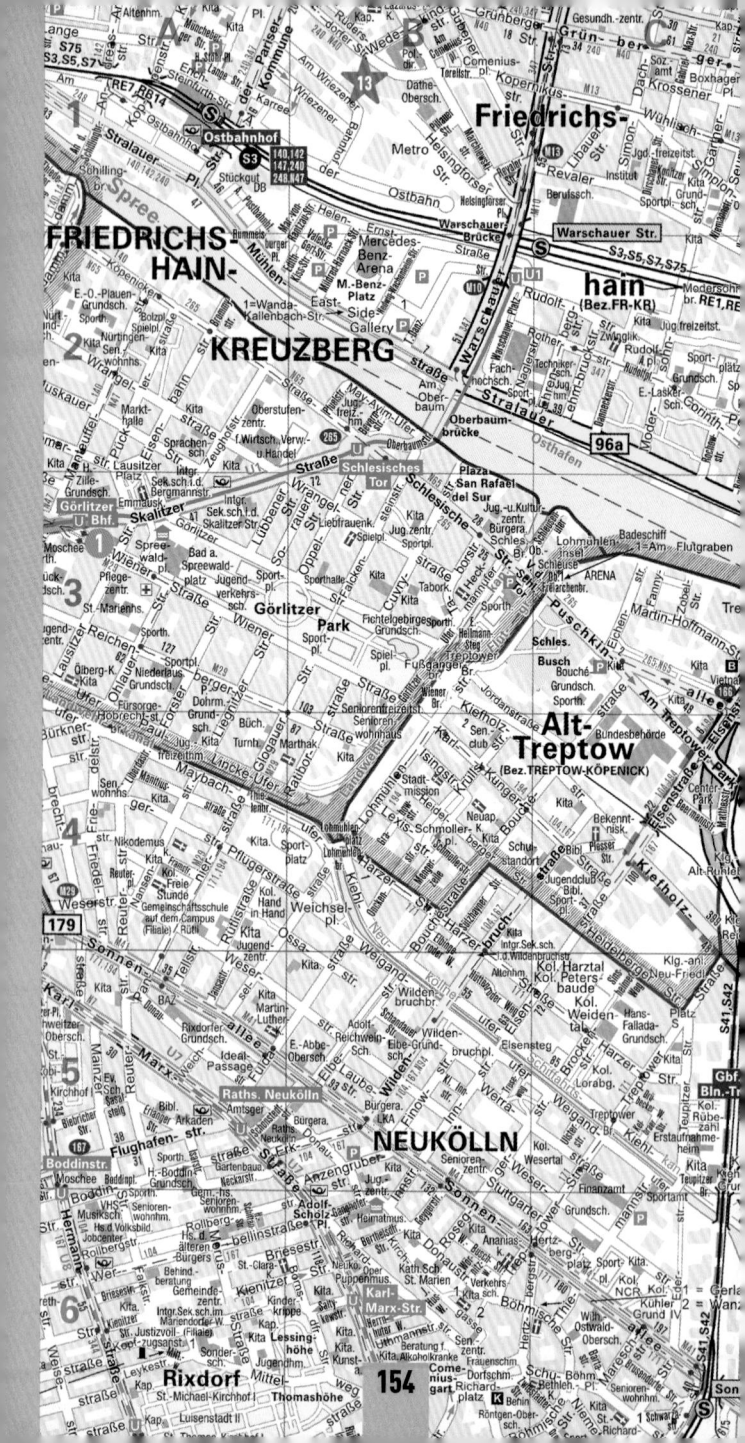
FRIEDRICHS-
HAIN-
KREUZBERG
Friedrichs-
hain
(Bez.FR-KB)
Alt-
Treptow
(Bez.TREPTOW-KÖPENICK)
NEUKÖLLN
Rixdorf
Ostbahnhof
Warschauer Str.
Warschauer Brücke
Oberbaumbrücke
Schlesisches Tor
Plaza San Rafael del Sur
Görlitzer Park
Schles. Busch
Treptower Park
Raths. Neukölln
Boddinstr.
Karl-Marx-Str.
Thomashöhe
Luisenstadt II
Michael-Kirchhof I
Lessinghöhe
Mittel-
Sonnen-
Weserstr.
Kienitzer
Hermannstr.
Flughafen-
Stralauer
Pariser
Kopenicker
Schillingbr.
Spree
Osthafen
Ostbahnhof
Mercedes-Benz-Arena
M.-Benz-Platz
Metro
Helsingforser
Helsingforser Pl.
Warschauer Straße
Revaler
Libauer
Str.
Simon-Dach-Str.
Wühlisch-
Simplon-
Grünberger
Boxhagener
Krossener
Pl.
Dathe-
Obersch.
Comenius-
Tereilstr.
Kopernikus-
Str.
Gesundh.-zentr.
Soz.amt
Grün-berger
Str.
Wiesener
Str.
Rudolf-
Rudolf-
Sport-
platz
Jug.freizeitst.
Grundsch.
E.-Lasker-
Sch.
Gürlitzer
Gürlitzer
Str.
Lausitzer
Platz
Emmauskirch.
Bergmannstr.
Intgr.
Sek.sch.i.d.
Skalitzer Str.
Skalitzer
Wiener
Pl.
Spree-
wald-
platz
Bad a.
Spreewald
Jugend-
verkehrs-
sch.
Sport-
pl.
Pflege-
zentr.
St.-Marienhs.
Oberstufen-
zentr.
Wirtsch. Verw.-
u. Handel
Liebfrauenk.
Jug. zentr.
Sportpl.
Sporthalle
Kita
Tabor
Fichtelgebirgs-
Grundsch.
Spiel-
pl.
Fußgänger-
Br.
Treptower
Br.
Lohmühlen-
insel
1=Am
Flutgraben
Badeschiff
Schleuse
Br. Ob.
ARENA
Friedrichsh.
Martin-Hoffmann-Str.
Pischkin-
Straße
Reichen-
berger
Str.
Grundsch.
Fürsorge-
Hobrecht-
Treizehnm.
Turnh.
Buch
Jug.
Kita
Marthak
Maybach-
Ufer
Senioren-
wohnhaus
Senioren-
zentr.
Jordanstraße
Kiefholz-
Str.
Sen.
club
Bundesbehörde
Am Treptower Park
Eisenstraße
Center-
Park
Bekennt-
nisk.
Str.
Schul-
standort
Jugendclub
Bibl.
Sport
pl.
Kiefholz-
Straße
Lohmühlen-
ufer
Lohmühlen-
Straße
Lexis-
Str.
Schmoller-
pl.
Stadt-
mission
Heider
Neuap.
K.
Kita
Kungerstr.
Bouchéstr.
Pflugerstraße
Ruthstraße
Kita
Sport-
platz
Weichsel-
pl.
Ossa-
straße
Weserstr.
Kol. Hand in Hand
Kita
Jugend-
zentr.
Weser-
Bouchéstraße
Herzberg-
straße
Kita
Intgr. Sek.sch.
i.d. Wildenbruchstr.
Altehrn.
Kol. Harztal
Kol. Peters-
baude
Kol. Weiden-
tal
Hans-
Fallada-
Grundsch.
Kig.-anl.
Neu-Fried.
Sonnen-
allee
Karl-
Marx-
Str.
Reuter-
platz
Sonnen-
allee
Weserstr.
BAZ
Kita
Martin-
Luther-
Str.
Rixdorfer
Grundsch.
Ideal-
Passage
E.-Abbe-
Obersch.
Adolf-
Reichwein-
Sch.
Wilden-
bruchhr.
Wilden-
bruchr.
Eisensteg
Elbe-Grund-
sch.
Kol.
Lorabg.
Treptower
Str.
Kol.
Wesertal
Finanzamt
Sportamt
Grundsch.
Kita
Teupitzer
Br.
Kol.
Rube-
zahl
Erstaufnahme-
heim
Gbf.
Bln.-Tr.
Bibl.
Sportp.
Arkaden
Amtsger.
Bürgera.
Burgera.
Kita
Gartenbaus.
Neukölln
Sportp.
H.-Boddin-
Grundsch.
Gem.-his.
Senioren-
wohnhm.
Musikch.
Hs. d. Volksbild.
Jobcenter
Rollbergstr.
Hs. d. ältereren
Bürgers
Behind.-
beratung
Gemeinde-
zentr.
Intgr. Sek.sch. im
Mariendorfer W.
St. Justizvoll. (Filiale)
Zugangst. 1
Kap.
Luisenstadt II
Kap.
Leykestr.
Kap.
Kita
Kinder-
krippe
Kap.
Kita Lessing-
höhe
Sonder-
sch.
Jugendhm.
Kita
Kunst-
Kita
Kita
Kita

Bln.-Lichtenberg
RB12,OE25
NE26,OE60
300m
328 yd
Nöldnerpl.
Ostkreuz
Nöldnerstr.
Rummelsburg
Rummelsburger See
Stralau
Treptower Park
Puschkin-
REPTOW-KÖPENICK
Treptower Park
Spreepark
Vergnügungs-und
Freizeitpark
(geschlossen)
Plänterwald
(Bez.TREPTOW-KÖPENICK)
Plänter-
wald
LSG
155

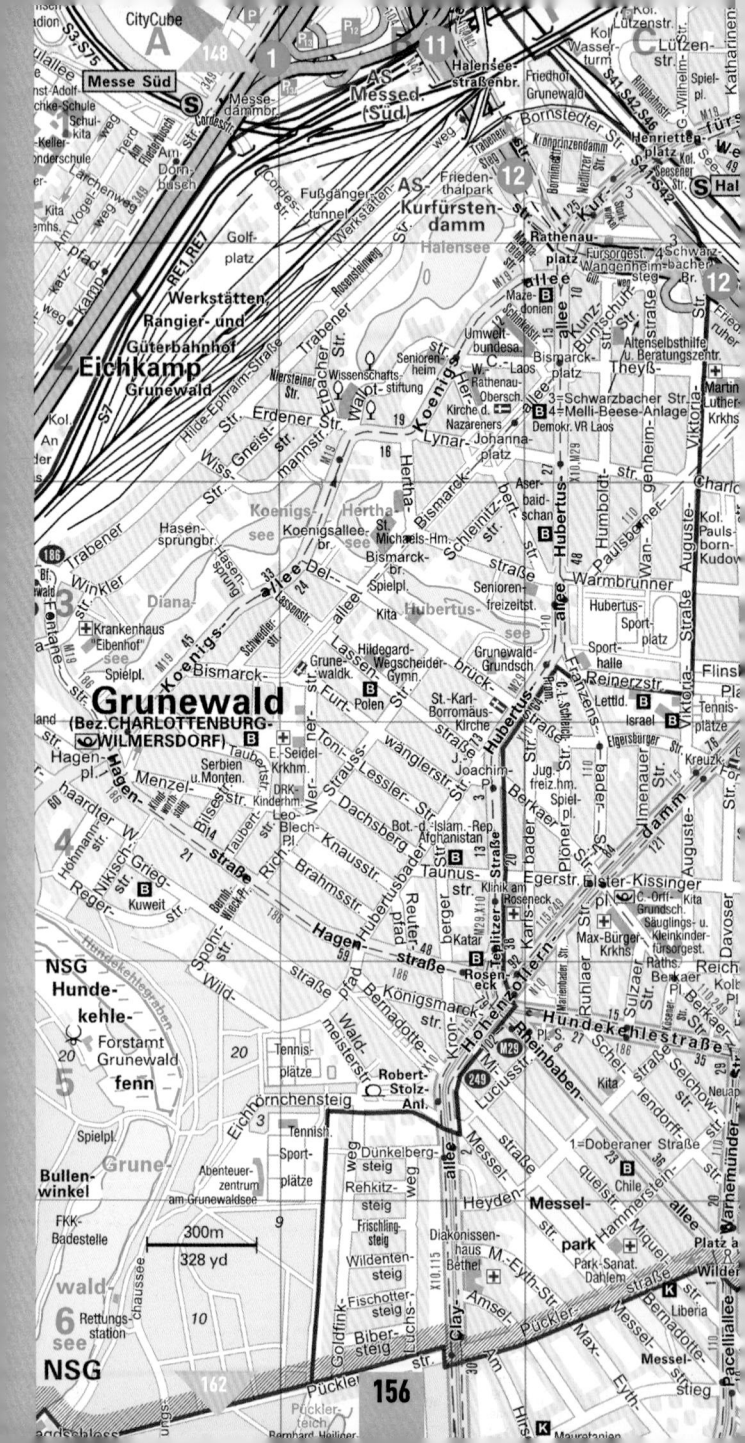
CityCube
Messe Süd
Messe-
gelände
Messed.
(Süd)
Halensee-
straßenbr.
Friedhof
Wasser-
turm
Lützen-
str.
Bornstedter Str.
Krongrinzendamm
Henriettenplatz
Friedenthalpark
Kurfürstendamm
Halensee
Rathenau-
platz
Werkstätten
Rangier- und
Güterbahnhof
Eichkamp
Grunewald
Golfplatz
Fußgängertunnel
Werkstätten
Rosenheimer
Trabener Str.
Wissenschafts-
stiftung
Seniorenheim
Umweltbundesa.
Bismarckplatz
Altenselbsthilfe
u. Beratungszentr.
Theyß-
Schwarzbacher Str.
Melli-Beese-Anlage
Demokr. VR Laos
Laos
Kirche d.
Nazareners
Johannaplatz
Hertha-
Bismarck-
Schleinitz-
Hubertus-
Humboldt-
Pauls-
Wan-
geniem-
Viktoria-
Auguste-
Hildegard-
Wegscheider-
Gymn.
Grunewald-
Grundsch.
Sport-
halle
Reinerzstr.
Lettld.
Israel
Tennis-
plätze
Grunewald
(Bez.CHARLOTTENBURG-
WILMERSDORF)
Krankenhaus
Eibenhof
Hasen-
sprungbr.
Koenigsallee-
br.
Koenigs-
see
Hertha-
see
St.
Michaels-Hm.
Bismarck-
br.
Spielpl.
Kita
Hubertus-
Senioren-
freizeitst.
Warmbrunner
Hubertus-
Sport-
platz
Diana
Polen
St.-Karl-
Borromäus-
Kirche
Joachim-
Jug.
freiz.hm.
Spielpl.
Serbien
u.Monten.
DRK-
Kinderhm.
Leo-
Blech-
Pl.
Islam.-Rep.
Afghanistan
Kuweit
Katar
Klinik am
Rosenecks
Max-Bürger-
Krkhs.
Egerstr.
Kissinger
pl.
Kita
Grundsch.
Säuglings- u.
Kleinkinder-
fürsorgest.
Davoser
Reichs-
Berkaer
Kolb
Ruhlaer
Sulzaer
Pl.
Hundekehlestraße
Hohenzollern-
Rheinbaben-
Königsmarck-
Bernadotte-
Wildmeisterstr.
Robert-
Stolz-
Anl.
Tennis-
plätze
Eichhörnchensteig
Spielpl.
Tennis-
Sport-
plätze
Abenteuer-
zentrum
am Grunewaldsee
Bullen-
winkel
FKK-
Badestelle
300m
328 yd
Rettungs-
station
NSG
Hunde-
kehle-
Forstamt
Grunewald
fenn
NSG
Dünkelberg-
steig
Rehkitz-
steig
Frischling-
steig
Wildenten-
steig
Fischotter-
steig
Biber-
steig
Diakonissen-
haus
Bethel
Heyden-
Messel-
park
Park-Sanat.
Dahlem
Liberia
Mauretanien
Pückler-
teich
Bernhard Heilinger
Pückler-
Clay-
Amsel-
Max-
Eyth-
Messel-
stieg
Pacelliallee
Wilder
Platz a
Hammerstein-
Miquel-
Bernadotte-
Messel-
Hirsch-
Lucius-
Schel-
Selchow-
Jendorff-
Neuap
Kita
1=Doberaner Straße
Hammerstein-
Miquel-
Bernadotte-
Messel-
Eyth-
Max-
Pückler-
Amsel-
Clay-
Goldfink-
Luchs-
Hirsch-
Pückler-
Messel-
Hundekehlegraben
Hundekehlegraben
Hundekehlegraben

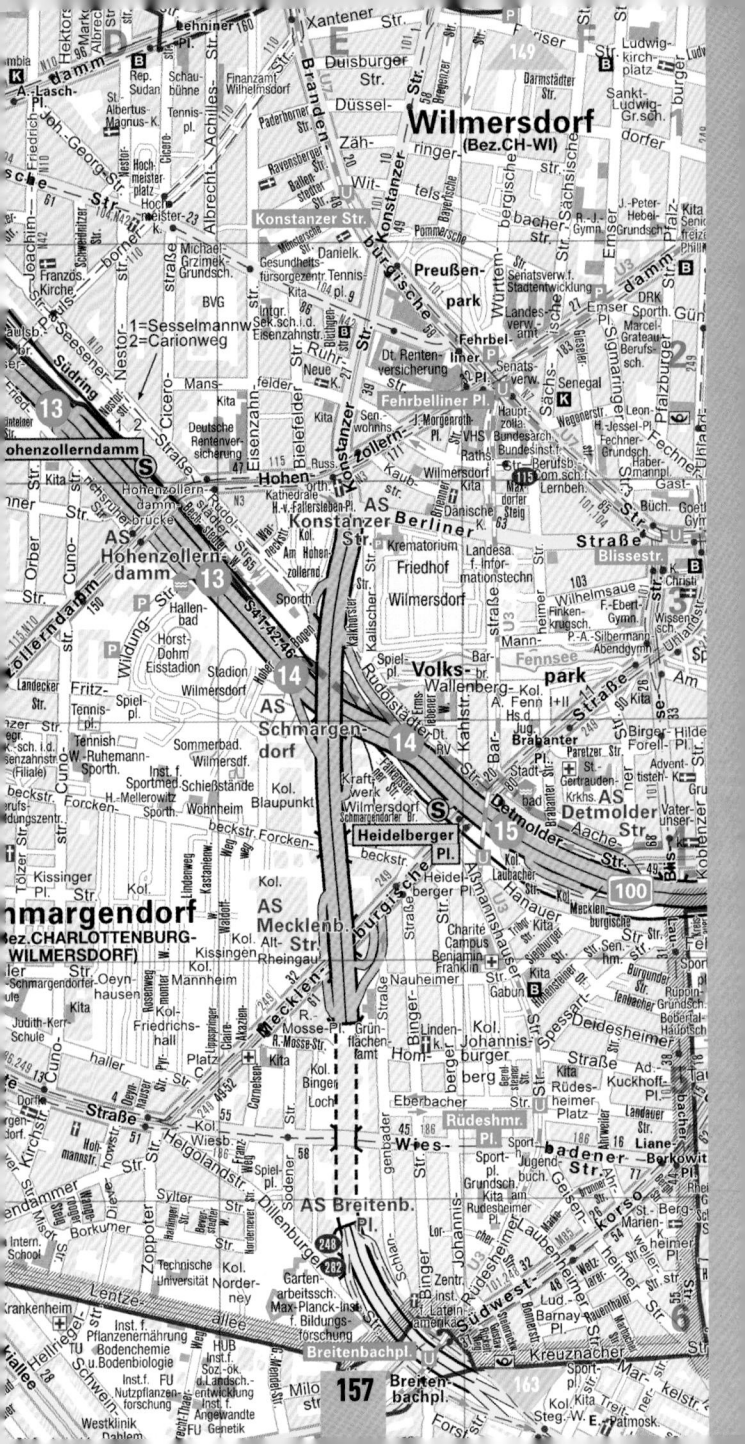
Wilmersdorf
(Bez.CH-Wl)
Konstanzer Str.
Preußen-
park
Fehrbelliner Pl.
Hohenzollerndamm
Hohenzollern-
damm
AS
Hohenzollern-
damm
Konstanzer Str.
Berliner
Straße
Blissestr.
Wilmersdorf
Friedhof
Krematorium
Volks-
park
Fennsee
Brabanter
Pl.
Detmolder
Str.
Heidelberger
Pl.
AS
Schmargen-
dorf
AS
Mecklenb.
Str.
AS Breitenb.
Pl.
Breitenbachpl.
Rüdesheimer
Platz
Wiesbadener
Str.
Kreuznacher
Str.
Sudwest-
korso
Sudring
Seesener
Str.
Nestor-
Str.
Cicero-
Str.
Brandenburgische
Str.
Bielefelder
Str.
Lentzeallee
Str.
Helgolandstr.
Dillenburger
Str.
Sylter
Str.
Zoppoter
Str.

Hohenzollernplatz
Spichernstr.
Nachod-
Viktoria-Luise-Pl.
Hohenstaufen-
Güntzelstr.
Wilmersdf.
Berliner Straße
Tunnel
Berliner
Badensche-
Blissestr.
Wilmers-
dorf
Bundesallee
Bundespl.
Detmolder
Wexstr.
Innsbrucker Pl.
Innsbrucker Platz
Friedenau
(Bez. TEMPELHOF-
u. SCHÖNEBERG)
Friedenauer Br.
Saarstr.
Friedenauer
Schmargendorfer
Friedrich-Wilhelm-Nied-
Wilhelmshöher
Hermann-Garten
Kaiser-eiche
Rheinstraße
Saarstraße
Rubens-straße
Martin-Luther-Str.
Hauptstraße
Stubenrauchstr.
Schmiljanstr.
Bayerischer Platz
Bayer.Pl.
Innsbruck.
Raths. Schöneberg
John-F.-Kennedy-Pl.
R.-Wilde-Park
Volks-park
Schoeler-park
Wilhelmsaue
Hohenzollern-
Prager Str.
Bamberger Str.
Grunewald
Hildegard-Forell-Pl.
Koblenzer
Bundesallee
Bundesplatz
Friedrich-Wilhelm-Platz
Perelsplatz
Friedenau
Schöneberg
Wilmersdorf
Tempelhof
Tempelhof-Schöneberg
Wilmersdorf
Tempelhof

Schöneberg
(Bez.TEMPELHOF-SCHÖNEBERG)
Park am Gleisdreieck
Yorckstr.
Großgörschenstr.
Kleistpark
Grunewald-straße
Kaiser-Wilh.-Pl.
J.-Leber-Br.
Kolonnenstr.
Kolonnenbr.
Duden-straße
Bayern-
Wilhelm-Kabus-Str.
Torgauer
Sachsen-damm
Tempelhofer
Südring
Südkreuz
Werner
Hansakorso
Kreuz Schöneberg
Damm
Vorarlberger
AS Alboinstr.
Eresburg
Burchard-
Egelingzeile
Obdachlosen-
Bessemer-
Albein-
Gärtnerweg
Friedrich-Ebert-
Sportanlage
Sporth.
Tennis-pl.
Magirus-str.
TÜV
Deutsche Post AG Briefzentrum
Baluschek-Park
NSG
Kinder-heim
Kaninchen-farm
Wiedervereinigung
Neue Zeit
Grüne Aue
Sonnen-land
Buren-land
Canova
Riemeischneider-
Heiterkeit
Sommer-hm.
Grünes Tal
Schönebg.
Frohsinn
Ideal
Lindenbm.
Friedhf. Priesterw.
Hans-
Lindenhain
Spree-wald
Kol. Feld-schlößchen
Kol. Luisen-gärten
Kol. Berg-frieden
Kol. Glück im Winkel
Tennispl.
Kol. Vorarlbg.
Sport-plätze
Turnh.
Kap.
Matthäifriedhofsweg
Priesterweg
Reichart-
Genest-
Druckenm.
Br.
Schönebgr.
Kol. Papestr. Bl. I
Kol. Papestr. Bl. II
Kol. Papestr.
Kol. Stein-grube
Kol. Pape-
R.-Koch-Institut
Wüsthoff-
St. Joseph-Krkhs.
H.-Gaudig-Sch.
Tempelherren-Sch.str.
Wintgens-
Hessen-
Gonter-
Voß-
Werner-
Berliner Wasserbetriebe
Sen.-whs.
Kol.
Hoeppner-
Sen.-reizeitst.
Jugend-club
Stadt-reinigung
Hilde-gard-Knef-Pl.
Goten-
Dohm-
Lotte-
Lasker-
Stein-
Werdauer-
W.-Br.
Sport-u. Lehrschwimm.
Damini-cus-Sport-pl.
Fr.-Gerlach-Br.
Sporth.
Zwölf-Apostel-Kirchhof II
Schöneb.
Stadtreinigung
Priesterweg
H.-Gans-wind-Br.
Torgauer
Ebersstr.
Feurig-
Ebers-
Gebenstr.
Naumannst.
Leuthener Pl.
Leuthener Str.
Intgr.Sek.sch. am Grazer Pl.
Sportpl.
GASAG
Cheruskerstr.
Gem.-hs.
Method.-K.
Bibl. Mus.
Kita
Jugendclub
Grundsch. Musiksch.
Roßbachstr.
Müller-pl.
Naumannst.
Zwölf-Apostel-Kirchhof I
Kön.-Luise-Ged.-K.
Elisabeth-K.
R.-Blum-Gymn.
Havelland-Grundsch.
Bautzener
Dt. Inst.f. Bautechn.
Sporth.
Sport-platz
Jug.-club
Gaßlerstr.
DIBT
Hohenfriedberg-str.
Brunhildstr.
Czerny-
Julius Leber-Br.
Post AG
Dt.
Turn-halle
Kita
Belziger
Vorbergstr.
Apostel-Paulus-K.
Spielpl.
Erd-mann-str.
Heim-
Crellestraße
Langenscheidtbr.
Langenscheidtstr.
Monumenten-
Monum.-b.
St.-Matthäus-Kirchhof I
Kulmer Str.
Neue Kulmer Str.
Neue Steinmetzstr.
Willmanndamm
Großgörschenstr.
Kaiser-
Bautzener Pl.
Kreuzberg-straße
Jesusk.
Viktor
Katzbach-
Boeckeh-straße
Kol. Papestr. Bl. I
Kol. Papestr. Bl. II
Kol. Papestr.
Kol. Stein-grube
Badener
Wolff-
Spiel-pl.
St. J.-Thaddaus-K.
Zeile
Sen.-reizeitst.
Jugend-club
Damm
Ru-
Berliner Wasserbetriebe
Sen.-whs.
Kol.
Hansakorso
Südring
Druckenm.
Br.
Schönebgr.
Kol. Feld-schlößchen
Kol. Luisen-gärten
Kol. Berg-frieden
Kol. Glück im Winkel
Tennispl.
Kol. Vorarlbg.
Sport-plätze
Turnh.
Kap.
Matthäifriedhofsweg
Priesterweg
Reichart-
Genest-
Kol. Ideal
Kol. Frohsinn
Kol. Lindenbm.
Friedhf. Priesterw.
Hans-
Lindenhain
Kol. Spree-wald
Kol. Heiterkeit
Kol. Sommer-hm.
Kol. Grünes Tal
Kol. Schönebg.
Kol. Grüne Aue
Kol. Sonnen-land
Kol. Buren-land
Kol. Canova
Kol. Wiedervereinigung
Kol. Neue Zeit
Kol. Kaninchen-farm
Kinder-heim
Riemeischneider-
Heiterkeit
Sommer-hm.
Grünes Tal
Schönebg.
Frohsinn
Ideal
Lindenbm.
Friedhf. Priesterw.
Hans-
Lindenhain
Spree-wald
Kol. Feld-schlößchen
Kol. Luisen-gärten
Kol. Berg-frieden
Kol. Glück im Winkel
Tennispl.
Kol. Vorarlbg.
Sport-plätze
Turnh.
Kap.
Matthäifriedhofsweg
Priesterweg
Reichart-
Genest-
Druckenm.
Br.
Schönebgr.
Kol. Papestr. Bl. I
Kol. Papestr. Bl. II
Kol. Papestr.
Kol. Stein-grube
Badener
Wolff-
Spiel-pl.
St. J.-Thaddaus-K.
Zeile
Sen.-reizeitst.
Jugend-club
Damm
Ru-
Berliner Wasserbetriebe
Sen.-whs.
Kol.
Hansakorso
Südring
Druckenm.
Br.
Schönebgr.
Kol. Feld-schlößchen
Kol. Luisen-gärten
Kol. Berg-frieden
Kol. Glück im Winkel
Tennispl.
Kol. Vorarlbg.
Sport-plätze
Turnh.
Kap.
Matthäifriedhofsweg
Priesterweg
Reichart-
Genest-
Kol. Ideal
Kol. Frohsinn
Kol. Lindenbm.
Friedhf. Priesterw.
Hans-
Lindenhain
Kol. Spree-wald
Kol. Heiterkeit
Kol. Sommer-hm.
Kol. Grünes Tal
Kol. Schönebg.
Kol. Grüne Aue
Kol. Sonnen-land
Kol. Buren-land
Kol. Canova
Kol. Wiedervereinigung
Kol. Neue Zeit
Kol. Kaninchen-farm
Kinder-heim
Riemeischneider-
Heiterkeit
Sommer-hm.
Grünes Tal
Schönebg.
Frohsinn
Ideal
Lindenbm.
Friedhf. Priesterw.
Hans-
Lindenhain
Spree-wald

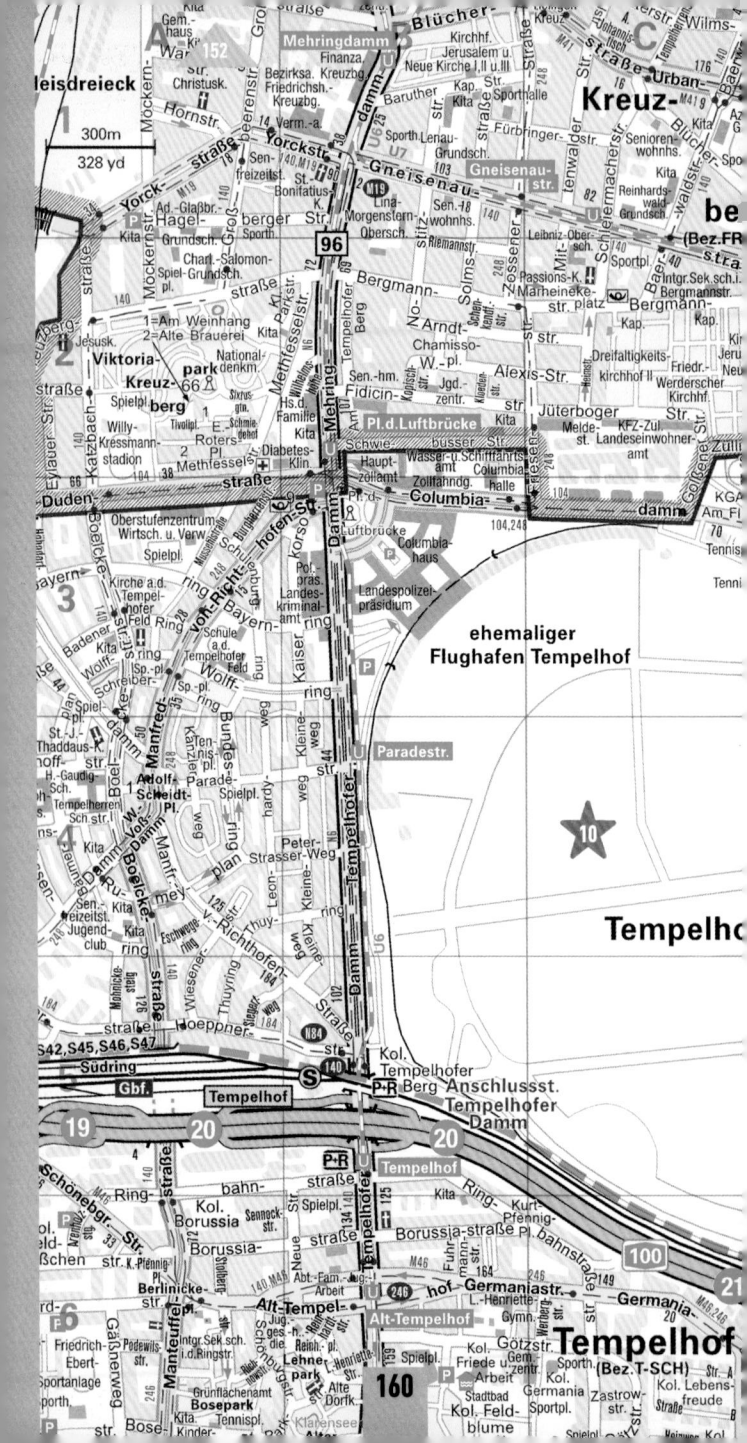
300m
328 yd
Mehringdamm
Blücher-
Kreuz-
Urban-
Gneisenau-
Yorck-
Hornstr.
Mockern-
Hagel-
Viktoria-
Kreuz-
berg
Mehring-
Pl.d.Luftbrücke
Schwie-
Columbia-
Duden-
Methfessel-
Bergmann-
Arndt-
Alexis-Str.
Jüteboger
Friesen-
Gneisenau-
Tempelhofer
Damm
Paradestr.
Kaiser-
Bayern-
Wolff-
Manfred-
Adolf-
Scheidt-
Pl.
Boelcke-
Richthofen-
Südring
Gbf.
Tempelhof
Anschlussst.
Tempelhofer
Damm
Kol.
Borussia
Berlinicke-
Alt-Tempel-
Alt-Tempelhof
Germania-
Tempelhof
(Bez.T-SCH)
Bosepark
Klausensee
ehemaliger
Flughafen Tempelhof
Landespolizei-
präsidium
Columbia-
haus
Luftbrücke
Leisdreieck
Tempelho
160
10
19
20
21
100
96

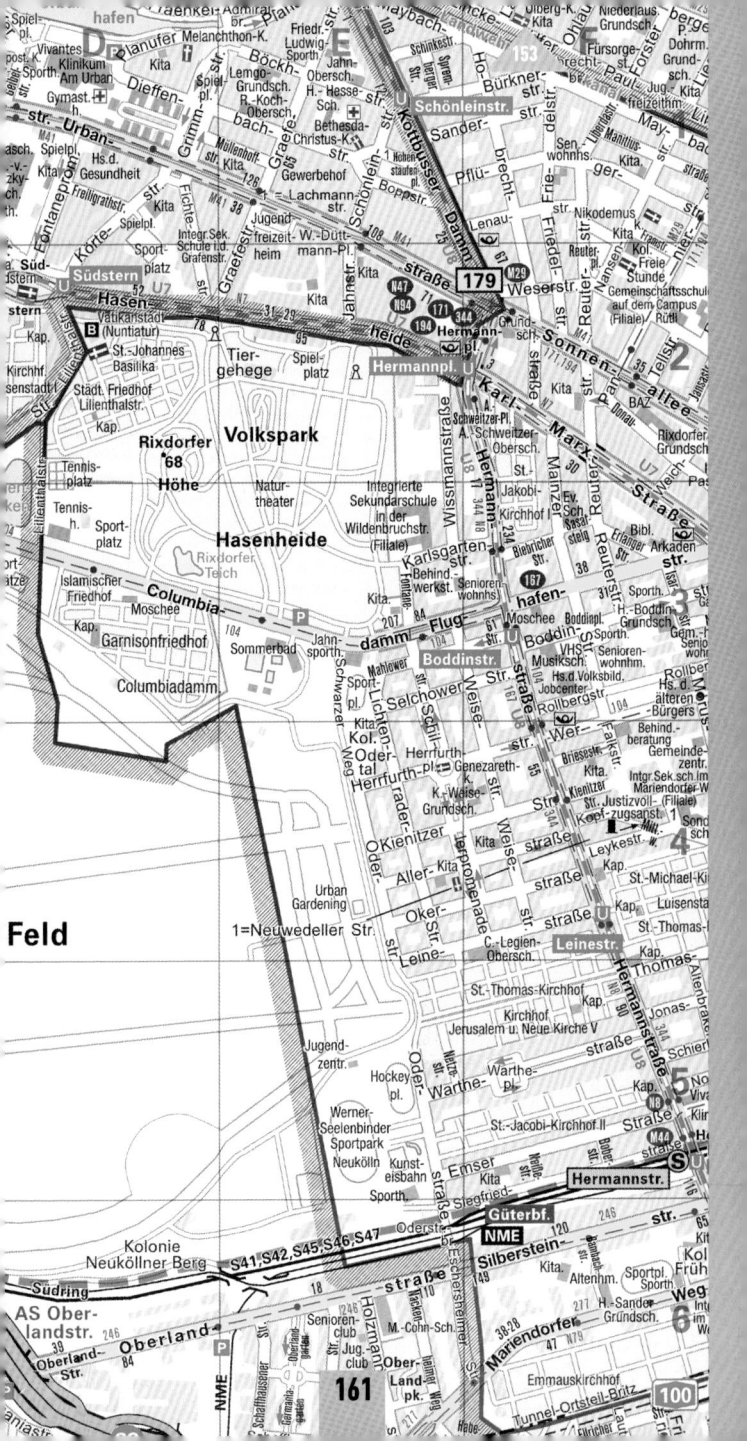
Schönleinstr.
Hermannplatz
Hermannstr.
Güterbf.
Leinestr.
Südstern
Hermannplatz
Volkspark
Rixdorfer Höhe
Hasenheide
Columbiadamm
Boddinstr.
Flughafen
Feld
Neukölln
Kolonie Neukölln Berg
Silberstein-straße
Mariendorfer
Oberland
Südring
S41,S42,S45,S46,S47
NME
161
100
179

300m
328 yd
1=Lohrbergweg
2=Löwenburgweg
3=Wolkenburgweg
Dahlem
(Bez.STEGLITZ-ZEHLENDORF)
Königin-Luise-Str.
Argentinische Allee
Saargemünder Str.
Clayallee
Berliner Straße
Sundgauer Str.
Freie Universität (FU)
Truman-plaza
Generalkonsulat der USA
Thielplatz
Thielallee
Dahlem-Dorf
Finken-park
Thiel-park
Dreipfuhl-park
Oskar-Helene-Heim
Waldfriedhof Dahlem
Alliierten Museum
Bundesinstitut für Risikobewertung
Max-Planck-Institut
Senioren Wohnanlage Rosenhof
Pflegewohnhm. Haus Nansen
Jugendverkehrsch.
Jugendfreizeithm.
Goerzbahn
Dahlemer
162

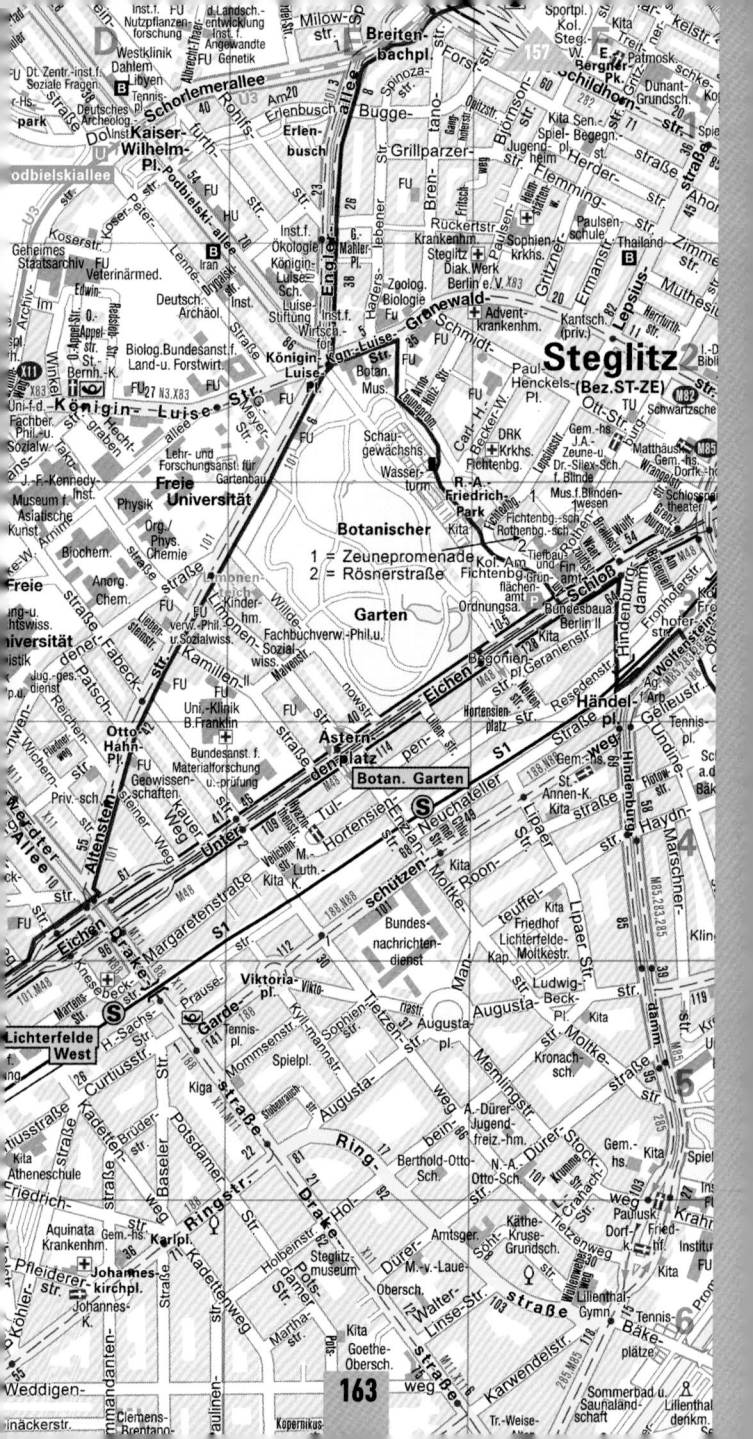
Steglitz
(Bez.ST-ZE)
Botanischer
Garten
Botan. Garten
1 = Zeunepromenade
2 = Rösnerstraße
Freie Universität
Königin-Luise-Str.
Königin-Luise-Pl.
Grunewald-
Breitenbachpl.
Schorlemerallee
Kaiser-Wilhelm-Pl.
Podbielskiallee
Lichterfelde West
Botanischer Garten
Astern-
Eichen-
Händel-pl.
Hindenburgdamm
Schloßstraße
Friedrich-Ring-
Ringstr.
Drakestr.
Alteisten-
Otto-Hahn-Pl.
Kamillen-
Limonen-
Hortensien-
Neuchateller
Moltke-
Augusta-
Viktoria-pl.
Garde-
Curtiusstr.
Karlpl.
Johannes-kirchpl.
Weddigen-
Kopernikus-
Tr.-Weise-
Sommerbad u. Saunalandschaft
Lillenthal-denkm.
Lillenthal-Gymn.
Tennis-plätze
Kita
Gem.-hs.
Spielpl.
Tennis-pl.
Bundesnachrichtendienst
Bundesbauamt Berlin II
Bundesanst. f. Materialforschung u.-prüfung
Geowissenschaften
Uni.-Klinik B.Franklin
Botan. Garten
Biolog.Bundesanst.f. Land-u. Forstwirt.
Deutsch. Archäol.
Veterinärmed.
Geheimes Staatsarchiv
Zoolog. Biologie
Botan. Mus.
Wasserturm
Schaugewächshs.
Krkhs. Richtenbg.
Sophien-krkhs.
Adventkrankenhm.
Krankenhm.
Diak.Werk Berlin e.V.
Kantsch. (priv.)
Paulsen-schule
Thailand
Sportpl. Kol. Steglitz
Patmosk-Grundsch.
Dunant-Grundsch.
Herder-straße
Hemming-straße
Grillparzer-straße
Bugge-straße
Erlen-busch
Forst-straße
Spinoza-straße
Bergner-Pk.
Schildhorn-str.
Lepsius-straße
Zimmer-straße
Ahornstr.
Kelstr.
Treitschke-straße
Gritzner-straße
Wolfenstein-damm
Hindenburg-damm
Lipaer-Str.
Haydn-straße
Matschiner-straße
Ludwig-Beck-Pl.
Kronach-sch.
Memlingstr.
Dürer-straße
Stock-weg
Tiefenweg
Walter-Linse-Str.
Karwendelstr.
Kathe-Kruse-Grundsch.
Amtsger.
Berthold-Otto-Sch.
N.-A.-Otto-Sch.
A.-Dürer-Jugendfreiz.-hm.
Gem.-hs.
Pauluskirch
Dorf-k.
Friedhof
Institut
Kita
Tennis-plätze
Sommerbad u. Saunalandschaft
Lillenthal-denkm.
Lillenthal-Gymn.
Tr.-Weise-
Kopernikus-
Clemens-Brentano-
Paulinen-
Mommsenstr.
Sophien-str.
Augusta-pl.
Augusta-straße
Kiga
Prause-
Viktoria-pl.
Garde-
Curtiusstr.
Kadettenweg
Kadettenbrüder-str.
Potsdamer-straße
Baseler-straße
Ringstr.
Drakestr.
Holbeinstr.
Steglitz-museum
Martha-str.
Kita Goethe-Obersch.
Kita Atheneschule
Aquinata Krankenhm.
Gem.-hs.
Johannes-K.
Friedrich-Wilhelm-Str.
Alteisten-
Eichen-
Margaretenstraße
Kaiser-straße
Otto-Hahn-Pl.
Kamillen-
Limonen-straße
Hortensien-straße
Neuchateller
Moltke-straße
Augusta-straße
Ringstr.
Friedrich-straße
Curtiusstr.

Hakenberg
Schlachtfeld Oberhavelland
Linum
Kremmen
Draisinenbetrieb
ORANIENBURG
Sachsen-hausen
Gedenks
Schloss
Dechtow
Linumer Bruch
Flatow
Staffelde
Schwante
Germendorf
Nikolauskirche
TURM
Lehni
Kuhhorst
Groß-Ziethen
Ober-
Velletanz
Leegebruch
Bärenklau
Kreuz Oranienburg
Tietzow
Kremmen
Oberkrämer
Deutschhof
Dreieck Havelland
Länd-chen
Karlsruh
Eichstädt
krämer
Velten
Hohen Neuendor
Ebereschenhof
Bornicke
Wolfslake
Marwitz
Hennigs-dorf
Kienberg
Grünefeld
Wolfslake
Glien
Perwenitz
-Glien
Dt. Tonstr.
Hertefeld
Bergerdamm
Deutsche Alleenstraße
Paaren im Glien
Bötzow
Stolpe
Stolper Heide
Am Weinberg
Pausin
Wansdorf
Stolpe Süd
Nauen
16 Schönwalde-
Hennigsdorf
Falkensee
Havelkanal
Schönwalde
HERMSDOF
Schulzen Str.
Lietzow
Siedlung Schönwalde
HEILIGENSEE
Schl. Tegel
Neukammer
Bredow
Brieselang
FALKENSEE
KONRADSHÖHE
Tegel
Holzhauser Str.
TEGELORT
Markee
Zeestow
Brieselang
K.-Schum
Wernitz
Finkenkrug
Seegefeld
SPANDAU
Flughafen Berlin-Tegel
Neugarten
Wustermark
Berlin-Spandau
Neuroehrbeck
Elstal
Zitadelle
Saarwinkler
Flughafen Tegel
Dallgow-
Hoppenrade
Hückendamm
Dr. Charlottenbg.
Schmargendorf
Trenmen
Berlin-Spandau
12 -Döberitz
STAAKEN
CHARLOTTENBURG
Olympia-stadion
Spandauer
Etzin
Buchow-Karpzow
Havelkanal
Priort
Seeburg
Neu-Falkenrehde
Falkenrehde
Kartzow
Finkenberg
Dr. Funkturm
Ketzin/-Havel
Paaren-Potsdam-Nord
Satzkorn
GATOW
Grune-wald
Paretz
Jetz-
Fahrland
Groß Glienicke
Luft-waffenmus.
Hüttenweg
Schmargow
Marquardt
KLADOW
Museum Dahle
Sacrow-
Grunewald
Neu Fahrland
Potsdamer Kanal
Leest
Leest
Nedlitz
Sacrow
Spanische Allee
ZEHLENDORF
Bot Gar
Töplitz
Grube
BORNIM
Schloss Cecilienhof
WANNSEE
Museumsdorf Düppel
Phöben
Kemnitz
Golm
BORNSTEDT
Schloss Sanssouci
Schloss Glienicke
Zehlen-dorf
Kleinmach
Derwitz
Phöben
Eiche
Neues Palais
BABELSBERG
ehem. Rathaus
Klein-machnow
Groß Kreutz
Plessow
Wildpark West
Filmpark Babelsberg
Teltow
Stahnsdorf
Neu-plötzin
Werder (Havel)
POTSDAM
Ruhlsdorf
Glindow
Geltow
Kl. Ravens-B
Drewitz
Babelsberg
Güterfelde
Plötzin
Glindower See
Petzow
Rehbrücke
P.-Drewitz
Dreieck Werder
Bliesendorf
Caputh
Kahen-B
Wilhelmshorst
Berghölz-Nuthe-tal
Schenkenhorst
Philippsthal
Sputendorf
Schwielowsee
Langerwisch
Saarmund
Nudow
Michendorf
Ferch
Fahrhorst
Ahrensdorf
Ludwigsfelde-Ost
Busendorf
Dreieck Potsdam
Michendorf
Dreieck Nuthetal
Wildenbruch
Ludwigsfelde West
Siethen
Fichtenwalde
Neuseddin
Seddiner See
Seddin
Kähnsdorf
Fresdorf
Gröben
Tremsdorf
Jütchendorf
Kleinbeuthen
Beelitz-Heilstätten
Beelitz-Heilstätten
Borkwalde
Oranier Route
Naturpark
Schlunkendorf
Stücken
Mietgendorf
Großbeuthen
Glau
Thyrow
Märkisch Wilmersdorf
Blankensee
Beelitz
Reesdorf
Borkheide
Schäpe
Schönefeld
Körzin
Schönhagen
Trebbin
164

BERLIN
Biesenthal
Melchow
Sydower Fließ
Klobbicke
Wandlitz
Lanke
Märkische Eiszeitstraße
Wandlitz See
Lobetal
Sydow
Grüntal
Danewitz
Tuchen
Beerbaum
5 km
3.1 mi
Zühlsdorf
Heidekrautbahn-Museum
Basdorf
Barnim
Naturpark
Rüdnitz
Ladeburg
Albertshof
Tempelfelde
Beiersdorf-
Summt
Mühlenbeck
Gorinsee
Schönow
Bernau b. Berlin
Schönfeld
Schönwalde
Zepernick
Befestigungsanlage
Börnicke
Willmersdorf
Mühlenbecker Land
Schönerlinde
Kolonie Röntgental
Panke-tal
Bernau-Süd
Weesow
Elisenau
Löhme
Birkholz
Birkholz-aue
Schwanebeck
Dreieck Barnim
Seefeld
Werneuchen
BUCH
Buchen-Str.
BLANKENFELDE
LÜBARS
NIEDER-SCHÖNHAUSEN
Pasewalker Str.
BLANKEN-BURG
Lindenberg
Neu Lindenberg
Blumberg
Berlin-Hohen-schönhausen
Krummensee
Wegendorf
Buchholz
MALCHOW
Brandenburg
Berlin
Ahrens-felde
Mehrow
Altlandsberg
PANKOW
Brenzl. Prom.
WEISSENSEE
REINICKEN-DORF
Eiche
Berlin-Marzahn
Seeberg-Dorf
Bruchmühle
Seeberg
WEDDING
PRENZLAUER BERG
Planetarium
HOHEN-SCHÖNHAUSEN
Hönow
MARZAHN
Hoppe-garten
Fredersdorf-
Neuenhagen
Reichstag
Museumsinsel
Zoo
Brandenburger Tor
LICHTENBERG
HELLERSDORF
Dahlwitz
Vogelsdorf
Gedächtnis-kirche
Gedenkst. KREUZBERG
Tierpark
MAHLS-DORF
Münchehofe
Berlin-Hellersdorf
Schulzenshöhe
Rüdersdorf
Tempelhofer Park
TREPTOW
KARLSHORST
Bln.Park-eisenb.
Schöneiche
Rüdersdorf
Museumspark
Tempeln. D. Balzer
OBER-SCHÖNEWEIDE
Wuhlhde.
Fichtenau
Woltersdorf
SCHÖNEBERG
TEMPELHOF
JOHANNISTHAL
Schloss KÖPENICK
Müggelsee
RAHNSDORF
Erkner
MARIENDORF
BUCKOW
LANKWITZ
RUDOW
ALT-GLIENICKE
WENDEN-SCHLOSS
MÜGGELHEIM
Müggelberge
GRÜNAU
Karutzhöhe
LICHTENRADE
Großziethen
Schönefeld
BOHNSDORF
Gosen
Neu Zittau
Birkholz
Waßmannsdorf
Flugh. B. Schönefeld
Flugh. Berlin Brandenburg Willy Brandt (Eröffnung noch offen)
Flugplatz Waldeck B.Brandenbg.
Schmöckwitz
Schulzen-dorf
Eichwalde
Wernsdorf
Mahlow
Selchow
Waltersdorf
Zeuthen
Miersdorf
Messe-gelände
Kiekebusch
Glasow
Rotberg
Wildau
Niederlehme
Diedersdorf
Groß Kienitz
Schönefelder Kreuz
Königs Wusterhsn.
Dahlewitz
Brusendorf
Dannenreich
Bad Saarow 25 km
Rangsdorf
Diepensee
Zernsdorf
Friedersdorf
Jühnsdorf
Am Fichtenplan
Ragow
Kablow
Löwenbruch
Rangsdorf
Groß Machnow
Schenkendorf
Senzig
Königs Wusterhausen
Bindow
Groß Schulzendorf
Mittenwalde
Bindow-Süd
Naturpark
Glienick
Körbiskrug
Gussow
Heidesee
Dabendorf
Telz
Gallun
Bestensee
Grabendorf
Dolgenbrodt
Nächst Neuendorf
Schönwalde
Pätz
Am Kahlberg
Heimatmuseum
Zossen
Horstfelde
165

This index lists a selection of the streets and squares shown in the street atlas.

A
Abbestraße **138/C1-149/F3**
Adalbertstraße **153/E5**
Adenauerplatz **138/A5-149/E6**
Adlerweg **142/A3**
Adolf-Scheidt-Platz **160/A4**
Afrikanische Straße **144/A1**
Agathe-Lasch-Platz **149/D6-157/D1**
Agricolastraße **150/A2**
Ahornallee **148/A5**
Akazienstraße **159/D2**
Albert-Schweitzer-Platz **161/E2**
Albrechtstraße **140/B2-152/A1**
Alexanderplatz **141/F2-153/D1**
Alexanderstraße **141/F2-153/D1-D2**
Alexanderufer **140/A2-151/F1**
Alexandrinenstraße **152/C6**
Alex-Wedding-Straße **153/D1**
Alfred-Döblin-Platz **153/D5**
Alice-Berend-Straße **151/D2**
Almstadtstraße **141/F2-153/D1**
Alte Jakobstraße **141/E6-152/C4**
Altensteinstraße **163/D4**
Alte Schönhauser Straße **141/E1-146/C6-152/C1**
Alt-Lietzow **138/A1-149/E3**
Alt-Moabit **150/B1-C1-A2**
Altonaer Straße **150/B2**
Alt-Stralau **155/D3**
Alt-Treptow **154/C4-155/E4**
Am Flutgraben (1) **154/C3**
Am Friedrichshain **147/E6**
Am Köllnischen Park **153/D3**
Am Kupfergraben **140/C2-152/B2**
Am Oberbaum **154/B2**
Am Ostbahnhof **153/F3-154/A1**
Am Postbahnhof **154/A1**
Amrumer Straße **144/B3**
Am Steinberg **147/E1**
Am Treptower Park **154/C3**
Amtsgerichtsplatz **149/D5**
Am Zeughaus **141/D3-152/B2**
Am Zirkus **140/C2-152/A1**
An der Kolonnade **140/B5-152/A3**
An der Putlitzbrücke **144/C5**
An der Spandauer Brücke **141/E2-152/C1**
An der Urania **150/C6**
Andreasstraße **153/F3-154/A1**
Anhalter Straße **152/A5**
Anklamer Straße **146/B5**
Anna-Louisa-Karsch-Straße **141/E3-152/C2**
Anneliese-u-Georg-Groscurth-Platz **148/A3**
Annenstraße **141/F5-153/D4**
Ansbacher Straße **139/F6-158/B1**
Apostel-Paulus-Straße **158/C2**
Arnswalder Platz **147/F5**
Aschaffenburger Straße **158/B1**
Askanischer Platz **151/F5-152/A5**
Augsburger Straße **139/D5-150/B5**
Augustenburger Platz **144/C4**
Auguste-Viktoria-Straße **156/C4**
Auguststraße **140/C1-141/D1-146/B6-152/B1**
Axel-Springer-Straße **141/E6-152/C4**

B
Babelsberger Straße **158/B3**
Bachstraße **139/E2-150/B3**
Badensche Straße **158/A3**
Baerwaldstraße **160/C2**
Bamberger Straße **158/B2**
Barbarossaplatz **158/C2**
Barbarossastraße **158/B2**
Barfusstraße **144/C2**
Bauhofstraße **141/D3-152/B2**
Bayerischer Platz **158/B2**
Bayerische Straße **157/E1**
Bayreuther Straße **139/F5-150/C6**
Bebelplatz **141/D4-152/B3**
Behmstraße **146/A2**
Behrenstraße **140/A4-C4-151/F3-152/A3-B3**
Bellermannstraße **145/F1-146/A1**
Bellevueallee **151/D3-E3**
Bellevuestraße **140/A5-151/F4**
Belziger Straße **158/C3**
Ben-Gurion-Straße **151/F4**
Bergmannstraße **160/B2**
Berkaer Platz **156/C5**
Berkaer Straße **156/B4**
Berliner Straße (Pank., Prenzl. Bg.) **147/D1**
Berliner Straße (Wilmdf.) **157/E3-158/A3**
Berliner Straße (Zehldf., Dahl.) **162/A6**
Bernauer Straße **146/A5**
Bernburger Straße **151/F5**
Bernhard-Weiß-Straße **153/D1**
Besselstraße **152/B5**
Beusselstraße **144/A5-A6-150/A2**
Birkenstraße **144/B6**
Bismarckallee **156/A3**
Bismarckplatz **156/B2**
Bismarckstraße **138/A2-149/D4-E4**
Bleibtreustraße **138/C6-149/F6**
Blissestraße **157/F4-158/A4**
Blücherstraße **152/B6-160/C1-B1**
Boddinstraße **154/A6-161/F3**
Bodestraße **141/D3-152/B2**
Böckhstraße **153/E6-161/E1**
Boelckestraße **159/F4-160/A4**
Bötzowstraße **147/F5-F6**
Bornholmer Straße **146/B1**
Borsigstraße **146/B6**
Bouchéstraße **154/B5**
Boxhagener Straße **154/C1**
Brabanter Platz **157/F4**
Brandenburgische Straße **138/A6-157/E1**
Breite Straße (Mitte) **141/E4-152/C3**
Breite Straße (Schmargdf.) **157/D5**
Breitscheidplatz **139/E4-150/B5**
Brückenstraße **153/D3**
Brüderstraße (Lichtfde.) **163/D5**
Brüderstraße (Mitte) **141/E4-152/C3**
Brümmerstraße **162/C4**
Brunnenstraße **146/A3**
Buchberger Straße **155/E1**
Budapester Straße **139/E4-F4-150/B5-C5**
Bülowstraße **151/D6**
Bundesallee **158/B4-B6-B5**
Bundesplatz **158/A4**
Burggrafenstraße **139/F4-150/C5**
Burgstraße **141/E2-152/C2**

C
Calvinstraße **150/C2**
Carmerstraße **138/C4-149/F5-150/A5**
Caroline-Herschel-Platz **155/D1**
Carpinusweg **162/A3**
Cauerstraße **138/B2-149/E3**
Charitéstraße **140/A2-151/F2**
Charlottenburger Ufer **149/D2**
Charlottenstraße **140/C3-152/B2**
Charlotte-Salomon-Hain (7) **155/E3**
Chausseestraße **140/B1-146/A6**
Claire-Waldoff-Promenade **151/D1**
Clara-Jaschke-Straße **151/E1**
Clara-Wieck-Straße **151/D4**
Clayallee **162/A6**
Columbiadamm **160/B3**
Courbièrestraße **150/C5**
Crellestraße **159/E2**
Cuxhavener Straße **150/B3**

D
Dänenstraße **146/C2**
Dahlienweg **142/B3**
Danziger Straße **147/D4**
Darmstädter Straße **138/B6-149/F6-157/F1**
Delbrückstraße **156/B3**
Demminer Straße **146/B4**
Dernburgstraße **148/B5**
Dessauer Straße **151/F5-152/A5**
Detmolder Straße **157/F4-158/A4**
Dieffenbachstraße **161/D1**
DIN-Platz **139/F4-150/C5**
Dircksenstraße **141/E2-152/C1**
Dominicusstraße **158/C3**
Donaustraße **154/A5-161/F2**
Dorotheenstraße **140/C3-A4-151/F2-152/A2-B2**
Dovestraße **149/F3**
Drakestraße (Lichtfde.) **163/D4**
Drakestraße (Tiergt.) **139/F3-150/C4**
Dresdener Straße **153/E5-D4**
Drontheimer Straße **145/F1**
Droysenstraße **149/D6**
Dudenstraße **159/F3-160/A3**
Düsseldorfer Straße **138/A6-157/E1**
Duisburger Straße **138/A6-149/E6-157/E1**

E
Eberswalder Straße **146/C4**
Ebertstraße **140/A5-151/F4**
Ede-und Unke-Weg **155/D1**
Edith-Kiss-Straße **154/A2**
Eichenallee **148/A3**
Eichendorffstraße **146/A6**
Einsteinufer **138/B1-C1-149/F3-150/A3**
Eisenacher Straße **159/D2**
Eisenzahnstraße **157/E2**
Eislebener Straße **139/E5-150/B6**
Elisabeth-Mara-Straße **141/E5-152/C4**
Ella-Kay-Straße **147/E4**
Ella-Trebe-Straße **151/E1**
Ellen-Eppstein-Straße **144/C5**
Else-Lasker-Schüler-Straße **151/D6**
Elsenstraße **154/C4-B5**
Emser Platz **157/F2**
Emser Straße **157/F2**
Engeldamm **153/E4**
Engelallee **163/E2**
Englische Straße **139/D2-150/A3**
Erich-Müller-Straße **155/E3**
Erich-Weinert-Straße **147/E2-D2**
Erkstraße **154/A5**
Erna-Samuel-Straße **144/A6**
Ernst-Reuter-Platz **138/C2-149/F4**
Ettaler Straße **139/E6-150/B6-158/B1**
Europaplatz **151/E1**
Exerzierstraße **145/E2**

F
Falkplatz **146/C3**
Fanny-Hensel-Weg **151/F5-152/A5**
Fasanenplatz **139/D6-150/A6**
Fasanenstraße **139/D5-150/A5-158/A1**
Fehrbelliner Platz **157/E2**
Fehrbelliner Straße **146/C5**
Feilnerstraße **141/D6-152/C4**
Fennstraße **145/D5**
Fichtenberg **163/F3**
Fischerinsel **141/F4-152/C3**
Flotowstraße (Hansav.) **139/E1-150/B3**
Flotowstraße (Lichtfde.) **163/F4**
Flottwellstraße **151/F6**
Flughafenstraße **154/A5-161/E3**
Föhrer Straße **144/C4**
Fontanestraße (Grwld.) **156/A3**
Fontanestraße (Nkln.) **161/E3**
Forckenbeckstraße **157/D4-E4**
Franklinstraße **138/C1-150/A3**

Franzensbader Straße **156/C3**
Französische Straße **140/C4-152/B3**
Fraunhoferstraße **138/B1-149/F3**
Friedelstraße **154/A4-161/F1**
Friedenstraße **147/E6-153/F1**
Friedrich-Hollaender-Platz **139/D5-150/A6**
Friedrichsberger Straße **153/F2**
Friedrichstraße (Krzbg, Mitte) **140/C3-C1-C4-C6-152/B4-B2-A1-B3**
Friedrichstraße (Lichtfde.) **163/D5**
Friedrich-Wilhelm-Platz **158/B5**
Friesenstraße (Kreuzbg., Tphf.) **160/C3**
Fromet-und-Moses-Mendelssohn-Platz (1) **152/B5**
Fünf Morgen **162/B3**
Fürstenbrunner Weg **148/A1**
Fuggerstraße **139/F5-150/C6**
Furtwänglerstraße **156/B3**

G

Gartenufer **139/E3-150/B4**
Gaußstraße **143/E6-149/E1**
Geisbergstraße **139/E6-F6-150/B6-158/B1**
Gendarmenmarkt **140/C5-152/B3**
Genthiner Straße **151/D5**
George-Grosz-Platz **138/B5-149/F6**
Georgenstraße **140/B3-152/A2**
Georg-Löwenstein-Straße **155/F3**
Gerichtstraße **145/D3**
Gerichtstraße **145/E3**
Gertraudenstraße **141/E5-152/C3**
Geschwister-Scholl-Straße **140/C2-152/B2**
Giesebrechtstraße **138/A5-149/E5**
Gipsstraße **141/D1-146/C6-152/C1**
Gisèle-Freund-Hain (10) **155/E3**
Gitschiner Straße **152/B6**
Gleimstraße **146/C3-B3**
Glinkastraße **140/C4-152/A3**
Glogauer Straße **154/A4**
Gneisenaustraße **160/B1**
Goebenstraße **159/E1**
Goethestraße (Charlbg.) **138/A3-B3-149/E4-F4**
Goethestraße (Weißs.) **147/F2**
Goltzstraße **159/D2**
Gontardstraße **141/F2-153/D1**
Gontermannstraße **159/F4**
Gormannstraße **141/E1-146/C6-152/C1**
Gotenstraße **159/E4-E3**
Gotlandstraße **147/D1**
Granseer Straße **146/C5**
Graunstraße **146/B3**
Grazer Damm **159/D5**
Greifswalder Straße **147/E6**
Grellstraße **147/E3**
Grieser Platz **156/C2**
Grolmanstraße **138/C3-149/F5**
Große Hamburger Straße **141/D1-146/B6-152/B1**
Große Querallee **151/E4**
Großer Stern **150/C3**
Grünberger Straße **154/B1**
Grüntaler Straße **146/A2**
Grunerstraße **141/F3-153/D2**
Grunewaldstraße (Schbg.) **158/B2-159/D2**
Grunewaldstraße (Stegl.) **163/E2**
Güntzelstraße **157/F2-158/A2-B2**
Guerickestraße **138/B1-149/E3**
Gürtelstraße **155/D1**
Gustav-Adolf-Straße **147/F2**
Gustav-Holzmann-Straße **155/F3**
Gustav-Mahler-Platz **163/E2**
Gustav-Meyer-Allee **145/F4-146/A4**
Gustav Rickelt-Weg **157/F6**
Gutenbergstraße (Charlbg.) **138/C1-150/A3**

H

Habelschwerdter Allee **162/C4**
Händelallee **139/E1-F1-150/B3**
Hagenstraße **156/B4-A4**
Halemweg **142/B6**
Hallesches Ufer **151/F5-152/A5-A6**
Hamburger Platz **147/F1**
Handjerystraße (Friedn.) **158/B4-B6**
Hannah-Karminski-Straße **139/D1-150/A3**
Hanne-Sobek-Platz (2) **146/A2**
Hannoversche Straße **140/A1-145/F6-151/F1**
Hansa-Ufer **139/E1-150/B3**
Hans-Otto-Straße **147/F5**
Hardenbergplatz **139/E3-150/B4**
Hardenbergstraße **138/C3-149/F4-150/A4**
Hasenheide **161/D2**
Hauptstraße (Lichtbg.) **155/D2**
Hauptstraße (Schbg., Friedn.) **158/C4-B5-159/D2**
Hausvogteiplatz **141/D5-152/B3**
Heckerdamm **142/A4-143/E4**
Hedwig-Dohm-Straße **159/E4**
Hedwig-Wachenheim-Straße **154/B2**
Heidelberger Platz **157/E4**
Heidestraße **145/D5**
Heilbronner Straße (Schbg.) **158/C1**
Heilbronner Straße (Wilmdf.) **148/C6**
Heilmannring **142/B5-C5**
Heinrich-Heine-Platz **153/D4**
Heinrich-Heine-Straße **153/D5**
Heinrich-von-Gagern-Straße **151/E3**
Helen-Ernst-Straße **154/B1**
Helgolandstraße **157/D5**
Helmholtzstraße **149/F2**
Helmstedter Straße **158/B2**
Henriettenplatz **156/C1**
Herderstraße (Charlbg.) **138/B3-149/F4**
Herderstraße (Stegl.) **163/F1**
Hermannplatz **161/E2**
Hermannstraße **154/A6-161/F2**
Herrfurthstraße **161/F4**
Hertha-Block-Promenade **159/E3**
Hertzallee **139/D3-150/A4**
Hessische Straße **140/B1-145/F6-146/A6**
Hilde-Ephraim-Straße **156/A2**
Hildegard-Knef-Platz **159/E4**
Hildegard-Marcusson-Straße (8) **155/E3**
Hindenburgdamm **163/F4**
Hinter der Katholischen Kirche **141/D4-152/B3**
Hirtenstraße **141/F1-147/D6-153/D1**
Hochmeisterplatz **157/D1**
Hochstraße **145/F4**
Hoffmann-von-Fallersleben-Platz **157/E3**
Hofjägerallee **150/C3**
Hohenstaufenplatz **161/E1**
Hohenstaufenstraße **158/B1**
Hohenzollerndamm **156/C3-B5-157/E2**
Hohenzollernplatz **158/A1**
Holsteinische Straße **158/A2**
Holtzendorffstraße **149/D5**
Holzmarktstraße **153/E3**
Hubertusallee **156/B4**
Hüttenweg **162/A3**
Hundekehlestraße **156/C5**
Huronseestraße **155/F3**
Hussitenstraße **145/F4-146/A4**
Huttenstraße **143/E6-149/E1**

I

Ida-von-Arnim-Straße **145/E5**
In den Ministergärten **140/A5-151/F3-152/A3**
Ingeborg-Drewitz-Allee **151/D2**
Innsbrucker Platz **158/C4**
Innsbrucker Straße **158/C2**
Inselstraße **141/F5-153/D3**
Invalidenstraße **151/D1**

J

Jägerstraße **140/C5-152/A3**
Jafféstraße **148/A6**
Jagowstraße **150/A3-B2**
Jebensstraße **139/D3-150/B5**
Jerusalemer Straße **141/D5-152/C3**
Joachim-Friedrich-Straße **157/D2**
Joachim-Karnatz-Allee **151/D2**
Joachimsthaler Platz **139/D5-150/A5**
Joachimsthaler Straße **139/D5-150/B6**
Joachimstraße **141/D1-146/C6**
Johannaplatz **156/B2**
Johannisstraße **140/C2-152/A1**
John-F.-Kennedy-Platz **158/C3**
John-Foster-Dulles-Allee **151/D3**
Jollenseglerstraße **155/D3**
Jüdenstraße **141/F3-153/D2**
Jungfernheideweg **142/A3**

K

Kaiserdamm **148/A5-C4**
Kaiser-Friedrich-Straße **149/D3**
Kaiserin-Augusta-Allee **149/E2**
Kaiser-Wilhelm-Platz (Dahl.) **163/D1**
Kaiser-Wilhelm-Platz (Schbg.) **159/D2**
Kalckreuthstraße **150/C6**
Kantstraße **138/C4-A4-149/D5-E5-150/A5**
Kapelle-Ufer **140/A2-151/F2**
Karl-August-Platz **138/A3-149/E5**
Karl-Heinrich-Ulrichs-Straße **151/D5**
Karl-Liebknecht-Straße **141/F2-E3-152/C2-153/D1**
Karl-Marx-Allee **153/D1**
Karl-Marx-Straße **154/A5-161/F2**
Karlplatz **163/D6**
Karlsgartenstraße **161/E3**
Karlshorster Straße (1) **155/E2**
Karl-Wilker-Straße (9) **155/F3**
Kastanienallee (Charlbg.) **148/A4**
Kastanienallee (Prenzl. Bg., Mitte) **146/C5**
Kastanienallee (Tiergt.) **151/D3**
Katzbachstraße **159/F3-160/A3**
Keithstraße **150/C5**
Kelheimer Straße **139/E6-150/B6-158/B1**
Kemperplatz **140/A5-151/E4**
Kiefholzstraße **154/B3**
Kirchstraße (Moab.) **150/C2**
Kirchstraße (Schmargdf.) **157/D5**
Kleine Rosenthaler Straße **146/C6**
Kleiner Stern **151/D3**
Kleiststraße **139/F5-150/C6**
Klingelhöferstraße **151/D4**
Klingsorplatz **163/F4**
Klopstockstraße **139/E1-150/B3**
Klosterstraße **141/F3-153/D2**
Knesebeckstraße (Charlbg.) **138/C5-149/F6-150/A6**
Knesebeckstraße (Lichtfde.) **163/D4**
Knobelsdorffstraße **148/C4-B4**
Kochstraße **140/C6-152/A4**
Königin-Elisabeth-Straße **148/B3**
Königin-Luise-Straße **162/B2-163/E2**
Köpenicker Chaussee **155/F3**
Köpenicker Straße **153/D3**
Köpenicker Straße **153/F4-154/A2**
Körtestraße **161/D2**
Kollwitzstraße **147/D5**
Koloniestraße **145/F1**
Kolonnenstraße **159/E2**
Kommandantenstraße **141/E5-152/C4**
Konstanzer Straße **138/B6-157/E3-E2**
Koppenplatz **141/D1-146/B6**
Koppenstraße **153/F3-154/A1**
Kottbusser Damm **161/E1**
Kottbusser Straße **153/E6**

Krausenstraße **141/D6-152/B4**
Krausnickstraße **141/D2-152/B1**
Kreuzberg **152/C5**
Kreuzbergstraße **159/F2**
Kronenstraße **140/C5-152/B4**
Krumme Straße (Charlbg.) **138/A4-A2-A3-149/E4-E5-E4**
Krumme Straße (Lichtfde.) **163/F5**
Kulmbacher Straße **139/E6-158/B1**
Kulmer Straße **159/E2**
Kurfürstendamm **138/A6-139/D5-149/D6-E6-150/A5-156/C1**
Kurfürstenstraße **139/F4-150/C5-151/E6-D5**
Kurstraße **141/E5-152/C3**
Kurt-Pfennig-Platz **160/B6**
Kurt-Schumacher-Damm **142/C6**
Kynaststraße **155/D3**

L

Landgrafenstraße **150/C5**
Landhausstraße **158/A2**
Landshuter Straße **158/B1**
Langenscheidtstraße **159/E2**
Langhansstraße **147/E1**
Laubacher Straße **157/F4-158/A4**
Lausitzer Platz **153/F5-154/A2**
Leberstraße **159/E4**
Lebuser Straße **153/F2**
Leibnizstraße **138/B5-B3-149/E6-E4**
Leipziger Platz **140/A6-151/F4-152/A4**
Leipziger Straße **140/B6-152/A4**
Lennéstraße **140/A5-151/F4**
Lessingstraße **150/B2**
Leuthener Straße **159/E3**
Levetzowstraße **150/B2**
Lewishamstraße **138/A5-149/D5**
Lichtenberger Straße **153/E3**
Lichtensteinallee **139/F3-150/C4**
Liesenstraße **145/F5**
Lietzenburger Straße **138/B6-139/E5-149/F6-150/A6**
Lilienthalstraße **161/D3**
Lindenstraße **152/B5**
Linienstraße **141/D1-146/C6**
Lise-Meitner-Straße **149/D1**
Littenstraße **153/D2**
Liverpooler Straße **144/B1**
Löhleinstraße **162/B4**
Loewenhardtdamm **159/F3**
Los-Angeles-Platz **139/E5-150/B5**
Loschmidtstraße **138/B1-149/E3**
Lotte-Laserstein-Straße **159/E5**
Ludwigkirchplatz **138/C6-149/F6-150/A6-157/F1-158/A1**
Ludwigkirchstraße **138/C6-149/F6-150/A6-157/F1-158/A1**
Lückstraße **155/F2**
Lüneburger Straße **151/D2**
Lützowplatz **151/D5**
Lützowstraße **151/E5-D5**
Lützowufer **150/C5-151/D5**
Luisenplatz **149/D3**
Luisenstraße **140/A1-B2-145/F6-146/A6-151/F1-F2-152/A2-A1**
Luxemburger Straße **144/C4**
Lynarstraße (Grwld.) **156/B2**
Lynarstraße (Wedd.) **145/D4**

M

Maaßenstraße **151/D6**
Märkisches Ufer **141/F5-153/D3**
Malmöer Straße **146/C1**
Manteuffelstraße **153/E6**
Marchstraße **138/C2-149/F3-150/A3**
Marheinekeplatz **160/B2**
Mariane-von-Rantzau-Straße **154/A2**
Marie-Curie-Allee **155/F2**
Marienburger Straße **147/E5**
Marienstraße **140/B3-151/F2-152/A2**
Markgrafenstraße **141/D4-152/B3**
Marktstraße **155/D2**
Marlene-Dietrich-Platz **140/A6-151/F4**
Marthashof **146/C4**
Martin-Hoffmann Straße **154/C3**
Martin-Luther-Straße **150/C6-158/C1-C2-C4**
Masurenallee **148/A5**
Mauerstraße **140/C5-152/B4**
Max-Beer-Straße **141/F2-152/C1**
May-Ayim-Ufer **154/B2**
Maybachufer **153/E6**
Medaillonplatz **155/E3**
Mehringdamm **160/B2**
Mehringplatz **152/B6**
Meierottostraße **139/D6-150/A6-158/A1**
Meinekestraße **139/D6-150/A6**
Memhardstraße **141/F2-153/D1**
Meraner Straße **158/B3**
Messedamm **148/A6**
Metzer Straße **147/D5**
Mierendorffplatz **149/D2**
Mierendorffstraße **149/D2**
Mildred-Harnack-Straße **154/B2**
Mittelstraße **140/B4-152/A2**
Mittenwalder Straße **160/C2**
Modersohnstraße **154/C2**
Möckernstraße **160/A2**
Mohrenstraße **140/B5-152/A3**
Molkenmarkt **141/F4-153/D2**
Mollstraße **147/D6-153/D1**
Mommsenstraße **138/B5-A5-149/E5**
Mommsenstraße **163/E5**
Monbijouplatz **141/D2-152/B1**
Monbijoustraße **141/D2-152/B2**
Monumentenstraße **159/E2**
Moritzplatz **153/D5**
Motzstraße **158/B1**
Mühlendamm **141/F4-152/C3**
Mühlenstraße **154/A2**
Müller-Breslau-Straße **139/D2-150/A4**
Müllerstraße **144/A1**
Münchener Straße **158/C1**
Münzstraße **141/E1-152/C1**
Mulackstraße **141/E1-146/C6-152/C1**

N

Nachodstraße **158/B1**
Nachtigalplatz **144/A1**
Nassauische Straße **158/A2**
Naumannstraße **159/E3-E4**
Nestorstraße **157/D1**
Neue Bahnhofstraße **155/D2**
Neue Grünstraße **141/E6-152/C4**
Neue Kantstraße **148/B5**
Neue Promenade **141/E2-152/C1**
Neue Roßstraße **141/F5-153/D3**
Neue Schönhauser Straße **141/E1-152/C1**
Neumannstraße **147/E1**
Neustädtische Kirchstraße **140/B3-152/A2**
Niebuhrstraße **138/A4-149/E5**
Niederkirchnerstraße **140/B6-151/F4-152/A4**
Niederlagstraße **141/D4-152/C3**
Niederwallstraße **141/D5-152/C3**
Nöldnerstraße **155/E2**
Nollendorfplatz **151/D6**
Nordufer **143/F4-144/A4**
Novalisstraße **146/A6**
Nürnberger Platz **139/E6-150/B6-158/B1**
Nürnberger Straße **139/E6-150/B6**

O

Oberbaumstraße **154/B2**
Oberwallstraße **141/D4-152/B2**
Olivaer Platz **138/B6-149/E6**
Olof-Palme-Platz **139/F4-150/B5**
Oranienburger Straße **140/C1-146/A6-152/A1**
Oranienburger Tor **140/B1-146/A6-152/A1**
Oranienstraße **141/E6-152/C4-153/E5**
Osloer Straße **145/E1**
Osnabrücker Straße **149/D1**
Ostender Straße **144/C4**
Ostseestraße **147/F2**
Otto-Braun-Straße **147/E6-153/D1**
Otto-Suhr-Allee **138/A1-149/E3**
Otto-von-Bismarck-Allee **140/A3-151/E2**

P

Pacelliallee **162/C2**
Paderborner Straße **138/A6-157/E1**
Pallasstraße **159/D1**
Pankstraße **145/E3**
Pannierstraße **154/A5-161/F2**
Pappelallee **147/D3**
Pariser Platz **140/A4-151/F3-152/A3**
Pariser Straße **138/B6-C6-149/F6-150/A6-157/F1-158/A1**
Parochialstraße **141/F3-153/D2**
Passauer Straße **139/F5-150/B6**
Pauline-Staegemann-Straße **147/E6-153/E1**
Paul-Löbe-Allee **140/A3-151/E2**
Paulsborner Straße **156/C3**
Paulstraße **151/D3**
Perleberger Straße **144/C6**
Pestalozzistraße **149/D5**
Petersallee **144/A2**
Pfalzburger Straße **138/C6-149/F6-150/A6-157/F2-F1-158/A2-A1**
Pflügerstraße **161/E1**
Philippistraße **148/C4**
Planckstraße **140/C2-152/B2**
Platz am Königstor **147/E6**
Platz vor dem Neuen Tor **145/F6**
Platz der Vereinten Nationen **153/F1**
Platz des 18. März **140/A4-151/F3**
Platz des 9. November 1989 **146/B1**
Plaza San Rafael del Sur **154/B2**
Podbielskiallee **156/C6**
Pommernweg **142/A3**
Poststraße **141/E3-152/C2**
Potsdamer Platz **140/A6-151/F4**
Potsdamer Straße (Lichtfde.) **163/D5**
Potsdamer Straße (Tiergt.,Schbg.) **140/A6-151/E6-E4-159/E2**
Prager Platz **158/B1**
Prenzlauer Allee **147/E3-D6-153/D1**
Prenzlauer Berg **147/D6**
Prinzenallee **145/F2-146/A2**
Prinzenstraße **153/D6**
Prinzregentenstraße **158/B2-B3**
Puschkinallee **154/C3-155/D4**
Putlitzbrücke **144/C5**
Putlitzstraße **144/B6**
Puttkamerstraße **152/B5**

Q

Quitzowstraße **144/B5**

R

Ramlerstraße **146/A3**
Rankestraße **139/D5-150/B6**
Rathausstraße **141/E3-152/C2**
Rathenauplatz **156/C1**
Rathenower Straße **144/C5-C6-151/D1**
Reichenberger Straße **153/D5**
Reichpietschufer **151/D4**
Reichstagufer **140/A3-151/F2**
Reichweindamm **143/D5**
Reinhardtstraße (Mitte) **140/A2-151/F2**
Reinhardtstraße (Tphf.) **160/B6**
Reinickendorfer Straße **145/E1**
Reuterplatz **154/A4-161/F2**
Revaler Straße **154/B1**
Rheinbabenallee **156/B5**
Rheinstraße **158/B6**
Richard-Wagner-Straße **138/A2-149/E4**
Ritterstraße **152/C5**
Robert-Koch-Platz **140/A1-145/F6-151/F1**
Rochstraße **141/E2-152/C1**

Röntgenstraße **138/B1-149/E3**
Rosa-Luxemburg-Platz **141/F1-147/D6-153/D1**
Rosa-Luxemburg-Straße **141/F1-153/D1**
Roseneck **156/B5**
Rosenheimer Straße **158/C2**
Rosensteinweg **156/B2**
Rosenstraße **141/E2-152/C2**
Rosenthaler Platz **146/C6**
Rosenthaler Straße **141/E2-152/C1**
Rudi-Dutschke-Straße **140/C6-152/B4**
Rudolstädter Straße **157/D3-E3**
Rückerstraße **141/E1-146/C6-152/C1**
Rückertstraße **163/E1**
Rügener Straße **146/B3**
Rungestraße **153/D3**

S

Saargemünder Straße **162/B4**
Saarstraße **158/B6**
Saatwinkler Damm **142/A3**
Saatwinkler Damm **143/F4-144/A4**
Sachsendamm **159/D4**
Sächsische Straße **138/C6-149/F6-157/F2-F1**
Saganer Straße **155/F3**
Salzufer **138/C1-150/A3**
Savignyplatz **138/C4-149/F5-150/A5**
Schadowstraße **140/B3-152/A2**
Schaperstraße **139/D6-150/A6-158/A1**
Scharounstraße **151/E4**
Scheidemannstraße **151/E3**
Scheringstraße **145/F4-146/A4**
Schildhornstraße **163/F1**
Schillerpromenade **161/E3**
Schillerstraße **138/B3-149/D4-E4**
Schillingbrücke **153/F4-154/A1**
Schillingstraße **153/E2**
Schillstraße **150/C5**
Schlegelstraße **146/A6**
Schleiermacherstraße **160/C2**
Schleswiger Ufer **139/E1-150/B3**
Schlichtallee **155/E2**
Schliemannstraße **147/D4**
Schloßplatz **141/E4-152/C3**
Schloßstraße (Charlbg.) **149/D3**
Schloßstraße (Stegl., Lichtfde.) **163/F3**
Schlüterstraße **138/B6-B4-149/F6-F5**
Schmiljanstraße **158/B5**
Schöneberger Straße **151/F6**
Schöneberger Ufer **151/E5**
Schönhauser Allee **147/D6**
Schönhauser Tor **146/C6**
Schorlemeralle **163/D1**
Schützenstraße (Mitte) **140/C6-152/B4**
Schützenstraße (Stegl.) **163/F3**
Schulstraße **145/D3**
Schulze-Boysen-Straße **155/E1**
Schulze-Delitzsch-Platz **141/F5-153/D3**
Schumannstraße **140/A2-151/F1-152/A1**
Schwäbische Straße **158/C1**
Schwarzbacher Straße (3) **156/C1**
Schwarzer Weg (Charlbg.) **149/E1**
Schwarzer Weg (Mitte) **145/F6**
Schwarzer Weg (Wilmdf.) **161/E3**
Schwedenstraße **145/E1**
Schwedter Straße **146/C2**
Sebastianstraße **141/F5-153/D4**
Seesener Straße **157/D2**
Seestraße **144/A5**
Sellerstraße **145/E5**
Sesenheimer Straße **138/A3-149/E4**
Seydelstraße **141/E5-152/C4**
Seydlitzstraße **151/D1**
Shakespeareplatz **138/A3-149/E4**
Sickingenstraße **143/E6-144/A6-149/E1**
Siegfriedstraße **161/E6**
Siegmunds Hof **139/E1-150/B3**
Siemensdamm **142/A5**
Siemensstraße (Moab.) **144/A6**
Simplonstraße **154/C1**
Singdrosselsteig **142/A3**
Singerstraße **153/E2**
Skalitzer Straße **153/D6**
Sömmeringstraße **149/D2**
Solinger Straße **150/B3**
Sonnenallee **154/A4-B5-161/F2**
Sophie-Charlotten-Straße **148/B2-C3**
Sophie-Charlotte-Platz **149/D4**
Sophienstraße (Lichtbg., Friedrfde.) **155/F1**
Sophienstraße (Lichtfde.) **163/E5**
Sophienstraße (Mitte) **141/D1-146/C6-152/C1**
Spandauer Damm **148/B3**
Spandauer Straße **141/E2-152/C2**
Spenerstraße **151/D2**
Spichernstraße **139/E6-158/B1**
Spittelmarkt **141/E5-152/C3**
Spreewaldplatz **153/F5-154/A3**
Spreeweg **150/C3**
Sprengelstraße **144/C4**
Stahlheimer Straße **147/D2**
Stallschreiberstraße **141/F6-152/C4**
Stargarder Straße **147/D3-D2**
Steinplatz **138/C3-150/A4**
Steinstraße **141/E1-146/C6-152/C1**
Stephanstraße **144/C6**
Stralauer Allee **154/B2**
Stralauer Straße **141/F4-153/D3**
Straße der Pariser Kommune **153/F4-154/A1**
Straße des 17. Juni **138/C2-139/E2-150/A4-B3**
Strausberger Platz **153/E2**
Stromstraße **150/B2**
Stülerstraße **150/C4**
Stuttgarter Platz **149/D5**
Suarezstraße **148/C6**
Südstern **161/D2**
Südwestkorso **157/F5-E6-158/A5**
Swinemünder Straße **146/B3**
Sybelstraße **138/B5-149/D6-E6**

T

Tamara-Danz-Straße **154/B2**
Taubenstraße **140/C5-152/A3**
Tauentzienstraße **139/E4-150/B5**
Tegeler Straße **145/D4**
Tegeler Weg **142/C6**
Tempelhofer Damm **160/B6-B4**
Tempelhofer Ufer **151/F5-152/A6-A5**
Tempelhofer Weg **159/D4**
Teplitzer Straße **156/B5**
Theanolte-Bähnisch-Straße **153/D1**
Theodor-Heuss-Platz **148/A5**
Thielallee **162/C5**
Thomas-Dehler-Straße **139/F2-150/C4**
Thomasiusstraße **150/C2**
Thulestraße **147/D1**
Tieckstraße **140/B1-146/A6**
Tiergartenstraße **151/D4**
Tiergartenufer **139/E2-150/B4**
Tile-Wardenberg-Straße **150/A2**
Toeplerstraße **142/B5**
Togostraße **144/A1**
Torfstraße **144/C4**
Torgauer Straße **159/D4**
Torstraße **140/C1-146/B6-152/B1**
Transvaalstraße **144/A3**
Trautenaustraße **158/A2**
Triftstraße **144/C4**
Tucholskystraße **140/C2-152/B1**
Tübinger Straße **158/B4**
Turmstraße **150/A1-C1**

U

Uhlandstraße **138/C5-150/A5-157/F2-F3-158/A3-A2-A1**
Universitätsstraße **140/C3-152/B2**
Unterbaumstraße **140/A2-151/F2**
Unter den Eichen **162/C5**
Unter den Linden **140/B4-151/F3-152/A3**
Urbanstraße **160/C1-161/D1**
Usedomer Straße **146/A4**

V

Valeska-Gert-Straße **154/B2**
Veteranenstraße **146/C5**
Viktoria-Luise-Platz **139/F6-158/C1**
Voltairestraße **153/D2**
Von-der-Heydt-Straße **151/D5**
Vorarlberger Damm **158/C5-159/D5**
Voßstraße **140/A5-151/F4-152/A4**

W

Waisenstraße **153/D2**
Waldemarstraße **153/E5**
Waldstraße **150/A1**
Wallstraße **141/E5-152/C3-153/D3**
Wanda-Kallenbach-Straße (1) **154/B2**
Warmbrunner Straße **156/C3**
Warnemünder Straße **156/C6**
Warschauer Straße **154/B2**
Washingtonplatz **151/E1**
Wassertorplatz **153/D6**
Waterloo-Ufer **152/B6**
Weimarer Straße **138/A4-149/E5**
Weinbergsweg **146/C6**
Weinmeisterstraße **141/E1-146/C6-152/C1**
Weitlingstraße **155/F2**
Welserstraße **139/F6-150/C6-158/C1**
Werbellinstraße **154/A6-161/F4**
Werderscher Markt **141/D4-152/C3**
Werner-Voß-Damm **159/E4-160/A4**
Westfälische Straße **156/C1**
Wexstraße **158/B4**
Wichertstraße **147/E2**
Wichmannstraße **150/C5**
Wiclefstraße **144/A6**
Wielandstraße (Charlbg.) **138/B6-149/F6**
Wielandstraße (Schbg.) **158/C6**
Wiener Straße **153/F5-154/A3**
Wiesbadener Straße **157/E5-158/A5**
Wiesenstraße **145/F3**
Wilhelmine-Gemberg-Weg **153/E4**
Wilhelm-Kabus-Straße **159/E4**
Wilhelmshavener Straße **144/B6**
Wilhelmstraße **140/B5-B6-152/A3-A4**
Willy-Brandt-Straße **151/E2**
Wilmersdorfer Straße **149/D3**
Wilmsstraße **152/C6-160/C1**
Windscheidstraße **149/D4**
Winterfeldtstraße **139/F6-151/D6-158/C1-159/D1**
Wisbyer Straße **147/D1**
Wittelsbacherstraße **157/E1**
Wörther Straße **147/D5**
Wolfensteindamm **163/F3**
Wolliner Straße **146/B4**
Württembergische Straße **157/F2**
Wullenweberstraße **150/A3**

X

Xantener Straße **138/A6-149/E6-157/E1**

Y

Yitzhak-Rabin-Straße **151/E3**
Yorckstraße **159/E1-160/A1**

Z

Zähringerstraße **157/E1**
Ziegelstraße **140/C2-152/A1**
Zietenplatz (1) **140/B5-152/A3**
Zillepromenade **155/E2**
Zillestraße **138/A2-149/D4-E4**
Zimmerstraße **140/C6-152/A4**
Zossener Straße **160/B2**

KEY TO STREET ATLAS

Autobahn mit Nummer
Motorway with number
Autoroute avec numéro

Nummer der Autobahnanschlussstelle
Motorway junction number
Numéro d'echangeur d'autoroute

Schnellstraße/ Bundesstraße
Expressway/ Federal road
Route express/ Route nationale

Durchgangsstraße
Main through road
Grande route

Übrige Straßen/ Weg
Other roads/ Footpath
Autres routes/ Sentier

Straßen in Bau/ Planung
Roads under construction/ projected
Routes en construction/ en projet

Fußgängerzone/ Einbahnstraße
Pedestrian zone/ One-way street
Zone piétonnière/ Rue à sens unique

Stadt- und Gemeindegrenze
Town and communal boundary
Limite de ville et commune

Umweltzone
Environmental zone
Zone environnement

Eisenbahn mit Bahnhof
Railway with station
Voie ferrée avec gare

Güter- und Industriebahn
Freight and industrial railway
Voie ferrée de marchandise et industrielle

S-Bahn mit Nummer und Station
Rapid transit train with number and station
Train en trafic suburbain avec numéro et gare

U-Bahn/ Stadtbahn
Underground/ Light Rail
Métro/ Métro Léger

Bus/ Straßenbahn mit Endhaltestelle
Bus/ Tramway with terminus
Autobus/ Tramway avec terminus

Parkplatz/ Parkhaus/ Tiefgarage
Car park/ Parking house/ Underground car park
Parking/ Garage/ Parking souterrain

Park+Ride/ Parkleitsystem
Park+Ride/ Parking control system
Park+Ride/ Système de signalisation

Hallenbad
Indoor swimming pool
Piscine couverte

Kirche
Church
Église

Krankenhaus
Hospital
Hôpital

Campingplatz/ Jugendherberge
Camping site/ Youth hostel
Camping/ Auberge de jeunesse

Post
Post office
Bureau de poste

Försterei
Forester's lodge
Maison forestière

Einzelne Bäume
Isolated trees
Arbres isolés

Wirtshaus/ Ausflugslokal
Inn/ Excursion-Inn
Auberge/ Café-Restaurant

Sendeanlage/ Leuchtturm
Transmitting station/ Lighthouse
Station d'émission/ Phare

Denkmal/ Turm
Monument/ Tower
Monument/ Tour

Windmühle/ Windrad
Windmill/ Windpower
Moulin à vent/ Éolienne

Tourist-Information
Tourist information center
Syndicat d'initiative

Konsulat/ Botschaft
Consulate/ Embassy
Consulat/ Ambassade

Wald/ Park, Friedhof
Forest/ Park, Cemetery
Fôret/ Parc, Cimetière

Weinberg
Vineyard
Vignoble

Heide/ Moor, Sumpf
Heath/ Marsh, Swamp
Lande/ Marais, Marécage

MARCO POLO Erlebnistour 1
MARCO POLO Discovery Tour 1
MARCO POLO Tour d'aventure 1

MARCO POLO Erlebnistouren
MARCO POLO Discovery Tours
MARCO POLO Tours d'aventure

MARCO POLO Highlight

FOR YOUR NEXT TRIP...

MARCO POLO TRAVEL GUIDES

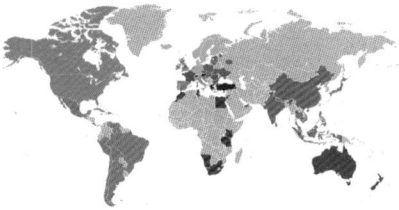

Algarve
Amsterdam
Andalucia
Athens
Australia
Austria
Bali & Lombok
Bangkok
Barcelona
Berlin
Brazil
Bruges
Brussels
Budapest
Bulgaria
California
Cambodia
Canada East
Canada West / Rockies & Vancouver
Cape Town & Garden Route
Cape Verde
Channel Islands
Chicago & The Lakes
China
Cologne
Copenhagen
Corfu
Costa Blanca & Valencia
Costa Brava
Costa del Sol & Granada
Crete
Cuba
Cyprus (North and South)
Dresden
Dubai
Dublin
Dubrovnik & Dalmatian Coast
Edinburgh
Egypt
Egypt Red Sea Resorts
Finland
Florence
Florida
French Atlantic Coast
French Riviera (Nice, Cannes & Monaco)
Fuerteventura
Gran Canaria
Greece
Hamburg
Hong Kong & Macau
Iceland
India
India South
Ireland
Israel
Istanbul
Italy
Jordan
Kos
Krakow
Lake Garda
Lanzarote
Las Vegas
Lisbon
London
Los Angeles
Madeira & Porto Santo
Madrid
Mallorca
Malta & Gozo
Mauritius
Menorca
Milan
Montenegro
Morocco
Munich
Naples & Amalfi Coast
New York
New Zealand
Norway
Oslo
Paris
Phuket
Portugal
Prague
Rhodes
Rome
San Francisco
Sardinia
Scotland
Seychelles
Shanghai
Sicily
Singapore
South Africa
Sri Lanka
Stockholm
Switzerland
Tenerife
Thailand
Turkey
Turkey South Coast
Tuscany
United Arab Emirates
USA Southwest (Las Vegas, Colorado, New Mexico, Arizona & Utah)
Venice
Vienna
Vietnam
Zakynthos & Ithaca, Kefalonia, Lefkas

The travel guides with Insider Tips

INDEX

This index lists all sights, museums and places, plus the names of important people featured in this guide. Numbers in bold indicate a main entry.

Admiralspalast 94
Ahrensfelde 116
Ahrensfelder Berge 118
Alexanderplatz 26, 31, **34**, 39, 40, 76, 86, 109, 122
Alliiertenmuseum 16, **56**
Altes Museum 28, **38**
Apartments 105
ARD-Hauptstadtstudio 113
Automobil-Forum Unter den Linden 31
Bahnhof Zoo 31
Barenboim, Daniel 96
Bauhaus-Archiv 41
Berlin-Marathon 125
Berlinale 124
Berliner Abgeordnetenhaus 112
Berliner Dom 16, **30**, 40
Berliner Ensemble 97
Berliner Mauer 14, 35, **48**, 52
Berlinische Galerie 52
Bernauer Straße 36
Berolinahaus 35
Bicycles 129
Biesdorfer Höhe 119
Bikini Berlin 53, 77, **81**
Black Box Kalter Krieg 52
Bodemuseum 28, 29, **38**
Bonbonmacherei 122
Botanischer Garten 56
Box offices 128
Brandenburger Tor 27, 29, 31, 40, **41**, 42, 69, 108, 113, 125
Brecht, Bertolt 31
Breitscheidplatz 56
Brücke-Museum 56
Brunnen der Völkerfreundschaft 35
Bundeskanzleramt 15, 46
BVG Cabriotour 122
Charlottenburg 24, 35, **53**, 76
Checkpoint Charlie 14, 35, **52**, 110
Chinesischer Garten 56
Chinesisches Teehaus (Potsdam) 62
Chipperfield, David 29, 38
Christopher Street Day 22, 124
Cinemas 93
City tours 129
City tours for kids 122
Classic Open Air on Gendarmenmarkt 125
Computerspielemuseum 30
Concert halls 94
Currywurst 65, 72
Dancing 96
DDR-Museum 31
Denkmal der Bücherverbrennung 31
Denkmal für die ermordeten Juden Europas **42**, 113
Design 22
Deutsche Oper 53, **94**
Deutscher Dom 16, 36, 47
Deutsches Historisches Museum 30, **31**
Deutsches Technikmuseum 52
Deutsches Theater 97
DMY International Design Festival Berlin 22
Döner Kebab 65, 72
Dorotheenstädtischer Friedhof 31
Eastside Gallery 48
Einstein, Albert 29
Eisenman, Peter 42
Embassy District 41
Fashion 22, 23
Fashion Week 23
Fernsehturm 29, **34**, 109
Fichte, Johann Gottlieb 31
Fleamarkets 80
Floating swimming pool 58
Flower Tower 118
Flughafen Tempelhof 60
Flussbadeanstalt Krokodil 62
Foster, Sir Norman 47
Französischer Dom 16, 36
Friedrich I 16, 55
Friedrich II (the Great) 62
Friedrich Wilhelm (crown prince) 28
Friedrich Wilhelm I 63
Friedrich Wilhelm II 59
Friedrich Wilhelm III 29, 55, 58
Friedrichshain 14, 24, **47**, 48
Friedrichstadtpalast 35, **94**
Friedrichstraße 27, **35**, 76
Friedrichswerdersche Kirche 35
Funkturm 53, 128
Galeries Lafayette 35, 76, **82**
Gärten der Welt **56**, 118
Gedenkstätte Berliner Mauer 35
Gedenkstätte Deutscher Widerstand 42
Gedenkstätte Stille Helden 36
Gemäldegalerie 44
Gendarmenmarkt 16, 30, **36**, 125
Gipsstraße 115
Glienicker Brücke 58
Glienicker Park 57
Government quarter 15, 26, 35, 41, **46**
Grips-Theater 94
Gropius, Walter 41, 53
Große Hamburger Straße 115
Grüne Woche 124
Grunewald 57
Grunewaldturm 121
Hackesche Höfe 22, **37**, 67, 77, 115
Hackescher Markt 30, 86
Hamburger Bahnhof **37**, 73
Handwerksvereinshaus 115
Hasenheide 24
Hauptbahnhof (main station) 15, **43**, 47, 128
Haus am Checkpoint Charlie **52**, 110
Haus der Kulturen der Welt 35, 41, **44**
Haus der Wannseekonferenz 58
Hebbel am Ufer 95
Heckmann-Höfe 22
Hegel, Georg Wilhelm Friedrich 31
Hertha BSC 55, 96
Holländisches Viertel (Potsdam) 63
Hostels 104
Hugenotten 16, 34, 36
Humboldt-Forum 15, 21, 109
Humboldt-Universität 21, 30, 40
Insel Scharfenberg 120
Internationale Funkausstellung 125
Internationale Luft- und Raumfahrtausstellung 124
Internationale Tourismusbörse (ITB) 124
Internationales Literaturfestival 125
Jagdschloss Grunewald 58
Jazzfest Berlin 125
Jüdische Kulturtage 125
Jüdischer Friedhof Weissensee 58
Jüdisches Museum Berlin 52
Kabarett & Varieté 91
KaDeWe 53, 76, 82, 109
Kaiser-Wilhelm-Gedächtniskirche **53**, 109
Karl-Marx-Allee 37

Karneval der Kulturen 124
Kästner, Erich 31
Kaulsdorf 119
Kienberg 57, 118
Kinderbad Monbijou 122
Kladow 121
Knobelsdorff, Georg Wenzeslaus von 62
Kollhoff-Tower 45, 112
Kollwitz, Käthe 48
Kollwitzplatz 48, 122
Konzerthaus am Gendarmenmarkt 95
Köpenick **61**, 119
Köpenicker Schloss 61
Kottbusser Tor 109
Kreuzberg 14, 15, 24, 25, 35, 44, **50**, 76, 109
Kronprinzenpalais 40
Kulturbrauerei **48**, 50
Kulturforum 29, 44
Kulturprojekte Berlin 122
Kunstgewerbemuseum 44
Kurfürstendamm 26, 53, **54**, 76
Kurt-Berndt-Höfe 22
Lange Nacht der Museen 125
Lange Nacht der Wissenschaften 25, 124
Langhans, Carl Gotthard 41
Leipziger Platz 108
Lenné, Peter Joseph 57
Libeskind, Daniel 52
Liebknecht, Karl 22
Liquidrom 44
Loxx (model railway) 123
Luftbrücke 16, 56
Luise (queen) 55
Luxemburg, Rosa 22
Mach mit! Museum 123
Madame Tussauds Berlin 37
Märchenbrunnen 50
main station (Hauptbahnhof) 15, **43**, 47, 128
Mann, Heinrich 31
Marie-Elisabeth-Lüders-Haus 46
Marmorpalais (Potsdam) 63
Martin-Gropius-Bau **53**, 111
Mauer-Gedenkstätte 16
Mauerpark 48
Max-Schmeling-Halle 96
Maxim Gorki Theater 97
Mercedes-Benz Arena 15, 96
Messegelände am Funkturm 53, 124
Mies van der Rohe, Ludwig 41, 45
Ministergärten 46
Mitte 13, **29**, 76, 77, 86
Molecule Men 49
Müggelsee 61, 62
Museum Berggruen 55
Museum für Film und Fernsehen 45
Museum für Kommunikation 38
Museum für Naturkunde 38
Museumsinsel 13, 16, 28, 29, 35, **38**, 40, 109
Musikfest Berlin 125
Musikinstrumenten-Museum 29, **44**
Nationalgalerie 28, 29, **38**
Neptunbrunnen 35
Neue Nationalgalerie 29, **45**
Neue Synagoge 16, 30, 37, **38**
Neuer Garten (Potsdam) 63
Neues Museum 28, **38**, 109
Neues Palais (Potsdam) 62
Neukölln 15, 25, 77, 86
Neuköllner Oper 95
Nikolaikirche 39
Nikolaiviertel 30, **39**
Oberbaumbrücke 24, 50, 86
Olympiastadium **55**, 96, 124
Oranienburger Straße 15, 37, 39, 116
Ostbahnhof 15, 27, 48, 86, 128
Palast der Republik 15, 20, 27, 41
Pariser Platz 27, 41
Paul-Lincke-Ufer 51
Paul-Löbe-Haus 46
Pergamonmuseum 28, **38**
Pfaueninsel **58**, 121
Philharmonie 95
Potsdam 62
Potsdamer Platz 15, 27, 41, **45**, 108, 112
Prenzlauer Berg 14, **47**, 48
Prinzessinnengärten 25
Private rooms 105
Pubs 93
Quartier 206 35, 76, **83**
Rathaus Köpenick 61
Rattle, Sir Simon 95
Rau, Johannes 31
Rauch, Christian Daniel 35
Reichstag building 15, 26, 41, **46**, 61, 66, 107, 113
Rixdorf 59
Ronneby promenade 121
Rotes Rathaus 26, 39
Schadow, Johann Gottfried 35, 38
Scharoun, Hans 95
Schaubühne 53, **97**
Schauspielhaus 16, 36, 95
Scheunenviertel 114
Schillertheater 53, 96
Schinkel, Karl Friedrich 31, 35, 36, 57, 58, 95
Schloss Bellevue 31
Schloss Cecilienhof (Potsdam) 63
Schloss Charlottenburg 53, **55**, 61
Schloss Sanssouci (Potsdam) 62
Schlossplatz 109
Schöneberg 77
Schöneberger Rathaus 40
Schönefeld Airport 24, 128
Sechstagerennen 124
Seghers, Anna 31
Siegessäule 31, 41, **47**
Solar boat tour 129
Sony-Center 15, 41, **45**, 113
Sophie Charlotte (electress) 55
Sophie-Gips-Höfe 22, 115
Sophienkirche 115
Sophiensaele 97
Sophienstraße 22, 115
Sowjetisches Ehrenmal 59
Spandau 120
Spandau citadel 121
Spandauer Vorstadt 114
St.-Hedwigs-Kathedrale 16, **40**
St.-Hedwig-Krankenhaus 115
Staatsoper Unter den Linden 16, 40, **96**
Stadtbad Mitte 61
Stadtschloss 15, 21, 27, 40, 41
Stasi prison Hohenschönhausen 59
Stüler, Friedrich August 38, 55
Sultan-Hamam 44
Tauentzienstraße 76
Tegel 119
Tegel Airport 24, 128
Tempelhofer Feld 25, **60**
Tempodrom 44
Teufelsberg 58
Teufelssee 57
The Story of Berlin 56
Theaters 97
Theater am Potsdamer Platz 96
Theater an der Parkaue 123
Theater des Westens 53, **96**
Theatertreffen 124
Tiergarten 41
Tierpark Friedrichsfelde **60**, 62
Topographie des Terrors **53**, 110
Treptow 49, 50
Treptower Park 59
Tucholsky, Kurt 31

CREDITS

TV tower 29, **34**, 109
Unter den Linden 29, **40**, 108
Velodrom 124
Villa Borsig 120
Virchow, Rudolf 29
Volksbühne 97
Volkspark Friedrichshain 24, 48, **50**
Wallot, Paul 46
Wannsee 24, 58
Wannsee (Lido) 24
Wedding 15, 24
Weekly markets 85
Weigel, Helene 31
Weltkugelbrunnen 56
Wilhelm I. 53
Wilhelm II. 35
Wilmersdorf 53
Wittenbergplatz 109
World-time clock 35
Wuhlesee 119
Wuhletal 117
Wuhlheide 96
Zeughaus 30, 31, 40
Zoologischer Garten 56
Zuckmayer, Carl 61

WRITE TO US

e-mail: info@marcopologuides.co.uk

Did you have a great holiday?
Is there something on your mind?
Whatever it is, let us know!
Whether you want to praise, alert us to errors or give us a personal tip – MARCO POLO would be pleased to hear from you.
We do everything we can to provide the very latest information for your trip.

Nevertheless, despite all of our authors' thorough research, errors can creep in. MARCO POLO does not accept any liability for this. Please contact us by e-mail or post.

MARCO POLO Travel Publishing Ltd
Pinewood, Chineham Business Park
Crockford Lane, Chineham
Basingstoke, Hampshire RG24 8AL
United Kingdom

PICTURE CREDITS

Cover photograph: Brandenburger Tor (huber-images/L. Da Ros)
Images: Corbis/Demotix: S. Struck (20/21); DuMont Bildarchiv: Freyer (72 right), Specht (5, 10, 76/77, 122, 125); eROCKIT GmbH: Stefan Gulas/Sascha Nolte (19 top); R. Freyer (66, 72 left, 92, 122/123, 123, 124, 124/125, 126 top); Getty Images: Nikada (4 top, 12/13), querbeet (23); J. Gläser (69); huber-images: M. Borchi (39), G. Cozzi (45), L. Da Ros (1, 26/27), M. Rellini (40, 133), R. Schmid (50); G. Knoll (75); Laif: A. Akhtar (64/65, 70), A. Back (9), H. Champollion (8), M. Danner (84, 104), T. Gerber (121), K. Harms (25), M. Jaeger (11), Th. Kierok (30), D. Schwelle (2/3, 14, 17, 18 top, 18 bottom, 36/37, 48, 59, 88), Wernet (117), G. Westrich (flap right, 7, 60); Laif/Gamma-Rapho/Hoa-Qui: S. Grandadam (95); Laif/hemis.fr: F. Guiziou (112); Laif/Le Figaro Magazine: Martin (4 bottom, 86/87); Laif/Zenit: Boening (98/99); Look: K. Johaentges (57); Look/age fotostock (55); mauritius images: W. Bibikow (52, 100); mauritius images/Alamy (42, 63, 81, 82, 126 bottom); mauritius images/imagebroker: Henkelmann (127), Reister (34), I. Schulz (103), L. Steiner (6), E. Wrba (46/47); picture-alliance/dpa (18 centre); picture-alliance/Eventpress Hoensch (97); picture-alliance/ZB (91); Smiling Berlin Verlag: Lasse Walter (19 bottom); Visum: M. Hanke (106/107), A. Kohls (flap left); M. Weigt (73, 78)

3rd Edition – fully revised and updated 2016
Worldwide Distribution: Marco Polo Travel Publishing Ltd, Pinewood, Chineham Business Park, Crockford Lane, Basingstoke, Hampshire RG24 8AL, United Kingdom. Email: sales@marcopolouk.com
© MAIRDUMONT GmbH & Co. KG, Ostfildern
Chief editor: Marion Zorn; Author: Christine Berger, Editor: Jochen Schürmann
Programme supervision: Susanne Heimburger, Tamara Hub, Nikolai Michaelis, Kristin Schimpf, Martin Silbermann
Picture editor: Gabriele Forst, Anja Schlatterer; What's hot: wunder media, Munich; Cartography street atlas: © MAIRDUMONT, Ostfildern; Cartography pull-out map: © MAIRDUMONT, Ostfildern; Design: milchhof : atelier, Berlin; Front cover, pull-out map cover, page 1: factor product munich; Discovery Tours: Susan Chaaban, Dipl.-Des. (FH)
Translated from the German by Robert McInnes; Susan Jones; editor of the English edition: Christopher Wynne
Prepress: writehouse, Cologne; InterMedia, Ratingen
Phrase book in cooperation with Ernst Klett Sprachen GmbH, Stuttgart,
Editorial by Pons Wörterbücher
All rights reserved. No part of this book may be reproduced, stored in a retrieval system or transmitted in any form or by any means (electronic, mechanical, photocopying, recording or otherwise) without prior written permission from the publisher.
Printed in China